GENERAL EDITOR: A. E. Dyson

PUBLISHED

Jane Austen: *Emma* DAVID LODGE

Jane Austen: *'Northanger Abbey'* and *'Persuasion'* B. C. SOUTHAM

Jane Austen: *'Sense and Sensibility'*, *'Pride and Prejudice'* and *'Mansfield Park'*
B. C. SOUTHAM

William Blake: *Songs of innocence and Experience* MARGARET BOTTRALL

Charlotte Brontë: *'Jane Eyre'* and *'Villette'* MIRIAM ALLOTT

Emily Brontë: *Wuthering Heights* MIRIAM ALLOTT

Browning: *'Men and Women'* and Other Poems*. J. R. WATSON

Bunyan: *Pilgrim's Progress* ROGER SHARROCK

Byron: *'Childe Harold's Pilgrimage'* and *'Don Juan'* JOHN JUMP

Chaucer: *Canterbury Tales* J. J. ANDERSON

Coleridge: *'The Ancient Mariner'* and Other Poems* ALUN R. JONES AND
WILLIAM TYDEMAN

Conrad: *The Secret Agent* IAN WATT

Dickens: *Bleak House* A. E. DYSON

Donne: *Songs and Sonets* JULIAN LOVELOCK

George Eliot: *Middlemarch* PATRICK SWINDEN

George Eliot: *'The Mill on the Floss'* and *'Silas Marner'* R. P. DRAPER

T. S. Eliot: *Four Quartets* BERNARD BERGONZI

T. S. Eliot: *'Prufrock'*, *'Gerontion'*, *'Ash Wednesday'* and Other Shorter Poems
B. C. SOUTHAM

T. S. Eliot: *The Waste Land* C. B. COX AND ARNOLD P. HINCHLIFFE

Farquhar: *'The Recruiting Officer'* and *'The Beaux' Stratagem'* RAYMOND A.
ANSELMENT

Henry Fielding: *Tom Jones* NEIL COMPTON

E. M. Forster: *A Passage to India* MALCOLM BRADBURY

Hardy: *The Tragic Novels* R. P. DRAPER

Gerard Manley Hopkins: *Poems* MARGARET BOTTRALL

Jonson: *'Every Man in his Humour'* and *'The Alchemist'* R. V. HOLDSWORTH

Jonson: *Volpone* JONAS A. BARISH

James Joyce: *'Dubliners'* and *'A Portrait of the Artist as a Young Man'* MORRIS
BEJA

John Keats: *Odes* G. S. FRASER

D. H. Lawrence: *Sons and Lovers* GĀMINI SALGĀDO

D. H. Lawrence: *'The Rainbow'* and *'Women in Love'* COLIN CLARKE

Marlowe: *Doctor Faustus* JOHN JUMP

The Metaphysical Poets GERALD HAMMOND

Milton: *'Comus'* and *'Samson Agonistes'* JULIAN LOVE[...]

Milton: *Paradise Lost*

John Osborne: *Look B[...]*

Peacock: *The Satirical Nove[...]*

Pope: *The Rape of the Lock* JO[...] N HUNT

Shakespeare: *Antony and Cleopatra*   JOHN RUSSELL BROWN
Shakespeare: *Coriolanus*   B. A. BROCKMAN
Shakespeare: *Hamlet*   JOHN JUMP
Shakespeare: *Henry IV Parts I and II*   G. K. HUNTER
Shakespeare: *Henry V*   MICHAEL QUINN
Shakespeare: *Julius Caesar*   PETER URE
Shakespeare: *King Lear*   FRANK KERMODE
Shakespeare: *Macbeth*   JOHN WAIN
Shakespeare: *Measure for Measure*   C. K. STEAD
Shakespeare: *The Merchant of Venice*   JOHN WILDERS
Shakespeare: *Othello*   JOHN WAIN
Shakespeare: *Richard II*   NICHOLAS BROOKE
Shakespeare: *The Sonnets*   PETER JONES
Shakespeare: *The Tempest*   D. J. PALMER
Shakespeare: *Troilus and Cressida*   PRISCILLA MARTIN
Shakespeare: *Twelfth Night*   D. J. PALMER
Shakespeare: *The Winter's Tale*   KENNETH MUIR
Shelley: *Shorter Poems and Lyrics*   PATRICK SWINDEN
Spenser: *The Faerie Queene*   PETER BAYLEY
Swift: *Gulliver's Travels*   RICHARD GRAVIL
Tennyson: *In Memoriam*   JOHN DIXON HUNT
Thackeray: *Vanity Fair*   ARTHUR POLLARD
Webster: *'The White Devil'* and *'The Duchess of Malfi'*   R. V. HOLDSWORTH
Virginia Woolf: *To the Lighthouse*   MORRIS BEJA
Wordsworth: *Lyrical Ballads*   ALUN R. JONES AND WILLIAM TYDEMAN
Wordsworth: *The Prelude*   W. J. HARVEY AND RICHARD GRAVIL
Yeats: *Last Poems*   JON STALLWORTHY

The English Novel: Developments in Criticism since Henry James   STEPHEN
HAZELL
The Romantic Imagination   JOHN SPENCER HILL

TITLES IN PREPARATION INCLUDE

Dickens: *'Hard Times', 'Great Expectations' and 'Our Mutual Friend'*   NORMAN
PAGE
Hardy: *Poems*   JAMES GIBSON AND TREVOR JOHNSON
Shakespeare: *'Much Ado about Nothing' and 'As You Like It'*   JOHN RUSSELL
BROWN
Sheridan: *'The Rivals', 'The School for Scandal' and 'The Critic'*   WILLIAM
RUDDICK

Drama Criticism: Developments since Ibsen   ARNOLD P. HINCHLIFFE
Poetry Criticism: Development since the Symbolists   A. E. DYSON

Shakespeare

Twelfth Night

A CASEBOOK

EDITED BY

D. J. PALMER

Selection and editorial matter © D. J. Palmer 1972

First edition 1972
Reprinted 1978

Published by
THE MACMILLAN PRESS LTD
London and Basingstoke
Associated companies in Delhi Dublin
Hong Kong Johannesburg Lagos Melbourne
New York Singapore and Tokyo

ISBN 0 333 12169 4

Printed in Hong Kong

CONTENTS

Acknowledgements   7
General Editor's Preface   9
Introduction   11

Part 1: *Performance, Adaptation and Comment, 1602–1912*

JOHN MANNINGHAM, p. 25 – LEONARD DIGGES,
p. 25 – SAMUEL PEPYS, p. 25 – WILLIAM
BURNABY, p. 25 – SAMUEL JOHNSON, p. 29
– WILLIAM HAZLITT, p. 29 – CHARLES LAMB,
p. 36 – JAMES BOADEN, p. 48 – E. MONTÉGUT,
p. 51 – SIR EDWARD RUSSELL, p. 54 – WILLIAM
WINTER, p. 55 – HARLEY GRANVILLE-BARKER,
p. 57 – JOHN MASEFIELD, p. 58.

Part 2: *Twentieth-Century Studies*

A. C. BRADLEY: Feste the Jester   63
H. B. CHARLTON: Shakespeare's Heroines and the
   Art of Happiness   72
LESLIE HOTSON: The Real Duke Orsino   78
JOSEPH H. SUMMERS: The Masks of *Twelfth
   Night*   86
JOHN HOLLANDER: The Role of Music in *Twelfth
   Night*   98
C. L. BARBER: Testing Courtesy and Humanity in
   Twelfth Night   112

BERTRAND EVANS: The Fruits of the Sport   137

PORTER WILLIAMS, JR: Mistakes in *Twelfth Night*
and Their Resolution   170

JOHN RUSSELL BROWN: Directions for *Twelfth Night*   188

D. J. PALMER: Art and Nature in *Twelfth Night*   204

M. C. BRADBROOK: Robert Armin and *Twelfth Night*   222

Select Bibliography   245

Notes on Contributors   247

Index   249

ACKNOWLEDGEMENTS

The editor and publishers wish to thank the following, who have kindly given permission for the use of copyright material: The Trustees of Harley Granville-Barker and Princeton University Press for 'On Producing *Twelfth Night*', from Preface to *Twelfth Night: An Acting Edition* (Heinemann, 1912); David Higham Associates for the John Masefield letter included in *Harley Granville-Barker* by C. B. Purdom (Rockliff, 1955); A. C. Bradley, 'Feste the Jester', from *A Miscellany* (Macmillan, 1929); Methuen & Co. Ltd for the extract from *Shakespearian Comedy* by H. B. Charlton (1938); Rupert Hart-Davis (Granada Publishing Ltd) for extracts from *The First Night of 'Twelfth Night'* by Leslie Hotson (1954); *University of Kansas City Review* for 'The Masks of *Twelfth Night*' by Joseph H. Summers, XXII (1955); Columbia University Press for the extract from '*Musica Mundana* and *Twelfth Night*' by John Hollander, from *Sound and Poetry: English Institute Essays 1956*, ed. Northrop Frye (1957); Princeton University Press for chap. 10 from *Shakespeare's Festive Comedy* by C. L. Barber (1959); the Clarendon Press for chap. iv from *Shakespeare's Comedies* by Bertrand Evans (1960); Modern Language Association of America for 'Mistakes in *Twelfth Night* and Their Resolution' by Porter Williams, Jr, *PMLA*, LXXVI (1961); Edward Arnold (Publishers) Ltd for 'Directions for *Twelfth Night*', from *Shakespeare's Plays in Performance* by John Russell Brown (1966); *Critical Quarterly* for 'Art and Nature in *Twelfth Night*', IX 3 (1967) by D. J. Palmer; Chatto & Windus Ltd and Barnes & Noble Inc., New York, for the extract from chap. IV of *Shakespeare the Craftsman* by M. C. Bradbrook (1969).

GENERAL EDITOR'S PREFACE

Each of this series of Casebooks concerns either one well-known and influential work of literature or two or three closely linked works. The main section consists of critical readings, mostly modern, brought together from journals and books. A selection of reviews and comments by the author's contemporaries is also included, and sometimes comments from the author himself. The Editor's Introduction charts the reputation of the work from its first appearance until the present time.

The critical forum is a place of vigorous conflict and disagreement, but there is nothing in this to cause dismay. What is attested is the complexity of human experience and the richness of literature, not any chaos or relativity of taste. A critic is better seen, no doubt, as an explorer than as an 'authority', but explorers ought to be, and usually are, well equipped. The effect of good criticism is to convince us of what C. S. Lewis called 'the enormous extension of our being which we owe to authors'. This Casebook will be justified only if it helps to promote the same end.

A single volume can represent no more than a small selection of critical opinions. Some critics have been excluded for reasons of space, and it is hoped that readers will follow up the further suggestions in the Select Bibliography. Other contributions have been severed from their original context, to which some readers may wish to return. Indeed, if they take a hint from the critics represented here, they certainly will.

A. E. DYSON

INTRODUCTION

I

In the grace and subtlety of its design, *Twelfth Night* is the crowning perfection of the sequence of comedies belonging to the first half of Shakespeare's career. Not printed until it appeared in the First Folio in 1623, the play was written some time between 1599, the date of Molyneux's 'new map with the augmentation of the Indies', to which Maria refers at III ii 74, and 2 February 1602, when John Manningham saw *Twelfth Night* performed in the Middle Temple and so left in his Diary the earliest reference to the play. Leslie Hotson believes that *Twelfth Night* was composed and first presented in honour of Virginio Orsino, Duke of Bracciano, when he was entertained at court by the Queen on Twelfth Night 1601. But although Shakespeare's company, the Lord Chamberlain's Men, was appearing at court on that day, there is no evidence to indicate what play they performed, while the amorous affectations of the stage Orsino hardly seem appropriate or decorous fare for the Virgin Queen and her guest of honour on that occasion. Even the traditional licence of Twelfth Night revels, reflected in the spirit and title of the comedy, would not have extended to such gross familiarity on the part of hired players. It is conceivable that if he wrote the play some time after the visit of this real-life Orsino, Shakespeare merely remembered his name as being suitably ducal. But if further speculation is nearly as fanciful as the play itself, we nevertheless owe much to Hotson's sagacity in unearthing documents which, by giving us a vivid picture of Twelfth Night celebrations at Elizabeth's court, illustrate the customary festivity which underlies the comedy.

The main plot of *Twelfth Night* is taken from 'Apolonius

and Silla', the second tale in Barnaby Riche's *Riche his Farewell to Militarie Profession* (1581). The story ultimately derives by way of French intermediaries from a very popular
anonymous Italian comedy, *Gl'Ingannati* ('The Deceived'),
which was first performed in Siena in 1531. Possibly this was
the play which Manningham had in mind when he observed
that Shakespeare's comedy was 'most like and neere to that
in Italian called *Inganni*', although there were two less well-
known and less similar plays of that title, by Nicolò Secchi
(1562) and by Curzio Gonzaga (1592). In any case, a plot
which turns upon a shipwreck, the separation and eventual
reunion of identical twins, a girl disguised in boy's clothes, and
the confusions of cross-wooing, is exploiting the characteristic
and well-worn devices of Plautine comedy and of romance,
materials which Shakespeare had often used in his previous
comedies. *Twelfth Night* reminded Manningham of *The
Comedy of Errors* as well of '*Inganni*', presumably because
Shakespeare's earlier play also presents twins who are separated
by shipwreck and constantly mistaken for each other, to the
confusion of those on stage and the merriment of the spectators.
Even more striking is the parallel between Viola's plight and
that of Julia in *The Two Gentlemen of Verona*; each heroine
disguises herself as a boy and serves the man she loves by wooing
her rival on his behalf. Julia, moreover, adopts the name of
Sebastian. In addition, the Antonio of *Twelfth Night*, who en-
trusts his money to Sebastian and puts his life at risk for his
friend, recalls his namesake in *The Merchant of Venice*, while
a resemblance to Falstaff has often been noted in Sir Toby's
degenerate knighthood and his roisterous dedication to cakes
and ale at someone else's expense.

More generally, in its blend of lyrical charm, wit, and moments of poignancy, *Twelfth Night* is placed with *As You Like
It* at the culminating point of this phase of Shakespearian
comedy. In the comedies that were to follow, *All's Well That
Ends Well* and *Measure for Measure*, Shakespeare turned to

a more urgent and analytical treatment of moral and social issues, of the depravity as well as the folly in human nature, and much of the earlier gaiety has gone. Yet beneath the light-hearted revelry of *Twelfth Night*, as if by anticipation, a more disturbing note of disenchantment is occasionally sounded; Antonio's bitter reproach when he supposes that Sebastian has betrayed him,·Feste's wry reflections on the way of the world, especially in his final song, the implacable hostility between Malvolio and his enemies, and the fortuitous basis of the marriages that conclude the play, leave one with an awareness that the play's sense of poise is fine because it is precarious. Twelfth Night, after all, is the last day of the Christmas festivities, and the melancholy which is never far below the surface of this consummation of Shakespeare's first phase of comedy is epitomised in Viola's reflection upon the fragility of woman's beauty : 'To die, even when they to perfection grow'.

II

Turning back to one of Shakespeare's earliest comedies, *The Taming of the Shrew*, we find in the dialogue of the Introduction, between Christopher Sly and the page pretending to be his wife, a suggestion of the elements that compose a Shakespearian comedy, festive and romantic, popular and courtly :

> *Sly:* . . . Is not a comonty a Christmas gambold or a tumbling-trick?
> *Page:* No, my good lord, it is more pleasing stuff.
> *Sly:* What, household stuff?
> *Page:* It is a kind of history.
> *Sly:* Well, we'll see't. Come, madam wife, sit by my side and let the world slip. (lines 133–40)

Twelfth Night, as the title implies, is a kind of 'Christmas gambold' as well as 'a kind of history', while the characteristic invitation to indulge the fancy and enter a world of make-

believe, which *Twelfth Night* shares with its predecessors, is epitomised in Sly's readiness to 'let the world slip'. But there is another element in *Twelfth Night* which reflects the advent of a different conception of comedy. For the influence of Ben Jonson's satirical 'humour' comedies (performed by Shakespeare's company in 1598 and 1599) is perceptible in the gulling of Malvolio, in the exposure, ridicule and punitive 'cure' of the steward's 'self-love'.

Significantly, during the seventeenth and early eighteenth centuries it was the putting-down of Malvolio which attracted most comment and admiration, as audiences (and readers) developed a taste for satirical rather than romantic comedy. Thus, although he was inattentive enough to mistake Olivia for a 'Lady widdowe', Manningham found the 'good practise' by which Malvolio is deceived to be the most effective and memorable part of the play. Other members of that Middle Temple audience might have felt so too, if the tastes of the Inns of Court are to be judged by Jonson's dedication to them of *Every Man Out of his Humour*. In 1640 Leonard Digges made special reference to Malvolio, 'that crosse garter'd Gull', in his commendatory verses on Shakespeare written for an edition of the *Poems*. Charles I himself, by a royal emendation to his copy of the Second Folio, substituted 'Malvolio' for Shakespeare's own title. The significance of Shakespeare's title certainly eluded Samuel Pepys, who thought the play 'silly'. And a continuity of attitude over the next century might be detected in Dr Johnson's Note on the play, in which the gulling of Malvolio is praised as 'truly comick' in a satirical sense, while the romantic perplexities of the final Act are condemned for their lack of 'credibility' and their failure to present a 'just picture of life'.

The critics of the Romantic period, of course, were to reverse the balance with a vengeance, but before coming to them, we should notice what William Burnaby did to *Twelfth Night* in *Love Betray'd: or, The Agreable Disappointment* (1703). This is not an adaptation of Shakespeare in the Restoration manner, but rather an original play made from Shakespeare's materials. In his Preface, Burnaby announces with the blandest confidence in his own talents:

Part of the Tale of this Play, I took from *Shakespear*, and about Fifty of the Lines; Those that are his, I have mark'd with Inverted Commas, to distinguish 'em from what are mine. I endeavour'd where I had occasion to introduce any of 'em, to make 'em look as little like Strangers as possible, but am afraid (tho' a Military Critick did me the honour to say I had plunder'd all from *Shakespear*) that they wou'd easily be known without my Note of distinction.

Love Betray'd is more an agreed failure than an agreeable disappointment, without anything to redeem it from oblivion except its interesting position in the history of attitudes to *Twelfth Night*. For, as the scene reprinted in this volume shows, the lines from Shakespeare's text which Burnaby inserted into his play are precisely those romantic passages which otherwise seem to have attracted little attention during the seventeenth and early eighteenth centuries. He is in fact attempting to write a sentimental comedy of the kind that was beginning to succeed the Restoration comedy of wit at the turn of the century, and while he relies on his own resources, such as they are, to provide the witty and satirical elements, he borrows from Shakespeare in an effort to boost the pathetical situations of his play. The result is a totally irreconcilable contradiction, not only between different styles, but between different conceptions of comedy as well, for Burnaby had none of Shakespeare's ability to blend varieties of comic mood with each other.

Burnaby represents a change in sensibility which responded as much to the sentiment as to the laughter in *Twelfth Night*. He might have endorsed Hazlitt's opinion over a century later, that 'the poetical and impassioned passages are the best parts'. Hazlitt, like Burnaby, quotes Viola's lines about the sister who

'never told her love', and enthusiastically exclaims, 'How long
ago it is since we first learned to repeat them; and still, still
they vibrate on the heart, like the sounds which the passing
wind draws from the trembling strings of a harp left on some
desert shore.' But with this extravagant image of the Aeolian
harp, the Romantic symbol of poetic inspiration, we are un-
mistakably in another age from Burnaby's. Hazlitt's famous
observation that *Twelfth Night* 'is perhaps too good-natured
for comedy' glances back at the neo-classical idea of comedy as
satire, but only in order to distinguish it from the uncensorious
spirit of Shakespearian comedy: 'Folly is indigenous to the
soil, and shoots out with native, happy, unchecked luxuriance.
Absurdity has every encouragement afforded it; and nonsense
has room to flourish in.' Hazlitt thus set the tone for a tradition
of interpretative commentary which was still thriving in 1938,
when H. B. Charlton wrote of the comedies: 'They entice to
a richer wisdom by alluring the imagination into desire for
larger delights. They are not mainly concerned to whip offenders into conventional propriety by scorn and by mockery.'

The Romantic view that the spirit of Shakespearian comedy,
and of *Twelfth Night* in particular, resides in sympathetic delight rather than in satirical laughter had its obvious implications for attitudes to Malvolio. Hazlitt's suggestion that 'poor
Malvolio's treatment . . . is a little hard' was corroborated a
few years later by his friend Charles Lamb's celebrated interpretation of the character: 'Malvolio is not essentially ludicrous. He becomes comic but by accident . . . his pride, or his
gravity, (call it which you will) is inherent, and native to the
man, not mock or affected, which latter only are the fit objects
to excite laughter.'

Perhaps deliberately, Lamb's conception is the very antithesis of Dr Johnson's. Certainly there is an element of conscious
idiosyncrasy in Lamb's interpretation, which sets its face against
the tradition, reaching back to Manningham, that Malvolio is
a funny character. Of the climax of the gulling scene Lamb

writes: 'you had no room for laughter'. Lamb claims that his conception of Malvolio derives from seeing the part acted by the late-eighteenth-century actor Robert Bensley: 'I confess that I never saw the catastrophe of this character, while Bensley played it, without a kind of tragic interest.' But, as Sylvan Barnet has shown in the essay referred to in the Select Bibliography at the end of this volume, Lamb was embroidering memory with imagination, for other witnesses of the same actor's performance found it essentially comic. James Boaden, for instance, described Bensley's Malvolio in his *Life of John Philip Kemble* (2 vols, 1825):

Mr Bensley here offers himself to my recollection as the only perfect representative of another character in the same comedy; the smiling, yellow stockened, and cross-gartered Malvolio. All his peculiarities of deportment here aided his exhibition of the steward – the sliding zig-zag advance and retreat of his figure fixed the attention to his stockings and his garters. His constrained smile, his hollow laugh, his lordly assumption, and his ineffable contempt of all that opposed him in the way to greatness were irresistibly diverting. (1 57)

And again, in his *Life of Mrs Jordan* (2 vols, 1831), Boaden recalled the visual comedy with which Bensley realised the character:

Bensley had been a soldier, yet his stage-walk eternally reminded you of the 'one, two, three, hop' of the dancing-master; this scientific progress of legs, in yellow stockings, most villainously cross-gartered, with a horrible laugh of ugly conceit to top the whole, rendered him Shakespeare's Malvolio at all points. (1 124)

The relationship between stage performance and literary interpretation is one of mutual influence, however, and in Boaden's description of Mrs Jordan's Viola ('the mere melody of her utterance brought tears into the eyes') the characteristic emphases of Romantic criticism are apparent. But to what extent that was indebted to Hazlitt, for whom 'the great and secret charm of *Twelfth Night* is the character of Viola', or to what extent the actors and actresses towards the end of the previous century anticipated and inspired the interpretations of the Romantic critics it is difficult to decide. There is little doubt, however, that Lamb's conception of Malvolio was the direct inspiration of Henry Irving's 'gaunt and sombre steward' later in the nineteenth century.

Not until 1912, with Harley Granville-Barker's production of the play, did the reaction set in against a nineteenth-century tradition of actresses who exploited their femininity in what Boaden called the 'infinite delicacy and enchanting eloquence' of Viola. Granville-Barker pointed out that Shakespeare wrote the part for a boy, not for a Victorian lady. To gauge the extent of Granville-Barker's revolt, we may compare William Winter's account of a very successful Viola, that of the American actress Ada Rehan ('Viola, when, as Cesario, she has captured the fancy of Olivia, although she may view that ludicrous dilemma archly, and even with a spice of innocent mischief, feels a woman's sympathy with the emotions of her sex, and her conduct toward Olivia is refined and considerate'), with Granville-Barker's strictures on actresses 'guilty of dramatic bad manners' : 'It is the common practice for actresses of Viola to seize every chance of reminding the audience that they are girls dressed up, to impress on one, moreover, by childish byplay as to legs and petticoats or the absence of them, that this is the play's supreme joke.' John Masefield's comment to Granville-Barker after seeing his production, that 'the women scenes were never once allowed to drop to the dreamy and emotional', is in itself a reflection upon the excesses of the tradition that began with Hazlitt.

III

Twentieth-century interpretations of *Twelfth Night* have found
its particular excellence, not in any single element of the play,
but in the integration of its parts to form one perfectly balanced
whole. This quality of balance is emphasised by H. B. Charlton,
who, if he is in one sense the last of the Romantic critics, is also
the founder of the modern interpretation of Shakespearian
comedy. According to Charlton, in this play and in *As You
Like It*, the equilibrium of feeling, intuition, and native wit in
the heroines provides a point of reference whereby 'the rich
variety of theme, of episode, and of person in these plays is knit
together and holds as a coherent structure'. The poise and
balance of the comedy are therefore an expression of the values
it upholds, not simply a matter of formal dramatic unity in the
narrower sense. A parallel conclusion is reached by C. L. Barber, whose study of the comedies is probably the most influential
since Charlton's. The equipoise and easy grace which Charlton
describes in *Twelfth Night* are referred by Barber to the Renaissance ideals of courtesy and decorum, and the play as he
sees it is 'an exhibition of the use and abuse of social liberty', in
which Malvolio comes off badly because he lacks that 'free
disposition' which is the basis of courtesy and of festive liberty,
as it is the saving grace of the other characters in their various
follies.

The image of the dance is used in Joseph Summers's interpretation of the play as a kind of maskers' revel, in which characters move to the discovery of their real identities through
playing a series of roles, deceiving themselves as often as each
other. Mistaken identity, one of the commonest motifs in comic
plotting, thus becomes in *Twelfth Night* not merely a fortuitous
device for complicating the action (though even at this level
its deployment is extraordinarily skilful), but a means of exposing the fantasies and secret desires nourished by those in the

state of deception. As Porter Williams Jr argues, Shakespeare
manipulates the series of comic errors in the play to reveal
rather than obscure those processes in human nature which
eventually enable the happy ending to be brought about. And
in relation to the play's elucidation of design and coherence
from confusion and contradiction, my own essay tries to show
how mutability and impermanence in nature is resolved into
that perfection and fixity of form which belongs only to art.

If Malvolio was singled out by the seventeenth century, and
Viola by the nineteenth, Feste has come into his own in the
present century. The attention he has received from modern
criticism may partly be due to a contemporary admiration for
his sceptical and detached intelligence, but our concern with
form and structure also brings him into prominence, since Feste
occupies a central position, linking main plot to sub-plot, and
bringing to the surface the play's major themes in his name,
his wit, and his songs. A. C. Bradley's essay somewhat senti-
mentalises the Fool in appealing to our sympathy for his
humiliating dependence upon insensitive patrons and for his
seeming incapacity to make personal attachments; but Bradley
also recognises the realism and sanity of Feste's attitude to
the world he lives in, and his total professional dedication to
his art. As an antidote to Bradley's concern with Feste's personal problems, we can turn to Miss Bradbrook's account of
Robert Armin, the professional fool for whom Shakespeare
created the part of Feste (and also those of Touchstone and
Lear's Fool): Miss Bradbrook suggests how much Shakespeare owed to Armin's particular brand of wise fooling (which
followed the learned tradition of Erasmus and More), not only
in conceiving Feste's role, but in placing it at the centre of universal folly. The songs of *Twelfth Night* also belong to Feste,
and, like his witty games with language and logic, they subtly
refract the situations of the dramatic action, both verbally and
musically. Music of several kinds pervades the play, and, as
John Hollander observes, its dramatic significance resides in its

power to move the passions (like Viola's rhetoric) as well as in its contribution to the spirit of revelry.

Such a finely balanced and yet richly orchestrated composition as *Twelfth Night* obviously accommodates interpretative approaches from many different angles. It is a play that offers some new revelation and fresh insight at each performance or reading. In the words of John Russell Brown, 'a single view of the play is continually growing in complexity and range, and in understanding', and his essay, exploring the text 'in the search for a comprehensive style' of stage production, reminds us that the vitality and charm of *Twelfth Night* depend upon visual as well as aural effects. The play, in its eloquence of wit, harmony and feeling, in its creation of a world of make-believe and revelry, and in its mobility of tone and mood, belongs essentially to the theatre. Even Dr Johnson's objections to its improbabilities conceded that they are 'well enough contrived to divert on the stage', and this is surely a fundamental though not a final test of its quality. Although literary criticism has its own idiom and evaluative techniques, critical interpretation of *Twelfth Night* is at its best when it respects and even enhances the experience of the play in the theatre.

D. J. PALMER

Note: Quotations and references to Shakespeare's plays throughout this Casebook have been standardised according to the text of *The Complete Works*, edited by Peter Alexander (1951).

PART ONE

Performance, Adaptation and Comment, 1602–1912

JOHN MANNINGHAM

At our feast wee had a play called 'Twelve Night, or What You Will', much like the Commedy of Errores, or Menechmi in Plautus, but most like and neere to that in Italian called *Inganni*. A good practise in it to make the Steward beleeve his Lady widdowe was in love with him, by counterfeyting a letter as from his Lady in generall termes, telling him what shee liked best in him, and prescribing his gesture in smiling, his apparaile, &c., and then when he came to practise making him beleeve they tooke him to be mad.

(from John Manningham's Diary, 2 February 1601/2)

LEONARD DIGGES

... loe in a trice
The Cockpit Galleries, Boxes, all are full
To heare *Malvoglio* that crosse garter'd Gull.
(from commendatory verses for Shakespeare's *Poems*,
1640)

SAMUEL PEPYS

To the Duke's house, and there saw Twelfth-Night acted well, though it be but a silly play, and not relating at all to the name or day.

(from Samuel Pepys's Diary, Twelfth Day, 6 January 1662/3)

WILLIAM BURNABY

Act II Scene i

Scene opens, and discovers Moreno *on a couch, and* Caesario *kneeling by.*

Caesario. (Sings.)

I

If I hear Orinda *swear,*
  She cures my jealous Smart;
The Treachery becomes the Fair,
  And doubly fires my Heart.

II

Beauty's Strength and Treasure,
  In Falsehood still remain;
She gives the greatest Pleasure,
  That gives the greatest Pain.

  Soft Musick, after which, Moreno *rises.*

Mor. 'If Musick be the Food of Love, play on!
  'Give me excess of it, that surfeiting
  'Thet Appetite may sicken, and so die.
  But oh! in vain, the pleasing Sounds once o'er
  Are lost for ever! – no Memory recalls
  The Pleasure past, but that which wounds us lives!
  How true a Wretch is Man!
  The mute Creation Nature has supply'd
  With Arts and Arms for their Defence and Safety;
  The Deer has Horns, and Subtlety the Fox,
  The Porcupine still bears upon his Back
  A Grove of Arrows to distress his Foe;
  But the unhappy Lord of all is made,
  With Darts turn'd inward on himself,
  His own Destroyer –
  His Passions and his Faculties are given,
  To war with his own Quiet – Oh Distraction!
  Let me embrace thee –
  For only they are happy who are Mad!
                    (*Throws himself on the Couch.*)

Caes. (*Aside.*) Alas! I pity his Distress,
  Tho' I'm overjoy'd at the occasion – My Lord try to sleep.
Mor. Poor *Caesario*! thou art too young for Cares,
  Or thou hadst known, they follow us in Sleep.
  Physicians poyson in their Sleep,
  Lawyers undoe in their Sleep,
  Courtiers get new Grants in their Sleep –
  Nothing in Nature's quite at rest,
  But the slick Prelate –
Caes. Right! my Lord, and the other Sex have their Fancies
too – Old Women Back-bite and Pray in their Sleep; Young-
ones Sigh and Dance in their Sleep; and Maids of thirty set
up for Virtue, and Dress in their Sleep.
Mor. Pretty Boy! Thy Manners are so soft, thy Sense so
quick at every Turn; thou should'st be older than thou seem'st
to be – Hast ever been in Love?
Caes. A little my Lord –
Mor. 'Tis that has form'd thy Mind.
  For Love, the kind refiner of the Soul,
  Softens harsh Nature's Work, and tempers Man:
  Without it, all are Salvages –
  What sort of Woman?
Caes. One very like your Lordship.
Mor. By so much the less meriting – Did she love you?
Caes. She kist me often, and told me so, but did not love me.
Mor. Trust 'em no more, they're all –
Caes. O! hold, my Lord, some are Just, and Love as well as
    we.
  'My Father had a Daughter lov'd a Man,
  'As it might be, perhaps, were I a Woman,
  'I shou'd your Highness.
Mor. And what's her Story?
Caes. 'A Blank, my Lord – She never told her Love,

'But let Concealment, like a Worm i' th' Bud,
'Feed on her Damask Cheek –
– – – She languish'd long,
Courting the Shade, the Night still found her weeping,
Nor cou'd the Sun e'er dry her Tears away,
'Till pining with distressful Melancholy
'She sate like Patience on a Monument, smiling at Grief.
Reduc'd to these extreams, at last I –

                                      (*She blushes.*)

Mor. How's that, *Caesario*?

Caes. I don't – you forget, my Lord, to send me to the Lady.
                                       (*Shewing a Letter.*)

Mor. Right! my dear Boy, go bear it to her now,
And plead thy self the Cause of Love and Me;
Thou hast a soft insinuating Way,
May sooth her Anger, and delude her Scorn.
But if her People shou'd deny thee entrance –

Caes. I warrant ye, my Lord, I get admittance; I'll Storm
the House, and Beat the Servants; my Youth, and your
Indulgence will protect me.

Mor. Nay! Women, Children, and Priests, they say, can
affront no body, so thou art safe.

Caes. O! very safe, my Lord, doubly safe.

Mor. Dear *Caesario*, take this and prosper, (*Kisses her.*)
Urge my Passion to her, and my Faith.

Caes. As zealously, as if your Favour depended on the Success; and if Fortune is but kind –

Mor. Invoke thy own good Stars, for I have none.

Caes. Most faithfully, my Lord, and hope this Affair will be
govern'd by 'em.

                 (*Exeunt severally.*)

            (from *Love Betray'd; or, The Agreable Disappointment,* 1703)

SAMUEL JOHNSON

This play is in the graver part elegant and easy, and in some of the lighter scenes exquisitely humorous. *Ague-cheek* is drawn with great propriety, but his character is, in a great measure, that of natural fatuity, and is therefore not the proper prey of a satirist. The soliloquy of *Malvolio* is truly comick; he is betrayed to ridicule merely by his pride. The marriage of *Olivia*, and the succeeding perplexity, though well enough contrived to divert on the stage, wants credibility, and fails to produce the proper instruction required in the drama, as it exhibits no just picture of life.

(Note from Johnson's edition of *The Works of William Shakespear*, 1765)

WILLIAM HAZLITT: The Comedy of Nature

This is justly considered as one of the most delightful of Shakespear's comedies. It is full of sweetness and pleasantry. It is perhaps too good-natured for comedy. It has little satire, and no spleen. It aims at the ludicrous rather than the ridiculous. It makes us laugh at the follies of mankind, not despise them, and still less bear any ill-will towards them. Shakespear's comic genius resembles the bee rather in its power of extracting sweets from weeds or poisons, than in leaving a sting behind it. He gives the most amusing exaggeration of the prevailing foibles of his characters, but in a way that they themselves, instead of being offended at, would almost join in to humour; he rather contrives opportunities for them to shew themselves off in the happiest lights, than renders them contemptible in the perverse construction of the wit or malice of others. – There is a certain stage of society in which people become conscious of their peculiarities and absurdities, affect to disguise what they are, and set up pretensions to what they are not. This gives rise to a corresponding style of comedy, the object of which is to detect

the disguises of self-love, and to make reprisals on these preposterous assumptions of vanity, by marking the contrast between the real and the affected character as severely as possible,
and denying to those, who would impose on us for what they
are not, even the merit which they have. This is the comedy of
artificial life, of wit and satire, such as we see it in Congreve,
Wycherley, Vanbrugh, &c. To this succeeds a state of society
from which the same sort of affectation and pretence are ban-
ished by a greater knowledge of the world or by their successful
exposure on the stage; and which by neutralising the materials
of comic character, both natural and artificial, leaves no comedy
at all – but *the sentimental.* Such is our modern comedy. There
is a period in the progress of manners anterior to both these, in
which the foibles and follies of individuals are of nature's plant-
ing, not the growth of art or study; in which they are therefore
unconscious of them themselves, or care not who knows them,
if they can but have their whim out; and in which, as there is
no attempt at imposition, the spectators rather receive pleasure
from humouring the inclinations of the persons they laugh at,
than wish to give them pain by exposing their absurdity. This
may be called the comedy of nature, and it is the comedy which
we generally find in Shakespear. – Whether the analysis here
given be just or not, the spirit of his comedies is evidently quite
distinct from that of the authors above mentioned, as it is in its
essence the same with that of Cervantes, and also very frequently of Molière, though he was more systematic in his
extravagance than Shakespear. Shakespear's comedy is of a
pastoral and poetical cast. Folly is indigenous to the soil, and
shoots out with native, happy, unchecked luxuriance. Absurdity has every encouragement afforded it; and nonsense has
room to flourish in. Nothing is stunted by the churlish, icy
hand of indifference or severity. The poet runs riot in a conceit, and idolises a quibble. His whole object is to turn the
meanest or rudest objects to a pleasurable account. The relish
which he has of a pun, or of the quaint humour of a low

character, does not interfere with the delight with which he described a beautiful image, or the most refined love. The clown's forced jests do not spoil the sweetness of the character of Viola; the same house is big enough to hold Malvolio, the Countess, Maria, Sir Toby, and Sir Andrew Ague-cheek. For instance, nothing can fall much lower than this last character in intellect or morals: yet how are his weaknesses nursed and dandled by Sir Toby into something 'high fantastical', when on Sir Andrew's commendation of himself for dancing and fencing, Sir Toby answers – 'Wherefore are these things hid? Wherefore have these gifts a curtain before 'em? Are they like to take dust, like mistress Mall's picture? Why dost thou not go to church in a galliard, and come home in a coranto? My very walk should be a jig; I would not so much as make water but in a sink-a-pace. What dost thou mean? Is it a world to hide virtues in? I did think by the excellent constitution of thy leg, it was form'd under the star of a galliard!' – How Sir Toby, Sir Andrew, and the Clown afterwards *chirp over their cups,* how they 'rouse the night-owl in a catch that will draw thee three souls out of one weaver!' What can be better than Sir Toby's unanswerable answer to Malvolio, 'Dost thou think, because thou art virtuous, there shall be no more cakes and ale?' – In a word, the best turn is given to every thing, instead of the worst. There is a constant infusion of the romantic and enthusiastic, in proportion as the characters are natural and sincere: whereas, in the more artificial style of comedy, every thing gives way to ridicule and indifference, there being nothing left but affectation on one side, and incredulity on the other. – Much as we like Shakespear's comedies, we cannot agree with Dr Johnson that they are better than his tragedies; nor do we like them half so well. If his inclination to comedy sometimes led him to trifle with the seriousness of tragedy, the poetical and impassioned passages are the best parts of his comedies. The great and secret charm of *Twelfth Night* is the character of Viola. Much as we like catches and cakes and ale,

there is something that we like better. We have a friendship for
Sir Toby; we patronise Sir Andrew; we have an understanding
with the Clown, a sneaking kindness for Maria and her
rogueries; we feel a regard for Malvolio, and sympathise with
his gravity, his smiles, his cross garters, his yellow stockings,
and imprisonment in the stocks. But there is something that
excites in us a stronger feeling than all this – it is Viola's confession of her love.

> *Duke.* What's her history?
> *Viola. A blank, my lord. She never told her love:*
>   But let concealment, like a worm i' th' bud,
>   Feed on her damask cheek. She pin'd in thought,
>   And with a green and yellow melancholy
>   She sat like Patience on a monument,
>   Smiling at grief. *Was not this love indeed?*
>   We men may say more, swear more, but indeed,
>   Our shows are more than will; for still we prove
>   Much in our vows, but little in our love.
> *Duke.* But died thy sister of her love, my boy?
> *Viola.* I am all the daughters of my father's house,
>   And all the brothers too – and yet I know not. –

Shakespear alone could describe the effect of his own poetry.

> O, it came o'er my ear like the sweet sound
> That breathes upon a bank of violets,
> Stealing and giving odour.

What we so much admire here is not the image of Patience
on a monument, which has been generally quoted, but the lines
before and after it. 'They give a very echo to the seat where love
is throned.' How long ago it is since we first learnt to repeat
them; and still, still they vibrate on the heart, like the sounds
which the passing wind draws from the trembling strings of a
harp left on some desert shore! There are other passages of not
less impassioned sweetness. Such is Olivia's address to Sebastian,
whom she supposes to have already deceived her in a promise
of marriage.

Blame not this haste of mine. If you mean well,
Now go with me and with this holy man
Into the chantry by; there, before him
And underneath that consecrated roof,
Plight me the full assurance of your faith,
That my most jealous and too doubtful soul
May live at peace.

We have already said something of Shakespear's songs. One
of the most beautiful of them occurs in this play, with a preface
of his own to it.

Duke. O, fellow, come, the song we had last night.
  Mark it, Cesario; it is old and plain;
  The spinsters and the knitters in the sun,
  And the free maids that weave their thread with bones,
  Do use to chant it; it is silly sooth,
  And dallies with the innocence of love,
  Like the old age.

SONG.

Come away, come away, death;
And in sad cypress let me be laid;
  Fly away, fly away, breath,
I am slain by a fair cruel maid.
  My shroud of white, stuck all with yew,
        O, prepare it!
My part of death no one so true
        Did share it.

Not a flower, not a flower sweet,
On my black coffin let there be strown;
  Not a friend, not a friend greet
My poor corpse where my bones shall be thrown;
  A thousand thousand sighs to save,
        Lay me, O, where
Sad true lover never find my grave,
        To weep there!

T.N.—B

Who after this will say that Shakespear's genius was only fitted for comedy? Yet after reading other parts of this play, and particularly the garden-scene where Malvolio picks up the letter, if we were to say that his genius for comedy was less than his genius for tragedy, it would perhaps only prove that our own taste in such matters is more saturnine than mercurial.

Enter MARIA.

Sir Toby. Here comes the little villain. How now, my metal of India!

Maria. Get ye all three into the box-tree. Malvolio's coming down this walk. He has been yonder i' the sun practising behaviour to his own shadow this half hour. Observe him, for the love of mockery, for I know this letter will make a contemplative idiot of him. Close, in the name of jesting! Lie thou there; for here comes the trout that must be caught with tickling.

[*They hide themselves. Maria throws down a letter, and Exit.*

Enter MALVOLIO.

Malvolio. 'Tis but fortune; all is fortune. Maria once told me she did affect me; and I have heard herself come thus near, that, should she fancy, it should be one of my complexion. Besides, she uses me with a more exalted respect than any one else that follows her. What should I think on't?

Sir Toby. Here's an overweening rogue!

Fabian. O, peace! Contemplation makes a rare turkey-cock of him; how he jets under his advanc'd plumes!

Sir Andrew. 'Slight, I could so beat the rogue –

Sir Toby. Peace, I say.

Malvolio. To be Count Malvolio!

Sir Toby. Ah, rogue!

Sir Andrew. Pistol him, pistol him.

Sir Toby. Peace, peace!

Malvolio. There is example for't; the Lady of the Strachy married the yeoman of the wardrobe.

Sir Andrew. Fie on him, Jezebel!

Fabian. O, peace! now he's deeply in; look how imagination blows him.

Malvolio. Having been three months married to her, sitting in my chair of state –

Sir Toby. O, for a stone-bow to hit him in the eye!

Malvolio. Calling my officers about me, in my branch'd velvet gown, having come from a day-bed – where I have left Olivia sleeping –

Sir Toby. Fire and brimstone!

Fabian. O, peace, peace!

Malvolio. And then to have the humour of state; and after a demure travel of regard, telling them I know my place as I would they should do theirs, to ask for my kinsman Toby –

Sir Toby. Bolts and shackles!

Fabian. O, peace, peace, peace! now, now.

Malvolio. Seven of my people, with an obedient start, make out for him. I frown the while, and perchance wind up my watch, or play with my – some rich jewel. Toby approaches; curtsies there to me –

Sir Toby. Shall this fellow live?

Fabian. Though our silence be drawn from us with cars, yet peace.

Malvolio. I extend my hand to him thus, quenching my familiar smile with an austere regard of control –

Sir Toby. And does not Toby take you a blow o' the lips then?

Malvolio. Saying 'Cousin Toby, my fortunes having cast me on your niece, give me this prerogative of speech' –

Sir Toby. What, what?

Malvolio. 'You must amend your drunkenness' –

Fabian. Nay, patience, or we break the sinews of our plot.

Malvolio. 'Besides, you waste the treasure of your time with a foolish knight' –

Sir Andrew. That's me, I warrant you.

Malvolio. 'One Sir Andrew'.

Sir Andrew. I knew, 'twas I; for many do call me fool.

Malvolio. What employment have we here?

[Taking up the letter.

The letter and his comments on it are equally good. If poor Malvolio's treatment afterwards is a little hard, poetical justice is done in the uneasiness which Olivia suffers on account of her mistaken attachment to Cesario, as her insensibility to the

violence of the Duke's passion is atoned for by the discovery
of Viola's concealed love of him.

(from Characters of Shakespear's Plays, 1817)

CHARLES LAMB: On Some of the Old Actors

The casual sight of an old Play Bill, which I picked up the
other day – I know not by what chance it was preserved so
long – tempts me to call to mind a few of the Players, who make
the principal figure in it. It presents the cast of parts in the
Twelfth Night, at the old Drury Lane Theatre two-and-thirty
years ago. There is something very touching in these old re-
membrances. They make us think how we *once* used to read a
Play Bill – not, as now peradventure, singling out a favourite
performer, and casting a negligent eye over the rest; but spell-
ing out every name, down to the very mutes and servants of
the scene; – when it was a matter of no small moment to us
whether Whitfield, or Packer, took the part of Fabian; when
Benson, and Burton, and Phillimore – names of small account
– had an importance, beyond what we can be content to attribute now to the time's best actors. – 'Orsino, by Mr Barrymore.'
– What a full Shakspearian sound it carries! how fresh to
memory arise the image, and the manner, of the gentle actor!

Those who have only seen Mrs Jordan within the last ten
or fifteen years, can have no adequate notion of her performance of such parts as Ophelia; Helena, in *All's Well that Ends
Well*; and Viola in this play. Her voice had latterly acquired
a coarseness, which suited well enough with her Nells and Hoy-
dens, but in those days it sank, with her steady melting eye, into
the heart. Her joyous parts – in which her memory now chiefly
lives – in her youth were outdone by her plaintive ones. There
is no giving an account how she delivered the disguised story
of her love for Orsino. It was no set speech, that she had foreseen, so as to weave it into an harmonious period, line necessarily following line, to make up the music – yet I have heard

it so spoken, or rather *read*, not without its grace and beauty –
but, when she had declared her sister's history to be a 'blank',
and that she 'never told her love', there was a pause, as if the
story had ended – and then the image of the 'worm in the
bud' came up as a new suggestion – and the heightened image
of 'Patience' still followed after that, as by some growing (and
not mechanical) process, thought springing up after thought,
I would almost say, as they were watered by her tears. So in
those fine lines –

> Write loyal cantos of contemned love –
> Hollow your name to the reverberate hills –

there was no preparation made in the foregoing image for that
which was to follow. She used no rhetoric in her passion; or
it was nature's own rhetoric, most legitimate then, when it
seemed altogether without rule or law.

Mrs Powel (now Mrs Renard), then in the pride of her
beauty, made an admirable Olivia. She was particularly excellent in her unbending scenes in conversation with the Clown.
I have seen some Olivias – and those very sensible actresses
too – who in those interlocutions have seemed to set their wits
at the jester, and to vie conceits with him in downright emula-
tion. But she used him for her sport, like what he was, to trifle
a leisure sentence or two with, and then to be dismissed, and
she to be the Great Lady still. She touched the imperious fantastic humour of the character with nicety. Her fine spacious
person filled the scene.

The part of Malvolio has in my judgment been so often
misunderstood, and the *general merits* of the actor, who then
played it, so unduly appreciated, that I shall hope for pardon,
if I am a little prolix upon these points.

Of all the actors who flourished in my time – a melancholy
phrase if taken aright, reader – Bensley had most of the swell
of soul, was greatest in the delivery of heroic conceptions, the
emotions consequent upon the presentment of a great idea to

the fancy. He had the true poetical enthusiasm – the rarest
faculty among players. None that I remember possessed even
a portion of that fine madness which he threw out in Hotspur's
famous rant about glory, or the transports of the Venetian
incendiary at the vision of the fired city. His voice had the dis-
sonance, and at times the inspiriting effect of the trumpet. His
gait was uncouth and stiff, but no way embarrassed by affectation; and the thorough-bred gentleman was uppermost in
every movement. He seized the moment of passion with the
greatest truth; like a faithful clock, never striking before the
time : never anticipating or leading you to anticipate. He was
totally destitute of trick and artifice. He seemed come upon the
stage to do the poet's message simply, and he did it with as
genuine fidelity as the nuncios in Homer deliver the errands of
the gods. He let the passion or the sentiment do its own work
without prop or bolstering. He would have scorned to mounte-
bank it; and betrayed none of that *cleverness* which is the bane
of serious acting. For this reason, his Iago was the only endur-
able one which I remember to have seen. No spectator from
his action could divine more of his artifice than Othello was
supposed to do. His confessions in soliloquy alone put you in
possession of the mystery. There were no by-intimations to
make the audience fancy their own discernment so much
greater than that of the Moor – who commonly stands like a
great helpless mark set up for mine Ancient, and a quantity
of barren spectators, to shoot their bolts at. The Iago of Bensley
did not go to work so grossly. There was a triumphant tone
about the character, natural to a general consciousness of
power; but none of that petty vanity which chuckles and cannot contain itself upon any little successful stroke of its knavery
– as is common with your small villains and green probationers
in mischief. It did not clap or crow before its time. It was not a
man setting his wits at a child, and winking all the while at
other children who are mightily pleased at being let into the
secret; but a consummate villain entrapping a noble nature

into toils, against which no discernment was available, where
the manner was as fathomless as the purpose seemed dark, and
without motive. The part of Malvolio, in the *Twelfth Night*,
was performed by Bensley, with a richness and a dignity, of
which (to judge from some recent castings of that character)
the very tradition must be worn out from the stage. No mana-
ger in those days would have dreamed of giving it to Mr
Baddeley, or Mr Parsons; when Bensley was occasionally absent
from the theatre, John Kemble thought it no derogation to
succeed to the part. Malvolio is not essentially ludicrous. He
becomes comic but by accident. He is cold, austere, repelling;
but dignified, consistent, and, for what appears, rather of an
over-stretched morality. Maria describes him as a sort of Puritan; and he might have worn his gold chain with honour in one
of our old round-head families, in the service of a Lambert, or
a Lady Fairfax. But his morality and his manners are misplaced
in Illyria. He is opposed to the proper *levities* of the piece, and
falls in the unequal contest. Still his pride, or his gravity, (call
it which you will) is inherent, and native to the man, not mock
or affected, which latter only are the fit objects to excite laughter. His quality is at the best unlovely, but neither buffoon nor
contemptible. His bearing is lofty, a little above his station, but
probably not much above his deserts. We see no reason why he
should not have been brave, honourable, accomplished. His
careless committal of the ring to the ground (which he was
commissioned to restore to Cesario), bespeaks a generosity of
birth and feeling. His dialect on all occasions is that of a gentleman, and a man of education. We must not confound him
with the eternal old, low steward of comedy. He is master of
the household to a great Princess; a dignity probably conferred
upon him for other respects than age or length of service.
Olivia, at the first indication of his supposed madness, declares
that she 'would not have him miscarry for half of her dowry'.
Does this look as if the character was meant to appear little or
insignificant? Once, indeed, she accuses him to his face – of

what? – of being 'sick of self-love', – but with a gentleness and considerateness which could not have been, if she had not thought that this particular infirmity shaded some virtues. His rebuke to the knight, and his sottish revellers, is sensible and spirited; and when we take into consideration the unprotected condition of his mistress, and the strict regard with which her state of real or dissembled mourning would draw the eyes of the world upon her house-affairs, Malvolio might feel the honour of the family in some sort in his keeping; as it appears not that Olivia had any more brothers, or kinsmen, to look to it – for Sir Toby had dropped all such nice respects at the buttery hatch. That Malvolio was meant to be represented as possessing estimable qualities, the expression of the Duke in his anxiety to have him reconciled, almost infers. 'Pursue him, and entreat him to a peace.' Even in his abused state of chains and darkness, a sort of greatness seems never to desert him. He argues highly and well with the supposed Sir Topas, and philosophises gallantly upon his straw.[1] There must have been some shadow of worth about the man; he must have been something more than a mere vapour – a thing of straw, or Jack in office – before Fabian and Maria could have ventured sending him upon a courting-errand to Olivia. There was some consonancy (as he would say) in the undertaking, or the jest would have been too bold even for that house of misrule.

Bensley, accordingly, threw over the part an air of Spanish loftiness. He looked, spake, and moved like an old Castilian. He was starch, spruce, opinionated, but his superstructure of pride seemed bottomed upon a sense of worth. There was something in it beyond the coxcomb. It was big and swelling, but you could not be sure that it was hollow. You might wish to see it taken down, but you felt that it was upon an elevation. He was magnificent from the outset; but when the decent sobrieties of the character began to give way, and the poison of self-love, in his conceit of the Countess's affection, gradually to work, you would have thought that the hero of La Mancha in person stood before you. How he went smiling to himself! with what ineffable carelessness would he twirl his gold chain! what a dream it was! you were infected with the illusion, and did not wish that it should be removed! you had no room for laughter! if an unseasonable reflection of morality obtruded itself, it was a deep sense of the pitiable infirmity of man's nature, that can lay him open to such frenzies – but in truth you rather admired than pitied the lunacy while it lasted – you felt that an hour of such mistake was worth an age with the eyes open. Who would not wish to live but for a day in the conceit of such a lady's love as Olivia? Why, the Duke would have given his principality but for a quarter of a minute, sleeping or waking, to have been so deluded. The man seemed to tread upon air, to taste manna, to walk with his head in the clouds, to mate Hyperion. O! shake not the castles of his pride – endure yet for a season bright moments of confidence – 'stand still ye watches of the element', that Malvolio may be still in fancy fair Olivia's lord – but fate and retribution say no – I hear the mischievous titter of Maria – the witty taunts of Sir Toby – the still more insupportable triumph of the foolish knight – the counterfeit Sir Topas is unmasked – and 'thus the whirligig of time', as the true clown hath it, 'brings in his revenges'. I confess that I never saw the catastrophe of this character, while Bensley played it, without a kind of tragic interest. There was good foolery too. Few now remember Dodd. What an Aguecheek the stage lost in him! Lovegrove, who came nearest to the old actors, revived the character some few seasons ago, and made it sufficiently grotesque; but Dodd was *it*, as it came out of nature's hands. It might be said to remain *in puris naturalibus*. In expressing slowness of apprehension this actor surpassed all others. You could see the first dawn of an idea stealing slowly over his countenance, climbing up by little and little, with a painful process, till it cleared up at last to the fulness of a twilight conception – its highest meridian. He seemed to keep back his intellect, as some have had the power to retard their pulsation. The balloon takes less time in filling, than it took to cover the expansion of his broad moony face over all its quarters with expression. A glimmer of understanding would appear in a corner of his eye, and for lack of fuel go out again. A part of his forehead would catch a little intelligence, and be a long time in communicating it to the remainder.

I am ill at dates, but I think it is now better than five and twenty years ago that walking in the gardens of Gray's Inn – they were then far finer than they are now – the accursed Verulam Buildings had not encroached upon all the east side of them, cutting out delicate green crankles, and shouldering away one of two of the stately alcoves of the terrace – the survivor stands gaping and relationless as if it remembered its brother – they are still the best gardens of any of the Inns of Court, my beloved Temple not forgotten – have the gravest character, their aspect being altogether reverend and law breathing – Bacon has left the impress of his foot upon their gravel walks – taking my afternoon solace on a summer day upon the aforesaid terrace, a comely, sad personage came towards me, whom, from his grave air and deportment, I judged to be one of the old Benchers of the Inn. He had a serious thoughtful forehead, and seemed to be in meditations of mortality. As I have an instinctive awe of old Benchers, I was passing him with that sort of subindicative token of respect which one is apt to demonstrate towards a venerable stranger, and which rather denotes an inclination to greet him, than any positive motion of the body to that effect – a species of humility and will-worship which I observe, nine times out of ten, rather puzzles than pleases the person it is offered to – when the face turning full upon me strangely identified itself with that of Dodd. Upon close inspection I was not mistaken. But could this sad thoughtful countenance be the same vacant face of folly which I had hailed so often under circumstances of gaiety; which I had never seen without a smile, or recognised but as the usher of mirth; that looked out so formally flat in Foppington, so froth-ily pert in Tattle, so impotently busy in Backbite; so blankly divested of all meaning, or resolutely expressive of none, in Acres, in Fribble, and a thousand agreeable impertinences? Was this the face – full of thought and carefulness – that had so often divested itself at will of every trace of either to give me diversion, to clear my cloudy face for two or three hours at least of its furrows? Was this the face – manly, sober, intelli-gent, – which I had so often despised, made mocks at, made merry with? The remembrance of the freedoms which I had taken with it came upon me with a reproach of insult. I could have asked it pardon. I thought it looked upon me with a sense of injury. There is something strange as well as sad in seeing actors – your pleasant fellows particularly – subjected to and suffering the common lot – their fortunes, their casualties, their deaths, seem to belong to the scene, their actions to be amen-able to poetic justice only. We can hardly connect them with more awful responsibilities. The death of this fine actor took place shortly after this meeting. He had quitted the stage some months; and, as I learned afterwards, had been in the habit of resorting daily to these gardens almost to the day of his decease. In these serious walks probably he was divesting himself of many scenic and some real vanities – weaning himself from the frivolities of the lesser and the greater theatre – doing gentle penance for a life of no very reprehensible fooleries, – taking off by degrees the buffoon mask which he might feel he had worn too long – and rehearsing for a more solemn cast of part. Dying he 'put on the weeds of Dominic'.[2]

If few can remember Dodd, many yet living will not easily forget the pleasant creature, who in those days enacted the part of the Clown to Dodd's Sir Andrew. – Richard, or rather Dicky Suett – for so in his life-time he delighted to be called, and time hath ratified the appellation – lieth buried on the north side of the cemetery of Holy Paul, to whose service his nonage and tender years were dedicated. There are who do yet remember him at that period – his pipe clear and harmonious. He would often speak of his chorister days, when he was 'cherub Dicky'.

What clipped his wings, or made it expedient that he should exchange the holy for the profane state; whether he had lost his good voice (his best recommendation to that office), like Sir John, 'with hallooing and singing of anthems'; or whether he was adjudged to lack something, even in those early years, of the gravity indispensable to an occupation which professeth to 'commerce with the skies' – I could never rightly learn; but we find him, after the probation of a twelvemonth or so, reverting to a secular condition, and become one of us.

I think he was not altogether of that timber, out of which cathedral seats and sounding boards are hewed. But if a glad heart – kind and therefore glad – be any part of sanctity, then might the robe of Motley, with which he invested himself with so much humility after his deprivation, and which he wore so long with so much blameless satisfaction to himself and to the public, be accepted for a surplice – his white stole, and *albe*.

The first fruits of his secularisation was an engagement upon the boards of Old Drury, at which theatre he commenced, as I have been told, with adopting the manner of Parsons in old men's characters. At the period in which most of us knew him, he was no more an imitator than he was in any true sense himself imitable.

He was the Robin Good-Fellow of the stage. He came in to trouble all things with a welcome perplexity, himself no whit troubled for the matter. He was known, like Puck, by his note – *Ha! Ha! Ha!* – sometimes deepening to *Ho! Ho! Ho!* with an irresistible accession, derived perhaps remotely from his ecclesiastical education, foreign to his prototype of, – *O La!* Thousands of hearts yet respond to the chuckling *O La!* of Dicky Suett, brought back to their remembrance by the faithful transcript of his friend Mathews's mimicry. The 'force of nature

could no further go'. He drolled upon the stock of these two
syllables richer than the cuckoo.

Care, that troubles all the world, was forgotten in his composition. Had he had but two grains (nay, half a grain) of it,
he could never have supported himself upon those two spider's
strings, which served him (in the latter part of his unmixed
existence) as legs. A doubt or a scruple must have made him
totter, a sigh have puffed him down; the weight of a frown
had staggered him, a wrinkle made him lose his balance. But
on he went, scrambling upon those airy stilts of his, with Robin
Good-Fellow, 'thorough brake, thorough briar', reckless of a
scratched face or a torn doublet.

Shakspeare foresaw him, when he framed his fools and
jesters. They have all the true Suett stamp, a loose and shamb-
ling gait, a slippery tongue, this last the ready midwife to a
without-pain-delivered jest; in words, light as air, venting
truths deep as the centre; with idlest rhymes tagging conceit
when busiest, singing with Lear in the tempest, or Sir Toby
at the buttery-hatch.

Jack Bannister and he had the fortune to be more of personal favourites with the town than any actors before or after.
The difference, I take it, was this : – Jack was more *beloved*
for his sweet, good-natured, moral pretensions. Dicky was more
liked for his sweet, good-natured, no pretensions at all. Your
whole conscience stirred with Bannister's performance of
Walter in *The Children in the Wood* – but Dicky seemed like
a thing, as Shakspeare says of Love, too young to know what
conscience is. He puts us into Vesta's days. Evil fled before him
– not as from Jack, as from an antagonist, – but because it could
not touch him, any more than a cannon-ball a fly. He was delivered from the burthen of that death; and, when Death came
himself, not in metaphor, to fetch Dicky, it is recorded of him
by Robert Palmer, who kindly watched his exit, that he received
the last stroke, neither varying his accustomed tranquillity, nor

tune, with the simple exclamation, worthy to have been recorded in his epitaph – *O La! O La! Bobby!*

The elder Palmer (of stage-treading celebrity) commonly
played Sir Toby in those days; but there is a solidity of wit in
the jests of that half-Falstaff which he did not quite fill out.
He was as much too showy as Moody (who sometimes took the
part) was dry and sottish. In sock or buskin there was an air of
swaggering gentility about Jack Palmer. He was a *gentleman*
with a slight infusion of *the footman*. His brother Bob (of re-
center memory) who was his shadow in every thing while he
lived, and dwindled into less than a shadow afterwards – was
a *gentleman* with a little stronger infusion of the *latter ingredi-
ent*; that was all. It is amazing how a little of the more or less
makes a difference in these things. When you saw Bobby in the
Duke's Servant,³ you said, what a pity such a pretty fellow was
only a servant. When you saw Jack figuring in Captain Absolute, you thought you could trace his promotion to some lady
of quality who fancied the handsome follow in his topknot,
and had bought him a commission. Therefore Jack in Dick
Amulet was insuperable.

Jack had two voices, – both plausible, hypocritical, and insinuating; but his secondary or supplemental voice still more
decisively histrionic than his common one. It was reserved for
the spectator; and the dramatis personæ were supposed to know
nothing at all about it. The *lies* of young Wilding, and the *sentiments* in Joseph Surface, were thus marked out in a sort of
italics to the audience. This secret correspondence with the company before the curtain (which is the bane and death of tragedy) has an extremely happy effect in some kinds of comedy,
in the more highly artificial comedy of Congreve or of Sheridan
especially, where the absolute sense of reality (so indispensable
to scenes of interest) is not required, or would rather interfere
to diminish your pleasure. The fact is, you do not believe in
such characters as Surface – the villain of artificial comedy –
even while you read or see them. If you did, they would shock

and not divert you. When Ben, in *Love for Love*, returns from sea, the following exquisite dialogue occurs at his first meeting with his father –

Sir Sampson. Thou hast been many a weary league, Ben, since I saw thee.

Ben. Ey, ey, been! Been far enough, an that be all. – Well, father and how do all at home? how does brother Dick, and brother Val?

Sir Sampson. Dick! body o' me, Dick has been dead these two years. I writ you word when you were at Leghorn.

Ben. Mess, that's true; Marry, I had forgot. Dick's dead, as you say – Well, and how? – I have a many questions to ask you –

Here is an instance of insensibility which in real life would be revolting, or rather in real life could not have co-existed with the warm-hearted temperament of the character. But when you read it in the spirit with which such playful selections and specious combinations rather than strict *metaphrases* of nature should be taken, or when you saw Bannister play it, it neither did, nor does wound the moral sense at all. For what is Ben – the pleasant sailor which Bannister gives us – but a piece of satire – a creation of Congreve's fancy – a dreamy combination of all the accidents of a sailor's character – his contempt of money – his credulity to women – with that necessary estrangement from home which it is just within the verge of credibility to suppose *might* produce such an hallucination as is here described. We never think the worse of Ben for it, or feel it as a stain upon his character. But when an actor comes, and instead of the delightful phantom – the creature dear to half-belief – which Bannister exhibited – displays before our eyes a downright concretion of a Wapping sailor – a jolly warm-hearted Jack Tar – and nothing else – when instead of investing it with a delicious confusedness of the head, and a veering un-directed goodness of purpose – he gives to it a downright daylight understanding, and a full consciousness of its actions;

thrusting forward the sensibilities of the character with a pretence as if it stood upon nothing else, and was to be judged by
them alone – we feel the discord of the thing; the scene is dis-
turbed; a real man has got in among the dramatis personæ,
and puts them out. We want the sailor turned out. We feel
that his true place is not behind the curtain but in the first or
second gallery.

(from *Elia's Essays*, 1823)

NOTES

1. *Clown.* What is the opinion of Pythagoras concerning wild
   fowl?
   Mal. That the soul of our grandam might haply inhabit a
   bird.
   Clown. What thinkest thou of his opinion?
   Mal. I think nobly of the soul, and no way approve his
   opinion.
2. Dodd was a man of reading, and left at his death a choice
collection of old English literature. I should judge him to have
been a man of wit. I know one instance of an impromptu which
no length of study could have bettered. My merry friend, Jem
White, had seen him one evening in Aguecheek, and recognising
Dodd the next day in Fleet Street, was irresistibly impelled to
take off his hat and salute him as the identical Knight of the preceding evening with a 'Save you, *Sir Andrew*'. Dodd, not at all
disconcerted at this unusual address from a stranger, with a cour-
teous half-rebuking wave of the hand, put him off with an 'Away,
Fool'.
3. *High Life Below Stairs.*

JAMES BOADEN: Mrs Jordan as Viola

She now was persuaded to indulge the town with a steadier
gaze at her male figure, and chose the part of Viola in Shakespeare's *Twelfth Night*, a character of infinite delicacy and
enchanting eloquence; one, in a word, where the great poet exhibits a sensibility so truly feminine, that in his world of wonders

it has scarcely yet excited sufficient critical praise. We were now to make the experiment how her '*provincial dialect*' would be borne in the music of the verse, such as even Shakespeare has seldom written. 'It was all well enough,' said the venerable stagers, 'while she could romp it away with a *jump* and a *laugh*; but what will they say to her in the loving and beloved Viola, who acts so tenderly and "speaks so masterly" all the science of passion, in words that "echo truly" all its best feelings?' What! Why, that the mere melody of her utterance brought tears into the eyes, and that passion had never had so modest and enchanting an interpreter. In a word, it was NATURE herself shewing us the *heart of her own mystery,* and at the same time thowing out a proud defiance to ART to approach it for a moment. She long continued to delight the town with her Viola, which she thus acted for the first time on the 11 November, 1785.

English audiences seldom know more of a play than is spoken from the stage, and the modern collection of English plays contains no more than the mutilators of the drama think proper to preserve of the author's text. I perceive in the passage above, that I have indulged in a favourite practice of throwing into a sentence some of the inimitable language of the poet, and usually in the play under consideration. The happy possessors of these stage copies have never either seen or heard the expressions so introduced, and I shall give a just notion of the injury done to our great poet by quoting the sentences connected with the lovely character of Viola. In the third scene of the second act, the Duke (Viola being present as Cesario) calls to his musicians to play the tune of an 'old and antique song', which had given more relief to his passion,

> . . . than light airs and recollected terms
> Of these most brisk and giddy-paced times.

He follows its repetition by this question to the youth at his side.

Duke.   How dost thou like this tune?
Vio. It gives a very echo to the seat
    Where love is thron'd.
Duke.   Thou dost speak masterly.

The player who dismissed this short passage, in the language of
Othello –

    Like the base Indian, threw a pearl away
    Richer than all his tribe.

And that, as it should seem, merely to relieve the gentlemen in
the orchestra from the trouble of playing a few bars of pathetic
and appropriate music.

    Who would not laugh, if such a man there be?
    Who would not *weep*, if ATTICUS were he?

In the original play, Feste, the jester, is brought in to sing the
song, and his appearance draws another beautiful remark from
the Duke to his young favourite.

    Mark it, Cesario; it is old and plain;
    The spinsters and the knitters in the sun,
    And the free maids that weave their thread with bones,
    Do use to chant it; it is silly sooth,
    And dallies with the innocence of love,
    Like the old age.

And then follows the song written by Shakespeare, 'Come away,
come away, death', which wandered about the pendulous world
a long while, until at last Kelly and Crouch bound it fast to the
Pizarro of Sheridan and Kotzebue; but the notes of the musician
echoing too faithfully the burthen of those feeble words 'come
away', the whole appeared too light for the occasion.

    It is in this scene too, that the tender poet has given us the
fine picture of a hopeless passion pining in thought, and gracing

a rooted grief with the faint smile, which Patience for ever wears upon some monument to the dead. Retaining this point for Viola, the wretched taste alluded to cut away all the essential preparation for such a thing, and marred the exquisite address of the poet. But enough.

In the great variety of the character, with the Duke, Olivia, and the drunken assailants, Mrs Jordan found ample field for her powers; and she long continued to delight the town in Viola, which she thus acted for the first time in Drury Lane theatre, on the 11 November, 1785.

(from *The Life of Mrs Jordan*, 1831)

E. MONTÉGUT: The Carnival World of *Twelfth Night*

Twelfth Night is a masquerade, slightly grotesque, as befits a play whereof the title recalls one of those festivals which were most dear to the jocund humour of our forebears. This festival was the day whereon in every family a king for the nonce was crowned after he had been chosen by lot; sometimes it fell to a child to be the ruler over the whole family, again a servant was crowned by his master, for the moment it was the world turned upside down, a rational hierarchy topsy-turvy, authority created by chance, and the more grotesque the surprise, the merrier the festival. You have seen it all depicted on the canvas of the jocose and powerful Jordaens, this jolly festival and its king with a large red face, his glass in his hand and his crown on his head, his fat and fair Flemish women excited by beer, good cheer, good health, and good humour; and their plump children so tempting to the taste of the Brillat-Savarin of cannibalism. In grotesqueness, *Twelfth Night* does not yield to the picture by Jordaens, and assuredly no caricature from the brush of this robust and popular master can match, either in comic power or as a reproduction of ancient manners, the characters of Uncle Toby and his comrades and the picture of their nocturnal drinking bouts. The whole episode of the wild orgy of Toby and of the crotchety Malvolio is drawn incomparably to the life; Shakespeare has there, so to speak, surpassed himself, for he has there shown himself a consummate master of a species of composition which has been many a time denied to him, namely, comedy. That Shakespeare, in the comedy of fancy, of caprice, of adventure, is without a peer is acknowledged by every one; but he has been gravely reproached with not being able to stand a comparison with those masters who draw their resources exclusively from those faculties whence alone true comedy springs; in a word, with not being sufficiently in his comedies exclusively comic. The episodes of Sir Toby and Malvolio correct this judgement of error; Rabelais is not more of a buffoon, and Molière not more exclusively comic than Shakespeare in these two episodes.

The sentimental and romantic portions of the play are stamped with that inimitable grace which especially characterises Shakespeare; but even here this comedy remains faithful to its title of *Twelfth Night*: for ambiguity still reigns sovereign mistress there, and treats the real world under its double form, the reality of nature and that of society, like a carnival farce. The characters instigated by their whims or the spitefulness of chance are deceived as to condition and sex and become involved in an imbroglio of charming and dangerous complications. Beneath the real piece, another can be read at the will of the reader, just as by certain artifices one image may be seen beneath another image, and herein lies the delicate point of this charming work for which that famous saying appears to have been expressly written : 'Glide, mortals, bear not heavily'. A surly reader or a stern critic might say that this poetic Viola is merely an amiable adventuress. And her brother, Sebastian, her living mirror, so charming that the friendships which he inspires cling to him like lichens on a rock – is he not too womanish? In sooth, he needed but the whim of donning woman's clothes to become *una feminuccia*, as the Italians say in their expressive diminutives. Of the Countess Olivia, with her singular mistakes, may we not also have some doubts? We might suspect that Toby, with his unmannerly perverted wit, who knew his world and fathomed his niece, was not far wrong when he said she was a 'Cataian', herein alluding to that land of Cathay whence came, with the Italian renaissance, and that princess Angelica through whom Medoro was made happy and Orlando desperate, all the magicians, sorceresses, enchantresses, and sirens who ruled all hearts in the chivalric literature of the sixteenth century. But, hush! youth, grace, beauty, with all their dreams, their illusions and their charms, enwrap these adventures. We are here in fairyland; why should we try to discover the real nature of these personages? They are the children of the imagination, of caprice, graceful fairies, sylphs and imps, *piccolini stregoni*.

In Shakespeare's plays philosophy is rarely lacking; is there then a philosophy in this poetic masquerade? Ay, there is one here, and to its fullest depth. In two words it is: we are all, in varying degrees, insane; for we are all the slaves of our defects, which are genuine chronic follies, or else we are the victims of dreams which attack us like follies at an acute stage. Man is held in leash by his imagination, which deceives him even to the extent of reversing the normal conditions of nature and the laws of reality. An image, ordinary but true, of man in every station is this silly Malvolio, whose folly unavowed and secretly cherished, bursts forth on a frivolous pretext. Malvolio is, no question, a fool, but this sly waiting-woman who ensnares him by an all-revealing stratagem, is she herself exempt from the folly of which she accuses Malvolio? And if the steward believes himself beloved by his mistress, does she not pursue the same ambitious dream of making a match with Sir Toby, who, however degraded and drunken, is at least a gentleman and the uncle of Olivia? It is the same dream under very different conditions which Viola pursues, – a dream which would never have come true, if luck had not extricated her from the *cul de sac* whither her temerity had led her. What is to be said of Olivia but that her imagination, suddenly smitten, could go so far astray as to stifle in her the instinct which should have revealed to her that Viola was one of her own sex? The friendship of Antonio for Sebastian, – a friendship which involves him in perils so easily foreseen, – is a sentiment exactly twin with the love of Olivia for Cesario-Viola. All dream, all are mad, and differ from one another only in the kind of their madness, – some have a graceful and poetic madness, others a madness grotesque and trivial. And after all, some of these dreams come true. Must we ascribe the honour of success to the good sense of the happy ones who see their secret desires crowned? Ah no, we must ascribe it to Nature. We all dream, – it is a condition of humanity; but in this multitude of dreams, Nature accepts only certain ones which are in harmony with grace, with poesy, and with beauty; for Nature is essentially platonic, and thrusts aside as a revolt and a sin, every dream wherein ugliness intrudes. Hence it is that Viola's secret dream comes true, while Malvolio's is condemned to remain for ever a grotesque chimera. Very humble indeed should all of us be, for we are only a little less mad than our neighbours; it is Nature alone who is our arbiter and decides which of us she wishes to pose as sages, and which of us she intends to retain in the rank of fools.

(1867; from H. H. Furness's Variorum Edition of
Twelfth Night, Philadelphia, 1901)

SIR EDWARD RUSSELL: Henry Irving as Malvolio

Lean, lank, with self-occupied visage, and formal, peaked Spanish beard; dressed in a close garb of black striped with yellow, and holding a steward's wand, in the lightness of which there is something of fantastic symbolism, he steps on the stage with nose in air and eyes half-shut, as if with singular and moody contemplation. He is visibly possessed of pride, of manners, and of intelligence. His pride, though intense, is not diseased, until the poison-dish of imagined love has been presented to him and has begun its work. Irving's gait; his abstraction of gaze, qualified by a polite observance of his lady, and a suspicious vigilance over his fellows in her service and her turbulent relations and followers; his sublime encounter with the Fool; his sententious observations on everything in general, and the infinite gravity yet imaginative airiness of his movements, carry the Malvolio of Shakespeare to a higher point of effect, probably than it has ever before reached on the stage. ... I do not wish, as Coleridge said, to flounder-flat a humorous image, but there is no evading certain results of the genuinely humanistic as opposed to the entirely humoristic rendering of certain of Shakespeare's characters. The gaunt and sombre steward is not, and is not likely to be, a purely amusing character. Even his tormentors at one point relent a little at the thought that they may carry their cruel joke too far, and for the nineteenth century it is carried too far to be entirely funny. Malvolio in the dark hole uttering sage, conscientious words to prove to the false Sir Topas that he is not mad, becomes a pathetic figure. The language evidently requires to be delivered with all Mr Irving's serious and significant earnestness.

(from *The Fortnightly Review*, 1 September 1884)

WILLIAM WINTER : Ada Rehan as Viola

After the action of the piece has opened, several comical situations are devised for Viola, together with several situations of serious perplexity, which mostly tend to create a comic effect for the auditor. In those situations Viola's gleeful spirit is liberated, – her irrepressible hilarity, on being expected to play the part of a masculine lover, and her feminine consternation, when confronted with the necessity of combat, being artfully contrasted, for the sake of humorous results. The true note of the character, however, is serious. Viola is a woman of deep sen-

sibility, and that way Miss Rehan comprehended and repro-
duced her, – permitting a wistful sadness to glimmer through
the gauze of kindly vivacity with which, otherwise, her bright
and gentle figure is artfully swathed. That was the pervading
beauty of the impersonation. Those frolic scenes in which Viola
participated are consonant with Miss Rehan's propensity for
mirth and with her faculty for comic action. She rejoiced in
them and she made the listener rejoice in them. But the underlying cause of her success in them was the profound sincerity
of her feeling, – over which her glee was seen to play, as moon-
light plays upon the rippling surface of the ocean depth. In that
embodiment, more than in any assumption of character
previously presented by her, she relied upon a soft and gentle
poetry of condition, discarding strong emphasis, whether of
colour, demeanour, or speech. Her action was exceedingly delicate, and if at any moment she became conspicuous in a scene
it was as the consequence of dramatic necessity, not of self-
assertion. Lovely reserve and aristocratic distinction blended
in the performance, and dignified and endeared it. The melody
of Shakespeare's verse, – especially in the passage of Viola's
renunciation, – fell from her lips in a strain of fluent sweetness that enhanced its beauty and deepened the pathos
of its tender significance. In such tones the heart speaks, and
not simply the warmth of an excited mind, and so the incom-
municable something that the soul knows of love and sorrow
finds an utterance, if not an intelligible expression. Subtlety
of perception naturally accompanies deep feeling. Viola, when,
as Cesario, she has captured the fancy of Olivia, although she
may view that ludicrous dilemma archly, and even with a spice
of innocent mischief, feels a woman's sympathy with the emotions of her sex, and her conduct toward Olivia is refined and
considerate. Miss Rehan was admirably true to the Shakespearian ideal in that particular, as also she was in expressing the
large generosity of Viola toward Olivia's beauty. It is only a
woman intrinsically noble who can be just toward her pros-

perous rival in matters of the heart. Miss Rehan, in her embodiment of Viola, obeyed the fine artistic impulse to make no
effort. Her elocution was at its best, – concealing premedita-
tion, and flowing, as the brook flows, with continuous music
and spontaneous, accidental variation. . . . Her witchery in
Viola did not consist in her action, – although that was appropriate, dignified, symmetrical, expressive, and winning, – but
in her assumption and preservation of a sweet, resigned
patience; not despairing, not lachrymose, – a gentle, wistful
aspect and state of romantic melancholy, veiled but not beneath an outward guise of buoyant, careless joy.

(from *Shadows of the Stage*, New York, 1895)

HARLEY GRANVILLE-BARKER: On Producing *Twelfth Night*

The most important aspect of the play must be viewed, to
view it rightly, with Elizabethan eyes. Viola was played, and
was meant to be played, by a boy. See what this involves. To
that original audience the strain of make-believe in the matter
ended just where for us it most begins, at Viola's entrance as a
page. Shakespeare's audience saw Cesario without effort as
Orsino sees him; more importantly they saw him as Olivia sees
him; indeed it was over Olivia they had most to make believe.
One feels at once how this affects the sympathy and balance of
the love scenes of the play. One sees how dramatically right is
the delicate still grace of the dialogue between Orsino and
Cesario, and how possible it makes the more outspoken passion
of the scenes with Olivia. Give to Olivia, as we must now do, all
the value of her sex, and to the supposed Cesario none of the
value of his, we are naturally quite unmoved by the business.
Olivia looks a fool. And it is the common practice for actresses
of Viola to seize every chance of reminding the audience
that they are girls dressed up, to impress on one moreover, by

childish byplay as to legs and petticoats or the absence of
them, that this is the play's supreme joke. Now Shakespeare
has devised one most carefully placed soliloquy where we are
to be forcibly reminded that Cesario is Viola; in it he has as
carefully divided the comic from the serious side of the matter.
That scene played, the Viola, who does not do her best, as far
as the passages with Olivia are concerned, to make us believe,
as Olivia believes, th... she is a man, shows, to my mind, a
lack of imagination and is guilty of dramatic bad manners,
knocking, for the sake of a little laughter, the whole of the play's
romantic plot on the head. ...

The Winter's Tale, as I see its writing, is complex, vivid,
abundant in the variety of its mood and pace and colour, now
disordered, now at rest, the product of a mind rapid, changing,
and overfull. I believe its interpretation should express all that.
Twelfth Night is quite other. Daily, as we rehearse together, I
learn more what it is and should be; the working together of
the theatre is a fine thing. But, as a man is asked to name his
stroke at billiards, I will even now commit myself to this: its
serious mood is passionate, its verse is lyrical, the speaking of it
needs swiftness and fine tone; not rush, but rhythm, constant
and compelling. And now I wait contentedly to be told that
less rhythmic speaking of Shakespeare has never been heard.

(from *Twelfth Night: An Acting Edition*, 1912)

POSTSCRIPT: John Masefield to Harley Granville-Barker

. . . much the most beautiful thing I have ever seen done on
the stage; the play which has delighted me most, quite perfectly done. The speaking of the verse was beautiful. Lillah
McCarthy often got most exquisite effects with a sort of clear
uplifting that carried us away, and I believe that the women
scenes were never once allowed to drop to the dreamy and
emotional; they were always high, clear, and ringing, coming
out of a passionate mood. ... You got the full flavour and power

from it and made one feel that one was listening to one of the world's masters at his happiest. One saw a great man's intention and also his strength. If I were asked what made me see it most plainly I should say your sudden and inspiring bit of vision at the end, when you made Feste blaze out at Malvolio and Malvolio flame up in reply. . . .

(1912; from C. B. Purdom, *Harley Cranville Barker,* 1955)

PART TWO

Twentieth-Century Studies

A. C. Bradley

FESTE THE JESTER (1916)

Lear's Fool stands in a place apart – a sacred place; but, of
Shakespeare's other Fools,[1] Feste, the so-called Clown in
Twelfth Night, has always lain nearest to my heart. He is not,
perhaps, more amusing than Touchstone, to whom I bow profoundly in passing; but I love him more.

Whether Lear's Fool was not slightly touched in his wits is
disputable. Though Touchstone is both sane and wise, we sometimes wonder what would happen if he had to shift for himself.
Here and there he is ridiculous as well as humorous; we laugh
at him, and not only *with* him. We never laugh at Feste. He
would not dream of marrying Audrey. Nobody would hint
that he was a 'natural' or propose to 'steal' him (*As You Like
It,* 1 i 46, 48; 1 iii 125). He is as sane as his mistress; his position
considered, he cannot be called even eccentric, scarcely even
flighty; and he possesses not only the ready wit required by
his profession, and an intellectual agility greater than it requires, but also an insight into character and into practical
situations so swift and sure that he seems to supply, in fuller
measure than any of Shakespeare's other Fools, the poet's own
comment on the story. He enters, and at once we know that
Maria's secret is no secret to him. She warns him that he will
be hanged for playing the truant. 'Many a good hanging,' he
replies, 'prevents a bad marriage'; and if Maria wants an
instance of a bad marriage, she soon gets it: 'Well, go thy way;
if Sir Toby would leave drinking, thou wert as witty a piece of
Eve's flesh as any in Illyria.' (Gervinus, on the contrary, re-
garded this marriage as a judgement on Sir Toby; but then
Gervinus, though a most respectable critic, was no Fool.) Maria
departs and Olivia enters. Her brother is dead, and she wears

the deepest mourning, and has announced her intention of
going veiled and weeping her loss every day for seven years.
But, in Feste's view, her state of mind would be rational only if
she believed her brother's soul to be in hell; and he does not
conceal his opinion. The Duke comes next, and, as his manner
ruffles Feste, the mirror of truth is held firmly before him too :
'Now, the melancholy god protect thee; and the tailor make
thy doublet of changeable taffeta, for thy mind is a very opal.'
In these encounters we admire the Fool's wisdom the more
because it makes no impression on his antagonists, who regard
it as mere foolery. And his occasional pregnant sayings and
phrases meet the same fate. His assertion that he is the better
for his foes and the worse for his friends the Duke takes for a
mere absurdity or an inadvertence of expression, though he is
tickled by Feste's proof of his affirmation through double nega-
tion.[2] The philosopher may speak to Sebastian of 'this great
lubber the world'; he may tell Viola how 'foolery, sir, does
walk about the orb like the sun – it shines everywhere'; he may
remark to the whole company how 'the whirligig of time brings
in his revenges'; but nobody heeds him. Why should any one
heed a man who gets his living by talking nonsense, and who
may be whipped if he displeases his employer?

All the agility of wit and fancy, all the penetration and wisdom, which Feste shows in his calling, would not by themselves
explain our feeling for him. But his mind to him a kingdom
is, and one full of such present joys that he finds content-
ment there. Outwardly he may be little better than a slave;
but Epictetus was a slave outright and yet absolutely free : and
so is Feste. That world of quibbles which are pointless to his
audience, of incongruities which nobody else can see, of flitting
fancies which he only cares to pursue, is his sunny realm. He is
alone when he invents that aphorism of Quinapalus and builds
his hopes on it; and it was not merely to get sixpence from Sir
Andrew that he told of Pigrogromitus and the Vapians passing
the equinoctial of Queubus. He had often passed it in that

company himself. Maria and Sir Toby (who do enjoy his more
obvious jests) are present when, clothed in the curate's gown
and beard, he befools the imprisoned Malvolio so gloriously;
but the prisoner is his only witness when, for his own sole delight, himself as Sir Topas converses with himself the Fool. But
for this inward gaiety he could never have joined with all his
heart in the roaring revelry of Sir Toby; but he does not need
this revelry, and, unlike Sir Toby and Sir Toby's surgeon, he
remains master of his senses. Having thus a world of his own,
and being lord of himself, he cares little for Fortune. His mistress may turn him away; but, 'to be turned away, let summer
bear it out'. This 'sunshine of the breast' is always with him
and spreads its radiance over the whole scene in which he
moves. And so we love him.

We have another reason. The Fool's voice is as melodious
as the 'sweet content' of his soul. To think of him is to remember 'Come away, come away, death', and 'O mistress mine',
and 'When that I was', and fragments of folk-song and ballad,
and a catch that 'makes the welkin dance indeed'. To think of
Twelfth Night is to think of music. It opens with instrumental
music, and ends with a song. All Shakespeare's best praise of
music, except the famous passage in *The Merchant of Venice*,
occurs in it. And almost all the music and the praise of music
comes from Feste or has to do with Feste. In this he stands alone
among Shakespeare's Fools; and that this, with the influence
it has on our feeling for him, was intended by the poet should
be plain. It is no accident that, when the Duke pays him for
his 'pains' in singing, he answers, 'No pains, sir; I take pleasure
in singing, sir'; that the revelry for which he risks punishment
is a revelry of song; that, when he is left alone, he still sings.
And, all this being so, I venture to construe in the light of it
what has seemed strange to me in the passage that follows the
singing of 'Come away'. Usually, when Feste receives his 'gra-
tillity', he promptly tries to get it doubled; but here he not only
abstains from any such effort but is short, if not disagreeably

sharp, with the Duke. The fact is, he is offended, even disgusted; and offended, not as Fool, but as music-lover and artist. We others know what the Duke said beforehand of the song, but Feste does not know it. Now he sings, and his soul is in the song. Yet, as the last note dies away, the comment he hears from this noble aesthete is, 'There's for thy pains'!

I have a last grace to notice in our wise, happy, melodious Fool. He was little injured by his calling. He speaks as he likes; but from first to last, whether he is revelling or chopping logic or playing with words, and to whomsoever he speaks or sings, he keeps his tongue free from obscenity. The fact is in accord with the spirit of this ever-blessed play, which could not have endured the 'foul-mouthed' Fool of *All's Well*, and from which Aldis Wright in his school edition found, I think, but three lines (not the Fool's) to omit. But the trait is none the less characteristic of Feste, and we like him the better for it.

It remains to look at another side of the whole matter. One is scarcely sorry for Touchstone, but one is very sorry for Feste; and pity, though not a painful pity, heightens our admiration and deepens our sympathy. The position of the professional jester we must needs feel to be more or less hard, if not of necessity degrading. In Feste's case it is peculiarly hard. He is perfectly sane, and there is nothing to show that he is unfit for independence. In important respects he is, more than Shakespeare's other fools, superior in mind to his superiors in rank. And he has no Celia, no Countess, no Lear, to protect or love him. He had been Fool to Olivia's father, who 'took much delight in him'; but Olivia, though not unkind, cannot be said to love him. We find him, on his first appearance, in disgrace and (if Maria is right) in danger of being punished or even turned away. His mistress, entering, tells him that he is a dry fool, that she'll no more of him, and (later) that his fooling grows old and people dislike it. Her displeasure, doubtless, has a cause, and it is transient, but her words are none the less signi-

ficant. Feste is a relic of the past. The steward, a person highly
valued by his lady, is Feste's enemy. Though Maria likes him
and, within limits, would stand his friend, there is no tone of
affection in her words to him, and certainly none in those of
any other person. We cannot but feel very sorry for him.

This peculiar position explains certain traits in Feste himself
which might otherwise diminish our sympathy. One is that he
himself, though he shows no serious malevolence even to his
enemy, shows no affection for any one. His liking for Maria
does not amount to fondness. He enjoys drinking and singing
with Sir Toby, but despises his drunkenness and does not care
for him. His attitude to strangers is decidedly cool, and he does
not appear to be attracted even by Viola. The fact is, he recognizes very clearly that, as this world goes, a man whom nobody
loves must look out for himself. Hence (this is the second trait)
he is a shameless beggar, much the most so of Shakespeare's
Fools. He is fully justified, and he begs so amusingly that we
welcome his begging; but shameless it is. But he is laying up
treasures on earth against the day when some freak of his own,
or some whim in his mistress, will bring his dismissal, and the
short summer of his freedom will be followed by the wind and
the rain. And so, finally, he is as careful as his love of fun will
allow to keep clear of any really dangerous enterprise. He must
join in the revel of the knights and the defiance of the steward;
but from the moment when Malvolio retires with a threat to
Maria, and Maria begins to expound her plot against him,
Feste keeps silence; and, though she expressly assigns him a
part in the conspiracy, he takes none. The plot succeeds magnificently, and Malvolio is shut up, chained as a lunatic, in a
dark room; and that comic genius Maria has a new scheme,
which requires the active help of the Fool. But her words, 'Nay,
I prithee, put on this gown and this beard', show that he
objects; and if his hesitation is momentary, it is not merely
because the temptation is strong. For, after all, he runs but

little risk, since Malvolio cannot see him, and he is a master
in the management of his voice. And so, agreeing with Sir
Toby's view that their sport cannot with safety be pursued to
the upshot, after a while, when he is left alone with the steward,
he takes steps to end it and consents, in his own voice, to provide the lunatic with light, pen, ink, and paper for his letter to
Olivia.

We are not offended by Feste's eagerness for sixpences and
his avoidance of risks. By helping us to realize the hardness of
his lot, they add to our sympathy and make us admire the more
the serenity and gaiety of his spirit. And at the close of the
play these feelings reach their height. He is left alone; for Lady
Belch, no doubt, is by her husband's bedside, and the thin-
faced gull Sir Andrew has vanished, and the rich and noble
lovers with all their attendants have streamed away to dream
of the golden time to come, without a thought of the poor jester.
There is no one to hear him sing; but what does that matter?
He takes pleasure in singing. And a song comes into his head;
an old rude song about the stages of man's life, in each of which
the rain rains every day; a song at once cheerful and rueful,
stoical and humorous; and this suits his mood and he sings it.
But, since he is even more of a philosopher than the author of
the song, and since, after all, he is not merely a Fool but the
actor who is playing that part in a theatre, he adds at the end a
stanza of his own :

> A great while ago the world begun,
>   With hey, ho, the wind and the rain,
> But that's all one, our play is done,
>   And we'll strive to please you every day.[3]

Shakespeare himself, I feel sure, added that stanza to the
old song; and when he came to write *King Lear* he, I think,
wrote yet another, which Feste might well have sung. To the
immortal words,

> Poor fool and knave, I have one part in my heart
> That's sorry yet for thee,

the Fool replies,

> He that has and a little tiny wit
>   With heigh-ho, the wind and the rain –
> Must make content with his fortunes fit,
>   Though the rain it raineth every day.

So Shakespeare brings the two Fools together; and, whether or no he did this wittingly, I am equally grateful to him. But I cannot be grateful to those critics who see in Feste's song only an illustration of the bad custom by which sometimes, when a play was finished, the clown remained, or appeared, on the stage to talk nonsense or to sing some old 'trash'; nor yet to those who tell us that it was 'the players' who tacked this particular 'trash' to the end of *Twelfth Night*. They may conceivably be right in perceiving no difference between the first four stanzas and the last, but they cannot possibly be right in failing to perceive how appropriate the song is to the singer, and how in the line

> But that's all one, our play is done,

he repeats an expression used a minute before in his last speech.[4] We owe these things, not to the players, but to that player in Shakespeare's company who was also a poet, to Shakespeare himself – the same Shakespeare who perhaps had hummed the old song, half-ruefully and half-cheerfully, to its accordant air, as he walked home alone to his lodging from the theatre or even from some noble's mansion; he who, looking down from an immeasurable height on the mind of the public and the noble, had yet to be their servant and jester, and to depend upon their favour; not wholly uncorrupted by this dependence, but yet superior to it and, also, determined, like Feste, to lay by the sixpences it brought him, until at last he could say the words, 'Our revels now are ended',[5] and could break – was it a magician's staff or a Fool's bauble?

SOURCE: *A Book of Homage to Shakespeare* (1916); reprinted in *A Miscellany* (1929) pp. 207–17

NOTES

1. I mean the Fools proper, i.e. professional jesters attached to a court or house. In effect they are but four, Touchstone, Feste, Lavache in *All's Well*, and Lear's Fool; for it is not clear that Trinculo is the court-jester, and the Clown in *Othello*, like the Fool (a brothel-fool) in *Timon*, has but a trivial part. Neither humorists like Launce and Launcelot Gobbo, nor 'low' characters, unintentionally humorous, like the old peasant at the end of *Antony and Cleopatra* or the young shepherd called 'clown' in *The Winter's Tale*, are Fools proper. The distinction is quite clear, but it tends to be obscured for readers because the wider designation 'clown' is applied to persons of either class in the few lists of Dramatis Personæ printed in the Folio, in the complete lists of our modern editions, and also, alike in these editions and in the Folio, in stage-directions and in the headings of speeches. Such directions and headings were meant for the actors, and the principal comic man of the company doubtless played both Launce and Feste. Feste, I may observe, is called 'Clown' in the stage-directions and speech-headings, but in the text always 'Fool'. Lear's Fool is 'Fool' even in the former.

2. Feste's statement of his proof (v i 20) can hardly be called lucid, and his illustration ('conclusions to be as kisses, if your four negatives make your two affirmatives') seems to have cost the commentators much fruitless labour. If anything definite was in the Fool's mind it may have been this. The gentleman asks for a kiss. The lady, denying it, exclaims 'No no no no'. But, as the first negative (an adjective) negates the second (a substantive), and the third in like manner the fourth, these four negatives yield two enthusiastic affirmatives, and the gentleman, thanks to the power of logic, gets twice what he asked for. This is not Feste's only gird at the wisdom of the schools. It has been gravely

surmised that he was educated for the priesthood and, but for some escapade, would have played Sir Topas in earnest.

3. Those who witnessed, some years ago, Mr Granville-Barker's production of *Twelfth Night*, and Mr Hayden Coffin's present-ment of the Fool's part, must always remember them with great pleasure, and not least the singing of this song.

4. 'I was one, sir, in this interlude; one Sir Topas, sir; *but that's all one.*'

5. *The Tempest,* IV i 148.

H. B. *Charlton*

SHAKESPEARE'S HEROINES AND THE ART OF HAPPINESS (1938)

... Shakespeare's enthronement of woman as queen of comedy is no mere accident, and no mere gesture of conventional gallantry. Because they are women, these heroines have attributes of personality fitting them more certainly than men to shape the world towards happiness. His menfolk, a Hamlet or a Macbeth or an Othello, may have a subtler intellect, a more penetrating imagination, or a more irresistible passion. But what they have more largely in one kind of personal endowment, they own only at the expense of other properties no less essential to the encountering of such varied circumstances as are presented by the act of living. These heroes, in effect, are out of harmony with themselves, and so are fraught with the certainty of tragic doom. Their personality is a mass of mighty forces out of equipoise : they lack the balance of a durable spiritual organism. It was in women that Shakespeare found this equipoise, this balance which makes personality in action a sort of ordered interplay of the major components of human nature. In his women, hand and heart and brain are fused in a vital and practicable union, each contributing to the other, no one of them permanently pressing demands to the detriment of the other, yet each asserting itself periodically to exercise its vitality, even if the immediate effect be a temporary disturbance of equilibrium, for not otherwise will they be potent to exercise their proper function when the whole of their owner's spiritual nature is struck into activity. Perhaps it was primarily because Shakespeare found women more sensitive to intuition and more responsible to emotion that he first promoted them to dominion in the realm of comedy. He found, moreover, in their instincts a kind of finely developed mother-wit, a variety of humanised common sense which, because it was impregnated with humane feeling, was more apt to lay hold of the essential realities of existence than was the more rarified and isolated intellect of man. But, though it was what to this extent may be called their essential femininity which gave his heroines their first claims to rulership in comedy, Shakespeare insisted in his maturest comedies that all the qualities which his heroines owed to the promptings of intuition and instinct were only certainly beneficent in human affairs when instinct and intuition were guided by a mind in which a sublimated common sense had established itself as the habitual director of action and behaviour.

It is unnecessary here to attempt to describe these heroines one by one, or even to name in detail all their generic traits. It will be enough to indicate one or two of their characteristic virtues. They have all the gift of inspiring and of returning affection. They have the good will of all who know them. They are simply human and patently natural in their response to emotional crises like that of falling in love. Rosalind's excitement when she first meets Orlando is as palpable as are her transparent endeavours to hide it. Their own passion still further sharpens the affection through which they seek the good of others. Once they are conscious of their own desire they are master-hands in reaching it. Rosalind is the main plotter of the flight to Arden; it is she who devises the means of ensuring Orlando's frequent company. Viola resolves at once to remedy her lot by taking service with the Duke; and immediately becomes his confidant and his private minister. She overcomes all the ceremonial obstacles which bar access to Olivia, using, when need be, the bluster and the rudeness which she learns from her opponents. She seizes a situation on the instant; and even when the outcome is not clearly to be foreseen, she acts in a manner which will save unnecessary suffering to others : 'she took the ring of me', is her lie to Malvolio, guessing at once how the distraught Olivia had tried to hide her device from her steward and messenger. In crises, all of them, Rosalind,

Viola, and Beatrice, are guided by intuitive insight, Beatrice
acclaims Hero's innocence in the face of damning evidence.
Viola judges her ship's captain by the same inner vision, and she
confides in him implicitly. Yet the instinct and the intuition
are always open-eyed and cautiously safeguarded against mere
casual vagary or whimsical sentimentality. When Viola judges
the captain's worth by his fair and outward character, she remembers that nature with a beauteous wall doth oft close in
pollution. Rosalind and Celia are equally immune from this
wide-spread romantic fallacy. They know that there is no certain and predictable relation between beauty and honesty in
mankind : they would have laughingly recommended all the
Tennysonian moralists of their day, who thought beauty to be
either truth or virtue, to stroll through the equivalent of their
West End after the theatres were shut and when the restaur-
ants were coming to the end of their cabarets. Yet, with all the
efficiency and savoir faire of which these heroines prove themselves to be possessed, they are amazingly modest. It is this
modesty which prevents them from endeavouring to compass
what is beyond mortal reach. Fortune, they know, is but a blind
worker; and she doth most mistake in her gifts to woman. Viola
undoubtedly is confident, but not over-confident : she will do
what she can, but

> O Time, thou must untangle this, not I;
> It is too hard a knot for me t' untie!

And Rosalind never forgets how full of briers is this work-a-
day world. But in the end, they triumph; and they triumph
because they are just what they are, the peculiar embodiment
in personality of those traits of human nature which render
human beings most loveable, most loving, and most service-
able to the general good.

But these ladies are not only doers and inspirers of action.
Merely by their presence in the play, they serve as standards

whereby degrees of worth and worthlessness in other characters are made manifest. Hence the rich variety of theme, of
episode, and of person in these plays is knit together and holds
as a coherent structure. The beneficence of emotion and of
intuition is no wise belittled by the revelation of the follies which
spring from feeling in less stable creatures than are the heroines.
So, *Twelfth Night* is largely occupied with the disclosure of
unbalanced sentiment. There is the enervating sentimentality
of Orsino, there is the unrestrained emotionalism of Olivia.
As You Like It handles an allied theme by its exposure of merely
conventional pastoralism. Indeed, once the positive construction of their larger world has been effected by the heroines, there
is now place, not only for their own safeguards for it, such as
this perpetual alertness to expose the dangers of unbalanced
sentiment, there is also place for the sort of direct satire and the
forthright comicality which were the manner of the older classical tradition. Just as Sir Toby finds his station in *Twelfth
Night*, so do Andrew and even Malvolio; there, in Andrew's
case, simply to display his own foolish inanity as do the witless in
all sorts of comedy; and in Malvolio's, to enter almost as Jonson
gave his characters entry, for a more subtle but still classical
kind of discomfiture. As Malvolio in *Twelfth Night*, so Jaques
in *As You Like It*, another of the few attempts of Shakespeare
to project malcontentism for comic purposes. Besides these,
traditional clowns may now also play their part, whether the
English Shakespearian ones of the tribe of Bottom, such as
Dogberry and Verges, or the more technical ones, Feste and
Touchstone, grown now by contact with natural Costards into
something more substantial and more homely than the mere
traditional corrupters of words, and therefore playing not the
part of an added funny interlude, but an essential role in the
orientation of the idea of comedy. 'Since the little wit that fools
have was silenced, the little foolery that wise men have makes
a great show.' The true fool's return is restorative. A fool of his
sort will use his folly like a stalking-horse, and under the pre-

sentation of that, will shoot his wit. Yet his range will necessarily be limited now. Only the crassest folly falls to such arrows, for those who have become expert in human traffickings can assume an easy indifference to simple and direct hits:

> He that a fool doth very wisely hit
> Doth very foolishly, although he smart,
> Not to seem senseless of the bob; if not,
> The wise man's folly is anatomiz'd
> Even by the squand'ring glances of the fool.

Thus the motley of romantic comedies is subtler than the slap-dash skittle-knocking of the satire in classical comedy. Their re-formatory way, too, is fundamentally different from the simple exposure of ludicrous abnormality which had been the ap-proved manner of older comedy. They entice to a richer wis-dom by alluring the imagination into desire for larger delights. They are not mainly concerned to whip offenders into, conven-tional propriety by scorn and by mockery. They persuade one to the better state by presenting it in all its attractiveness: they depict a land of heart's desire, and, doing that, reveal the way of human and natural magic by which it is to be attained.

Hence, in the last resort, the greatness of these greatest of Shakespeare's comedies will be measured by the profundity and the persuasiveness of the apprehension of life which they embody, by the worth, that is, of their underlying worldly wis-dom. What then is this comic idea of which these plays are the dramatic revelation?

Something of the answer has already been given in estimat-ing the characteristics of the heroines. But the conclusions may be made more general: in the first place, however, it must be noted that though these romantic comedies break through the traditional scope of classical comedy, their sphere is still rigor-ously confined within the proper orbit of comedy. They limit themselves to acquaintance with life here and now; the world, and not eternity, is their stage. It is, of course, a world presenting many more woeful pageants than comedy is capable of transmuting to happiness : and comedy must confine itself to those threats of fate and those rubs of circumstance which can be reconciled with man's reach for assured joy in living. In these ripest of Shakespeare's comedies, comedy is seeking in its own artistic way to elucidate the moral art of securing happiness by translating the stubbornness of fortune into a quiet and a sweet existence.

It finds that this art comes most easily to those who by nature are generous, guiltless, and of a free disposition, just, indeed, as are Shakespeare's heroines. It finds the art crippled, if not destroyed, in those who lack the genial sense of fellowship with mankind. A Malvolio, sick of self-love, thanking God that he is not of the element of his associates, sees the rest of men merely as specimens of the genus 'homo', – 'why, of mankind'. The springs of sympathy are dried up within him. He becomes merely a time-server, planning only for his own selfish gain. The aptitude to do this successfully had been a positive asset to the earlier, even to the Falstaffian, kind of comic hero. But now, in the radiance of these maturer plays, it is seen in truer light. Malvolio has lost the art of life; his very genius is infected.

SOURCE: *Shakespearian Comedy* (1938) pp. 285–90

Leslie Hotson

THE REAL DUKE ORSINO (1954)

I. DON VIRGINIO ORSINO, DUKE OF BRACCIANO

But what of the Italian Duke, Orsino? No Shakespeare's insight is needed to recognize in this 'most brilliant nobleman of his day' the favoured guest. It was notorious that the Queen delighted to meet accomplished *cavalieri* from the land of Castiglione. Eighteen months before this, the Italian-educated Count of Anhalt had arrived. Lord Nottingham's opinion of him was, 'he is the most properest and the best brought up gentleman that I have ever seen, of that country or of any other. I know her Majesty will like him well, for he hath been brought up in Italy.' Queen Elizabeth justly prided herself on her supreme mastery of the Tuscan tongue: the princely Florentine Orsino, patron of Torquato Tasso, could savour the delicate artistry of her speech.

She liked the Italian manners and customs to the point of protesting on occasion that she herself was, 'as it were, half Italian' – and she loved to be nicknamed 'the Florentine'. Not such a far-fetched notion even in a Queen who was certainly *mere English*; for 'the English humour', as the seventeenth-century Henry Belasyse remarked, 'is somewhat like unto that of the Italians, and a middling humour between the too much of the French and the too little of the Spaniard. It neither melts away like a snowball, nor stands out dully like a stone.' Unquestionably, as we shall find, Elizabeth had every political reason for making much of Don Virginio Orsino. But also unquestionably she enjoyed the challenge his visit presented. Was it possible for any woman of sixty-seven to charm and delight a young man of twenty-eight? Let no one answer in scorn or disbelief before Elizabeth of England makes the trial.

Don Virginio's story, as it later unfolded itself, proved absorbing in the extreme; but the present and crucial problem was to trace him at the time of his visit to England. First, we must introduce him briefly. Son of Paolo Giordano Orsino, Duke of Bracciano, and of Isabella de' Medici, and orphaned at the age of thirteen, Virginio Orsino had been brought up at Florence by his uncle Ferdinand I, Grand Duke of Tuscany, along with the Grand Duke's niece Maria de' Medici, who was less than a year younger than her cousin Virginio. It was later whispered that the two had a fondness for each other; but however that may have been, they were 'great states', and in those days of political alliances by marriage, it was inconceivable that they should marry. Ferdinand grew deeply and sincerely attached to his nephew, and treated him as a son. Virginio reciprocated the affection of the prudent and able Medici ruler, and long after he had married and had children of his own he continued to pass most of his life assisting his uncle at the Pitti Palace in the government of Tuscany rather than at his own castle of Bracciano near Rome. Late in 1600 his cousin Maria was married in Florence by proxy to Elizabeth's 'Antichrist of ingratitude', the Catholic-converted and divorced French King Henri IV, and Virginio Orsino escorted the royal bride in state to France, where she saw her husband for the first time in her life, at Lyons. Leaving that city in December, the young Duke pursued his way to England, and to his Twelfth Night at Whitehall. . . .

II. ORSINO'S ACCOUNT OF TWELFTH NIGHT AT COURT,
FROM HIS LETTER TO HIS WIFE

On the Tuesday morning she [*the Queen*] sent her coaches and two great ones [*Lord Darcy, Mr William Cecil*] to take me and carry me to court. Arrived there, I found at the gate the Earl of

Rutland (*Rotelan*), one of the first nobles of the realm, who assisted me to alight. He received me in her Majesty's name, and led me to a lodging appointed for me [*Lord Worcester's, Deputy Master of the Horse*]. I stayed there very little, and then went abovestairs, where I found a hall [*Presence Chamber, King's side*] all filled with waiting gentlewomen; another within [*Privy Chamber*], full of ladies and gentlemen; in the third [*Withdrawing Chamber, King's side*] were all the officers of the Crown, and the Knights of the Garter, all dressed in white – as was the whole Court that day – but with so much gold and jewels, that it was a marvellous thing.

These all came to greet me, the most part speaking Italian, many, French, and some, Spanish. I answered all as well as I knew how, in the tongue which I heard spoken; and I am sure that at the least I made myself understood. I found no more than two gentlemen who knew no other tongue than the English; and with these I employed other gentlemen as interpreters. All these brought me near the door where the Queen was to enter. Over against me was the Muscovite Ambassador, who had come as an Extraordinary, to 'compliment with' her Majesty.

The Queen came to the door, and I presently approached in all humility to do her reverence; and she drew near me with most gracious cheer, speaking Italian so well, uttering withal such fine conceits, that I can maintain that I might have been taking lessons from Boccaccio or the [*Cruscan*] Academy. Her Majesty was dressed all in white, with so many pearls, broideries, and diamonds, that I am amazed how she could carry them. When I had done her reverence, Signore Giulio and Signore Grazia did the like; and then all the Court set forward in order toward the chapel. The order is such that I am having the whole noted in writing; nor do I believe I shall ever see a court which, for order, surpasses this one.

I attended her Majesty to a room next the chapel, where I stayed, in company with many gentlemen; and as we stood in excellent conversation, we heard a wondrous music.

Here we must break in on Don Virginio's letter for a moment. For at this point he smoothly omits to mention a circumstance which soon was common knowledge: namely, that *he looked through the window at the service below, and watched*

the Queen make her Epiphany offering. What was this but
'going with the Queen to church'? Was this behaviour proper
in a Prince Assistant to the Papal Throne? What the Catholics
thought of it may be gathered from a letter of Father Anthony
Rivers to Father Robert Parsons:

She invited him to go with her to her closet over the chapel,
having before given order that the Communion table should be
adorned with basin and ewer of gold and evening tapers and other
ornaments (some say also with a crucifix), and that all the minis-
try should be in rich copes. The Duke, of curiosity, accompanied
her, and she was very pleasant thereat, saying she would write
to the Pope not to chide him for that fact, with other like dis-
courses; and so, service ended, they returned. But herewithal
many Papists are much scandalized.

Scandalous it was, but very human. The Pope's decree had
offered him, the Orsino, a shameful public *disgrazia* when he
had come out to attend the Cardinal at Florence. Should he
now refuse to attend the great Queen who showed him *honori
particolarissimi*, out of fear of what that Pope would say? Or
of 'a kiss of the Inquisition'? He was very curious, charmed
and flattered, and a bit reckless. In his shoes, who would not
have been? And Elizabeth dared him. But let him get on with
his story:

At the end of half an hour her Majesty returned, with all the
Court two by two according to their quality and degrees before
her, and all the countesses and ladies after; and while I accompanied her she was ever discoursing with me, as she had also done
before.
When her Majesty had entered her chamber, I was conducted
into the hall where her Majesty was to dine: the which hall, together with many other rooms, was hanged with tapestries of
gold. On a dais at the head was her Majesty's table; at the opposite end, a great court-cupboard all of vessels of gold; on the right
hand, a great cupboard of vessels with gold and jewels; and on

the left, a low table with three little services for the Muscovite
ambassador and two who were with him : it being the custom of
Muscovy that if he had not been seen eating in the Queen's presence, his Great Duke would have had him beheaded.

Meanwhile came the viands of her Majesty, borne by knights,
and the Sewer was of the great Order [*i.e. of St George, the Garter*]. These did the same honour to her Majesty's chair of state
as they would have done had she been present; and as soon as
the table was prepared came the Queen. I reserve for telling by
word of mouth the manner of the many cloths, and of her hand-
washing, for this description alone would fill four sheets. Presently after her Majesty had sat down to table, the Muscovite
Ambassador (of whose ridiculous manners I shall give an account)
fell to dining; and I was conducted by the Lord Admiral (to
whom the Queen had given the office of High Steward, but only
for that day) and by many other great officers of the Crown and
Knights of the Order, into a hall [*the Council Chamber, adjoin-
ing*] where there was prepared for me a most noble banquet, at
the end of which appeared a good music.

As soon as the banquet was ended I rose from the table and
went to her Majesty, who was already on her feet; and talking
now with me, and now with the Muscovite Ambassador, she tar-
ried a while, and then was attended by me to her room. Those
gentlemen who were appointed to wait upon me, with many
others whose acquaintance I had made, conducted me to my
lodging [*Lord Worcester's*] so that I might rest myself; but after
a little the chief among them began coming to visit me; and then
there was music, of some instruments to my belief never heard in
Italy, but miraculous ones [*i.e. the hautboys, played no doubt by
the Waits of London*]; so that with good entertainment we came
to the hour of supper, which was made ready in a hall in my
own lodging [*the Queen had provided Jean Mouchy, Stafford's
French cook*]. To sup with me came the Master of the Horse
[*Lord Worcester*], and also the Earl of Cumberland (*Comber-
lan*); and with him I had some speech which will be to the taste
of his Highness [*the Grand Duke, his uncle Ferdinand*], since
that man is the greatest corsair in the world. Presently after supper I was taken to the lodgings of her Majesty, where in a hall
[*the Closet, or Withdrawing Room?*] the Secretary of State [*Sir
Robert Cecil*] caused me to salute all the ladies of title after the
French fashion [*first, kiss the fingers; next, kiss the lips; then*

embrace the waist]. With one I spoke Italian, with divers French; and with the rest he himself played the interpreter for me.

Hereupon the Queen came in, and commanded me to go along discoursing with her. [*Along the King's side, and down out, back of the Great Chamber, to the Hall stairs.*] Her Majesty mounted the stairs, amid such sounding of trumpets that methought I was on the field of war, and entered a public hall [*the Noon-hall*], where all round about were rising steps with ladies, and diverse consorts of music. As soon as her Majesty was set at her place [*the canopied throne on the dais before the grandstand at the South*], many ladies and knights began a Grand Ball. When this came to an end, there was acted a mingled comedy, with pieces of music and dances (*una commedia mescolata, con musiche e balli*), and this too I am keeping to tell by word of mouth [*Alas!*]. The Muscovite Ambassador was not present. I stood ever near her Majesty, who bade me be covered, and withal caused a stool to be fetched for me; and although she willed me a thousand times to sit, I would however never obey her. She conversed continually with me; and when the comedy was finished . . . .

Here we must beg to interrupt Don Virginio: to remind ourselves that for him this was the grand climax. The greatest Queen in the world had *publicly ranked him as her peer* by bidding him wear his hat in her presence. He accepted that rare honour; but courteously declined the still greater one – to be seated in public by her side. *She conversed continually with me.* Besides pointing out the deft and ingeniously-contrived compliments in Shakespeare's comedy, what did Queen Elizabeth chat about in her skilful Italian with Don Virginio? I find evidence of one topic at least: her own relationship with his ancient House, the Casa Orsina. She said that her Tudor Rose, embroidered in gold and silver on the scarlet coats of her Guard, and the Rose in the Orsini coat of arms were one and the same. For an Italian heraldic manuscript in the British Museum contains the following memorandum, based obviously on Don Virginio's own information :

By Queen Elizabeth of England, at a public ball, it was given
to the Duke, Virginio Orsini, to sit under the state (*sotto il trono*);
and the Queen said that the Rose, which is in her royal arms,
took its origin from the House of Orsini, and treated him as kin
(*lo trattò come parente*); and afterwards had her Historio-
grapher (*Archevesta*) send the Duke an authentical certificate
(*fede autentica*) of her descent.

I have not seen Queen Elizabeth's Orsini-Tudor genealogical
tree, engrossed especially for Don Virginio. But it is carefully
preserved today in Rome, among the treasured muniments of
Prince Virginio Orsini, 21st Duke of Gravina. Little wonder
that Don Virginio felt that even Shakespeare's graceful compliments were surpassed by Queen Elizabeth's claiming him for
her cousin. But we have interrupted his letter long enough, and
must go back to allow him to follow the glorious thread.

She conversed continually with me; and when the comedy
was finished, I waited upon her to her lodgings, where there was
made ready for her Majesty and for the ladies a most fair colla-
tion, all of confections. [*Mr Controller Knollys had seen to it
that it was 'made of better stuff fit for men to eat, and not of
paper shows as it is wont to be'.*] The Queen, having first taken
but two morsels, gave order that it should all be put to the spoil
(*tutta saccheggiata*); which was done amid a graceful confusion
(*con una confusione galante*). After the Queen had gone into
her chamber, those ladies who could speak Italian and French
fell into conversation with me, and at the end of half an hour we
took our leave of one another, and I went away home, it being
already two hours after midnight.

On seeing Don Virginio to bed – to the passing bellman's
cry, 'Past two o'clock and almost three, My masters all, good
day to ye!' – one's first unregenerate impulse is to wring his
neck for not planning to put more about the comedy into his
letter. But second thought reminds us that he acted precisely
as we should have done in his place: that is, he saved the best
and most fascinating detail – such as the Muscovite's *costumi*

ridicolosi, the Queen's rare dinner-ceremony, and the *commedia mescolata* in which the quick comedians extemporally had staged him to the life – to tell to his wife by gesture and by word of mouth.

SOURCE: *The First Night of 'Twelfth Night'* (1954)
pp. 30–2, 198–204

Joseph H. Summers

THE MASKS OF *TWELFTH NIGHT* (1955)

Love and its fulfillment are primary in Shakespeare's comedies. Its conflicts are often presented in terms of the battle of the generations. At the beginning of the plays the bliss of the young lovers is usually barred by an older generation of parents and rulers, a group which has supposedly experienced its own fulfillment in the past and which is now concerned with preserving old forms or fulfilling new ambitions. The comedies usually end with the triumph of young love, a triumph in which the lovers make peace with their elders and themselves assume adulthood and often power. The revolutionary force of love becomes an added element of vitality in a re-established society.

Twelfth Night does not follow the customary pattern. In this play the responsible older generation has been abolished, and there are no parents at all. In the first act we are rapidly introduced into a world in which the ruler is a love-sick Duke – in which young ladies, fatherless and motherless, embark on disguised actions, or rule, after a fashion, their own households, and in which the only individuals possibly over thirty are drunkards, jokesters, and gulls, totally without authority. All the external barriers to fulfillment have been eliminated in what becomes almost a parody of the state desired by the ordinary young lovers, the Hermias and Lysanders – or even the Rosalinds and Orlandos. According to the strictly romantic formula, the happy ending should be already achieved at the beginning of the play : we should abandon the theater for the rites of love. But the slightly stunned inhabitants of Illyria discover that they are anything but free. Their own actions provide the barriers, for most of them know neither themselves, nor others, nor their social world.

For his festival entertainment, Shakespeare freshly organized all the usual material of the romances – the twins, the exile, the impersonations – to provide significant movement for a dance of maskers. Every character has his mask, for the assumption of the play is that no one is without a mask in the serio-comic business of the pursuit of happiness. The character without disguises who is not ridiculous is outside the realm of comedy. Within comedy, the character who thinks it is possible to live without assuming a mask is merely too naïve to recognize the mask he has already assumed. He is the chief object of laughter. As a general rule, we laugh with the characters who know the role they are playing and we laugh at those who do not; we can crudely divide the cast of *Twelfth Night* into those two categories.

But matters are more complicated than this, and roles have a way of shifting. All the butts except perhaps Sir Andrew Aguecheek have moments in which they are the masters of our laughter; yet all the masters have moments in which they appear as fools. In our proper confusion, we must remember the alternative title of the play, 'What You Will'. It may indicate that everyone is free to invent his own title for the proceedings. It also tells the author's intention to fulfill our desires: we wish to share in the triumphs of love and we wish to laugh; we wish our fools occasionally to be wise, and we are insistent that our wisest dramatic figures experience our common fallibility. Most significantly, the title may hint that what 'we' collectively 'will' creates all the comic masks – that society determines the forms of comedy more directly than it determines those of any other literary genre.

At the opening of the play Orsino and Olivia accept the aristocratic (and literary) ideas of the romantic lover and the grief-stricken lady as realities rather than as ideas. They are comic characters exactly because of that confusion. Orsino

glories in the proper moodiness and fickleness of the literary
lover; only our own romanticism can blind us to the absurdities
in his opening speech. Orsino first wishes the music to continue
so that the appetite of love may 'surfeit'; immediately, however,
he demands that the musicians stop the music they are playing
to repeat an isolated phrase – an awkward procedure and a
comic bit of stage business which is rarely utilized in productions. Four lines later the music must stop entirely because the
repeated 'strain' no longer *is* sweet, and the appetite is truly
about to 'surfeit'. He then exclaims that the spirit of love is
so 'quick and fresh' that like the sea (hardly a model of fresh-
ness)

> nought enters there,
> Of what validity and pitch soe'er,
> But falls into abatement and low price,
> Even in a minute.

Orsino is a victim of a type of madness to which the most admirable characters are sometimes subject. Its usual causes are
boredom, lack of physical love, and excessive imagination, and
the victim is unaware that he is in love with love rather than
with a person.

In the same scene, before we ever see the lady, Olivia's state
is as nicely defined. Valentine, Orsino's messenger, has acquired
something of his master's extraordinary language, and his report on his love mission manages both to please the Duke and
to convey his own incredulity at the excess of Olivia's vow for
her brother. In his speech the fresh and the salt are again confused. It is impossible to keep fresh something so ephemeral
as grief; Olivia can make it last and 'season' it, however, by
the process of pickling –the natural effect of 'eye-offending
brine'. Orsino feels unbounded admiration for the depth of
soul indicated by Olivia's vow and at the same time he assumes
that the vow can easily be broken by a lover. He departs for

'sweet *beds* of flow'rs' which are somehow to provide a *canopy* for 'love-thoughts'.

Both Orsino and Olivia have adopted currently fashionable literary postures; yet neither of them is a fool. We are glad to be reassured by the Captain that Orsino is 'A noble duke, in nature as in name', and that his present infatuation is only a month old. Sir Toby's later remark 'What a plague means my niece, to take the death of her brother thus?' indicates that Olivia too had seemed an unlikely candidate for affectation. She is also an unconvincing practitioner. Although at our first glimpse of her she is properly the grief-stricken lady ('Take the fool away'), her propriety collapses under Feste's famous catechism. We discover that Olivia is already bored and that she really desires to love. Outraged nature has its full and comic revenge when Olivia falls passionately in love with a male exterior and acts with an aggressiveness which makes Orsino seem almost feminine. Still properly an actor in comedy, Olivia quickly changes from the character who has confused herself with a socially attractive mask to one who fails to perceive the mask which society has imposed on another.

Viola's situation allows time for neither love- nor grief-in-idleness. A virgin, shipwrecked in a strange land, possessing only wit and intelligence and the Captain's friendship, she must act immediately if she is to preserve herself. She, like Olivia, has 'lost' a brother, but the luxury of conventional mourning is quickly exchanged for a *willed* hope that, as she was saved, 'so perchance may he be'. With Viola's wish for time to know what her 'estate is', before she is 'delivered to the world', we are reminded that society often requires a mask, neither for the relief of boredom nor the enjoyment of acting, but merely for self-preservation. While Antonio, 'friend to Sebastian', almost loses his life because of his failure to assume a disguise, Viola suffers from no failure of discretion or imagination. She must assume a disguise as a boy and she must have help in preparing it.

Although she knows the ways of the world, Viola takes the necessary chance and wills to trust the Captain:

> There is a fair behaviour in thee, Captain.
> And though that nature with a beauteous wall
> Doth oft close in pollution, yet of thee
> I will believe thou hast a mind that suits
> With this thy fair and outward character.

We have in this second scene not only the beginning of one strand of the complicated intrigue, but also the creation of the one character active in the intrigue who provides a measure for the comic excesses of all the others. (Feste's role as observer is analogous to Viola's role as 'actor'.) Although Viola chooses to impersonate Cesario from necessity, she later plays her part with undisguised enjoyment. She misses none of the opportunities for parody, for confession, and for *double entendre* which the mask affords, and she never forgets or lets us forget the biological distance between Viola and Cesario. Except in the fencing match with Sir Andrew Aguecheek, she anticipates and directs our perception of the ludicrous in her own role as well as in the roles of Orsino and Olivia.

Sebastian is the reality of which Cesario is the artful imitation. Viola's twin assumes no disguises; Viola and the inhabitants of Illyria have assumed it for him. He is, to the eye, identical with Viola, and his early scenes with Antonio serve to remind us firmly of his existence as well as to introduce an initial exhilarating confusion at the entrance of either of the twins. When he truly enters the action of the play in Act IV he is certainly the object of our laughter, not because he has confused himself with an ideal or improper mask, but because he so righteously and ineffectually insists on his own identity in the face of unanimous public opposition. Our attitude quickly changes, however, to a mixture of amused patronization and identification: we do, after all, *know* so much more than does Sebastian; yet, within the context of the play, we can hardly

keep from identifying with the gentleman who, practically if
not idealistically, decides not to reject the reality of a passionate
Olivia just because he has never seen her before :

> Or I am mad, or else this is a dream.
> Let fancy still my sense in Lethe steep;
> If it be thus to dream, still let me sleep !

The other characters in the play do not truly belong to an
aristocracy of taste and leisure. For some of them, that is the
chief problem. Malvolio and Sir Andrew Aguecheek are ruled
by their mistaken notions of the proper role of an upper-class
gentleman, and they fail to perceive the comic gaps between
themselves and their ideal roles, and between those ideals and
the social reality. Sick with self-love as he is, Malvolio is also
sick with his desire to rise in society : 'an affection'd ass that
cons state without book and utters it by great swarths; the best
persuaded of himself, so cramm'd, as he thinks, with excellen-
cies that it is his grounds of faith that all that look on him love
him'. Although he knows it without, he has learned his 'state'
by book – but such a pupil inevitably distorts the text. He
dreams of ruling a thrifty and solemn household while he plays
with 'some rich jewel', a dream characteristically attractive to
the *arriviste* and absolutely impossible to the *arrivé*. We, like
Maria, 'can hardly forbear hurling things at him'. His is as
absurd as the reverse image which possesses Sir Andrew, a
carpet-knight rightly described by Sir Toby as 'an ass-head and
a coxcomb and a knave, a thin-faced knave, a gull !' In the
gallery of false images Sir Andrew's roaring boy hangs opposite Malvolio's burgher. Although in a low moment Sir Andrew
may think that he has 'no more wit than a Christian or an ordinary man has', he never has such grave self-doubt for long.
Like a true gull, he tries to assume the particular role which,
of all others, he is most poorly equipped to play : drinker,
fighter, wencher.

Sir Andrew, however, would hardly exist without Sir Toby Belch: the gull must have his guller. Sir Toby may fulfill Sir Andrew's idea of what a gentleman should be, but Sir Toby himself has no such odd idea of gentility. (Sir Andrew may be 'a dear manikin to you, Sir Toby', but Sir Toby has a superlatively good reason for allowing him to be: 'I have been dear to him, lad, some two thousand strong, or so.') Even at his most drunken, we are delightfully unsure whether we laugh at or with Sir Toby, whether he is or is not fully conscious of the effects as well as the causes of his 'mistakes', his verbal confusions, and even his belches. Like another drunken knight, and like Viola, Toby possesses a range of dramatic talents and he enjoys using them. He is equally effective as the fearless man of action, as the practitioner of noble 'gentleness' with the 'mad' Malvolio, and as the experienced alcoholic guide to Sir Andrew. His joy is in the jest as well as in the bottle, and he can bring himself to abandon the latter long enough to marry Maria simply in admiration for her ability as an intriguer. But like other knowing players, Sir Toby is vulnerable to deception. He is object rather than master of our laughter from the time when he mistakes Sebastian for Cesario and attempts to assert his masculine ability as a swordsman.

In the business of masking, Feste is the one professional among a crowd of amateurs; he does it for a living. He never makes the amateur's mistake of confusing his personality with his mask – he wears not motley in his brain. Viola recognizes his wisdom and some kinship in the fact that each 'must observe their mood on whom he jests'. But though Feste may have deliberately chosen his role, society determines its conditions. Now that he is growing old, the conditions become difficult: 'Go to, y'are a dry fool; I'll no more of you. Besides, you grow dishonest.' While all the other characters are concerned with gaining something they do not have, Feste's struggle is to retain his mask and to make it again ingratiating. He is able to penetrate all the masks of the others, and he succeeds in retaining his own.

However fanciful its dreams of desire, the play moves within a context of an almost real world, from one disguise and half-understood intrigue to another, until all its elements are whirled into a complexly related and moving figure. With the constant contrasts and parallels and reversals in character, situation, and intrigue, we find ourselves at last, along with Malvolio and Olivia and Viola and the rest, in a state of real delirium. Until the concluding scene, however, we can largely agree with Sebastian : if we dream, we do not wish to wake; if this is madness, it is still comic madness, and we do not envy the sane. The attempts at false and inflexible authority are being defeated, the pretentious are being deflated, and the very sentimentality of the likable sentimentalists has led them close to biological reality. We are particularly delighted with Viola. Young, intelligent, zestful, she is a realist. She cuts through the subterfuges and disguises of the others with absolute clarity, and she provides us with a center for the movement, a standard of normality which is never dull. In her rejection of the artificial myths of love, moreover, Viola never becomes the advocate of a far more terrifying myth, the myth of absolute rationality. In a completely rational world, Shakespeare never tires of pointing out, what we know as love could not exist. We have never desired such a world.

From the time of her first aside to the audience after she has seen Orsino ('Yet a barful strife ! / Whoe'er I woo, myself would be his wife'), Viola directly admits her irrational love. She differs, then, from Orsino and Olivia not in any invulnerability to blindness and passion, but in the clarity and simplicity with which she recognizes and accepts her state. Reason is not abandoned : she rationally admits her irrationality and her inability to cope with the situation :

> O Time, thou must untangle this, not I ;
> It is too hard a knot for me t'untie !

Viola needs a miracle. Although she may imagine herself as 'Patience on a monument, smiling at grief', she remains as close as possible to her loved one and waits for the miracle to happen. Since we have seen Sebastian, we know that the miracle will occur; yet through our identification with Viola we come to know the comic burden, the masker's increasing weariness of the mask which implies that love is still pursued rather than possessed.

The burden becomes comically unbearable only in the final scene, when it is cast off. Here Shakespeare underscores all those possibilities of violence and death which are usually submerged in comedy. Antonio is arrested and in danger of his life. Orsino, finally recognizing the hopelessness of his suit to Olivia, shows the vicious side of sentimentality. After considering the possibility of killing Olivia 'like to the Egyptian thief', he determines to do violence to 'Cesario' :

> Come, boy, with me; my thoughts are ripe in mischief :
> I'll sacrifice the lamb that I do love,
> To spite a raven's heart within a dove.

Olivia is hysterical at what seems to be the baseness of Cesario. Sir Toby has a broken pate to show for his one major failure to penetrate a mask. The dance must stop. The miracle must occur.

The entrance of Sebastian is 'what we will'. It is the most dramatic moment of the play. The confrontation of Sebastian and Cesario-Viola, those identical images, concludes the formal plot and provides the means for the discarding of all the lovers' masks. The moment must be savored and fully realized. As Viola and Sebastian chant their traditional formulas of proof, both the audience and the other characters on the stage undistractedly view the physical image of the duality which has made the confusion and the play. The masks and the play are to be abandoned for a vision of delight beyond delight, in which lovers have neither to wear nor to penetrate disguises since they are at last invulnerable to error and laughter.

Yet the play does not resolve into a magic blessing of the world's fertility as does *A Midsummer Night's Dream*. We have been promised a happy ending, and we receive it. We are grateful that the proper Jacks and Jills have found each other, but the miracle is a limited miracle, available only to the young and the lucky. Not every Jack has his Jill even in Illyria, and after the general unmasking, those without love may seem even lonelier. Malvolio, of course, is justly punished. He has earned his mad scene, and with the aid of Feste he has made it comic. As a result of his humiliation he has also earned some sort of redress. Yet he is ridiculous in his arrogance to the end, and his threatened revenge, now that he is powerless to effect it, sustains the comedy and the characterization and prevents the obtrusion of destructive pathos.

It is Feste rather than Malvolio who finally reminds us of the limitations and the costs of the romantic vision of happiness with which we have been seduced. However burdensome, masking is his career, and romantic love provides no end for it. Alone on the stage at the end of the play, he sings a song of unfulfilled love which shows the other side of the coin. For Feste, as for his audience, the mask can never be finally discarded : the rain it raineth every day. His song has those overtones, I believe, but they are only overtones. The music, here and elsewhere in the play, provides an element in which oppositions may be resolved. And the song itself, like the movement which must accompany it, is crude and witty as well as graceful and nostalgic. However far it may have missed the conventionally happy ending, Feste's saga of misfortunes in love is comic, even from his own point of view. The exaggeration so often operative in the refrains of Elizabethan lyrics emphasizes that the watery as well as the sunny vision can become funny : it doesn't rain every day by a long shot.

The song, which begins as the wittiest observer's comment on the denouement of the play, ends as a dissolution of the dramatic fiction :

> A great while ago the world begun,
>   With hey, ho, the wind and the rain,
> But that's all one, our play is done,
>   And we'll strive to please you every day.

The audience has been a participant in the festivity. As the fictional lovers have unmasked to reveal or realize their 'true' identities, it is only proper that the clown, the only character who might move freely in the environs of Bankside, as well as in the realm of Illyria, should unmask the whole proceeding for the imitation of a desired world which it has been. The audience must be returned from 'What You Will' to its own less patterned world where the sea rarely disgorges siblings given up for lost, where mistaken marriages rarely turn out well, where Violas rarely catch Dukes, and where Malvolios too often rule households with disturbing propriety. The lovers have met, and Feste announces that present laughter has come to an end. But the actors, those true and untiring maskers, will continue to 'strive to please' us. They will find few occasions in the future in which their efforts will be more sure of success.

Twelfth Night is the climax of Shakespeare's early achievement in comedy. The effects and values of the earlier comedies are here subtly embodied in the most complex structure which Shakespeare had yet created. But the play also looks forward : the pressure to dissolve the comedy, to realize and finally abandon the burden of laughter, is an intrinsic part of its 'perfection'. Viola's clear-eyed and affirmative vision of her own and the world's irrationality is a triumph and we desire it; yet we realize its vulnerability, and we come to realize that virtue in disguise is only totally triumphant when evil is not in disguise – is not truly present at all. Having solved magnificently the problems of this particular form of comedy, Shakespeare was evidently not tempted to repeat his triumph. After *Twelfth Night* the so-called comedies require for their happy resolutions more radical characters and devices – omniscient and omnipresent Dukes, magic, and resurrection. More obvious miracles are needed for comedy to exist in a world in which evil also exists, not merely incipiently but with power.

SOURCE : *University of Kansas City Review,* XXII (1955) 134-43

John Hollander

THE ROLE OF MUSIC IN *TWELFTH NIGHT* (1957)

When seen in the light of the richness of sixteenth-century musical thought, the modern academic question of 'Shakespeare and Music' tends to be more blinding than the glittering of its generality would warrant. With the aid of the musicological studies of the past thirty years, we are better able than ever before to reconstruct the actual music performed, and referred to, in Shakespeare's plays. The growth of study in the History of Ideas has given us models for understanding how words and customs that have misleadingly retained their forms to this day reverberated differently in various historical contexts. The forays of sixteenth- and seventeenth-century poets into *musica speculativa*, consequently, can now be understood as more than either the fanciful conceits or the transmissions of quaint lore that many nineteenth-century readers took them to be. But the recent critical traditions that read all of Shakespeare with the kind of attention previously devoted to other kinds of poetry has tended to create a third, queer category of symbolic music. G. Wilson Knight in particular has employed the images of tempest and music in his criticism to suggest the universal themes of disorder and resolving, reconciling order. These concepts stem largely from his invaluable early work on the last plays, in which, trivially speaking, storm and music do appear to alternate in profound and general ways. But more recently, Professor Knight has elevated his rather *symboliste* construction of the word 'music' to the heights proclaimed in Verlaine's manifesto: '*De la musique avant toute chose*'. One result of this has been, I feel, to credit Shakespeare's imagination with the creation of what, for hundreds of years, had been fairly widely received ideas. Worse than this, however, has been the failure to see exactly to what degree Shakespeare's poetic intelligence utilized these received ideas about music, both speculative and practical, analyzing and reinterpreting them in dramatic contexts. Finally, and perhaps worst of all, some of Shakespeare's amazingly original contributions to *musica speculativa* have been lost sight of.

Twelfth Night represents, I feel, an excellent case in point. Probably written late in 1600, its treatment of the theme of music is considerably more complex than that of the plays preceding it. By and large, the bulk of the references in all the plays is to practical music, which is cited, satirized, and praised in various contexts like any other human activity. Of particular interest to Shakespeare always was the richness of various technical vocabularies, and much of the wit in all but the later plays consists of puns and twisted tropes on technical terminology, often that of instrumental music. Two well-known passages of *musica speculativa* in the earlier plays, however, deserve some comment.

The first of these is Richard II's great speech in Pomfret castle. After likening his prison to the world and to his own body, the King hears music offstage :

> Music do I hear?
> Ha, ha ! keep time. How sour sweet music is
> When time is broke and no proportion kept !
> So is it in the music of men's lives.
> And here have I the daintiness of ear
> To check time broke in a disorder'd string;
> But, for the concord of my state and time,
> Had not an ear to hear my true time broke. (v v 41–8)

'Proportion' here is used in its immediate sense of time-signature, and 'time broke in a disordered string' refers to the music he hears playing. But the 'disordered string' is also himself, an emblem of the unruled, unruly state. 'The concord of my state

and time' invokes the musical connotations of 'concord' as well
– for centuries the word had reverberated with the old pun on
'heart' and 'string'. What the King is saying is that now, in his
broken state, he is sensitive to all the nuances of musical order,
but formerly, lulled by the metaphorically musical order of
his earlier reign, he had been unable to hear the tentative tempi
in his own *musica humana*. In this passage an occurrence of
practical music is interpreted in perfectly traditional terms, and
human and worldly musics are made to coincide, both in
Richard's own rhetoric and in the hierarchical imagery
throughout the play. The.conventional multiplicity of exten-
sions of the term 'music' are employed directly, and Richard,
aside from the tireless progression of his thoughts, is talking
like something out of an Old Book.

The final irony of Richard's soliloquy:

> This music mads me. Let it sound no more;
> For though it have holp madmen to their wits,
> In me it seems it will make wise men mad.
> Yet blessings on his heart that gives it me!
> For 'tis a sign of love; and love to Richard
> Is a strange brooch in this all-hating world. (v v 61–6)

is reinforced by the fragmentation of 'music' into its various
categories. The music is maddening because its human and
universal roles have not coincided for the King, whose necessary identity with the proper order of the state has been called
into question by the fact of his deposition and imprisonment.
Bolingbroke, the discord, the untuner, will himself become the
well-tuned regulating instrument of state. And finally, the practical music is sundered from its speculative form in Richard's
gratitude for the instrumental sounds themselves, which he
takes as the evidence of someone's thoughtful care.

I believe that it is this same conventional use of the emblematic stringed instrument in a political context that is at
work during a moment in Brutus' tent in Act iv, scene iii of

Julius Caesar. The boy Lucius has fallen asleep over his instrument after singing for Brutus, and the latter has taken it away from him lest it drop to the ground and break. After the ominous appearance of Caesar's ghost, Brutus cries out, and the boy half-awakens, murmuring, 'The strings, my lord, are false'. Brutus, missing the import of this, comments, 'He thinks he still is at his instrument', and shakes Lucius fully awake, inquiring after the phantom. But the meaning, I think, is clear, and the false strings are the discordant conspirators, now jangling and out of tune even among themselves. Brutus, who 'in general honest thought/ And common good to all, made one' of the varying faction he led, meets the prophetic truth of the boy's half-dreamed image with a benevolently naturalistic interpretation of it.

The even better known music at Belmont in *The Merchant of Venice* shows a more dramatically sophisticated use of *musica speculativa.* In general, the dramatic structure of the whole play hinges on the relationship between Venice, the commercial city where gold is ventured for more gold, and the symbolically golden Belmont, where all is hazarded for love. Belmont is full of practical music in one of its most common sixteenth-century forms. Music used for signalling, the tuckets, flourishes, and sennets familiar to modern readers through stage directions, were not confined to the uses of dramaturgy; it was a matter of actual practice for distinguished persons to be accompanied by their private trumpeters. It is almost as a signal that the song 'Tell me where is fancy bred' is employed. Like a nursery-rhyme riddle, it advises against appearances, and cryptically urges the choice of the lead. In a speech preceding the song, Portia's wit analyses and interprets the ceremonial music she has ordered :

> Let music sound while he doth make his choice;
> Then, if he lose, he makes a swan-like end,
> Fading in music. That the comparison

May stand more proper, my eye shall be the stream
And wat'ry deathbed for him. He may win;
And what is music then? Then music is
Even as the flourish when true subjects bow
To a new-crowned monarch. (III ii 43–50)

Here Portia makes the point that the same music can play many
roles, that the institution emerges from the fact as the result of
an intellectual process. She selects two polar institutions, in-
cidentally : music as signal, which plays little or no part in traditional musical speculation, and the myth of the dying swan, a
stock image in romantic lyrics throughout the century. Portia
reaffirms this later on, when she remarks of the music that
Jessica and Lorenzo hear on the bank, 'Nothing is good, I see,
without respect;/ Methinks it sounds much sweeter than by
day.' Nerissa replies that 'Silence bestows that virtue on it',
invoking one of the dominant Belmont themes of the deception of ornament, of the paleness more moving than eloquence.
It is the same theme that prefaces Lorenzo's initiation of Jessica
into the silent *harmonia mundi* :

> Soft stillness and the night
> Become the touches of sweet harmony.
> Sit, Jessica. Look how the floor of heaven
> Is thick inlaid with patines of bright gold;
> There's not the smallest orb which thou behold'st
> But in his motion like an angel sings,
> Still quiring to the young-ey'd cherubins;
> Such harmony is in immortal souls,
> But whilst this muddy vesture of decay
> Doth grossly close it in, we cannot hear it. (v i 56–65)

This is the vision of Plato's Er and Cicero's Scipio. It is significant that the one instance of Shakespeare's troping of the
doctrine is Lorenzo's explanation of the inaudible character of
the heavenly music. Neither of the traditional reasons (accli-
matization, or the physical thresholds of perception) is given.'

Instead, the unheard music is related to immortality, and by extension, to a prelapsarian condition, a world which, like heaven, need not conceal its ultimate gold, which even Belmont must do. This approaches Milton's treatment of the subject in *At a Solemn Musick*.

Then enter the musicians, to play at Lorenzo's bidding. 'I am never merry when I hear sweet music', says Jessica. She may, of course, be referring to the concentration demanded by the soft, 'indoor' music of Portia's house musicians, as opposed to the more strident character of 'outdoor' instruments. Lorenzo, at any rate, answers this with an instructive, though standard, disquisition on music and the affections, ending on a note of *musica humana* with all of its ethical and political connotations :

> The reason is your spirits are attentive ;
> For do but note a wild and wanton herd,
> Or race of youthful and unhandled colts,
> Fetching mad bounds, bellowing and neighing loud,
> Which is the hot condition of their blood –
> If they but hear perchance a trumpet sound,
> Or any air of music touch their ears,
> You shall perceive them make a mutual stand,
> Their savage eyes turn'd to a modest gaze
> By the sweet power of music. Therefore the poet
> Did feign that Orpheus drew trees, stones, and floods;
> Since naught so stockish, hard, and full of rage,
> But music for the time doth change his nature.
> The man that hath no music in himself
> Nor is not mov'd with concord of sweet sounds,
> Is fit for treasons, stratagems, and spoils;
> The motions of his spirit are dull as night
> And his affections dark as Erebus.
> Let no such man be trusted. Mark the music. (v i 70–88)

Innuendoes of *musica mundana*, golden, silent, and inaccessible, are intimated at Belmont, where actual music is heard, and where the Venetian incompatibilities of gold and love are finally reconciled, almost as much in the golden music as in the golden ring.

In *Twelfth Night*, however, the role of music is so obviously fundamental to the spirit of the play that it is momentarily surprising to find so little speculative music brought up for discussion. But I think that, on consideration of the nature of the play itself, the place of both active and intellectual music, and the relations ·between them, emerge as something far more complex than Shakespeare had hitherto cause to employ. *Twelfth Night* is, in very serious ways, a play about parties and what they do to people. Full of games, revels, tricks, and disguises, it is an Epiphany play, a ritualized Twelfth Night festivity in itself, but it is much more than this : the play gives us an analysis, as well as a representation, of feasting. It developes an ethic of indulgence based on the notion that the personality of any individual is a function not of the static proportions of the humors within him, but of the dynamic appetites that may more purposefully, as well as more pragmatically, be said to govern his behavior. Superficially close to the comedy of humors in the characterological extremes of its *dramatis personae*, the play nevertheless seems almost intent on destroying the whole theory of comedy and of morality entailed by the comedy of humors.

The nature of a revel is disclosed in the first scene. The materials are to be music, food and drink, and love. The basic action of both festivity in general, and of the play itself, is declared to be that of so surfeiting the appetite that it will sicken and die, leaving fulfilled the tempered, harmonious self. The movement of the whole play is that of a party, from appetite, through the direction of that appetite outward toward something, to satiation, and eventually to the condition when, as the Duke hopes for Olivia, 'liver, brain and heart/These sovereign thrones, are all supplied, and filled/Her sweet perfections with one self king'. The 'one self king' is the final harmonious state to be achieved by each reveller, but it is also, in both the

Duke's and Olivia's case, Cesario, who kills 'the flock of all affections else' that live in them, and who is shown forth in a literal epiphany in the last act.

The Duke's opening speech describes both the action of feasting, and his own abundant, ursine, romantic temperament. But it also contains within it an emblematic representation of the action of surfeiting :

> If music be the food of love, play on,
> Give me excess of it, that, surfeiting,
> The appetite may sicken and so die.
> That strain again ! It had a dying fall;
> O, it came o'er my ear like the sweet sound
> That breathes upon a bank of violets,
> Stealing and giving odour ! Enough, no more;
> 'Tis not so sweet now as it was before. (1 i 1–8)

The one personage in the play who remains in a melancholy humor is the one person who is outside the revels and cannot be affected by them. Olivia's rebuke cuts to the heart of his nature : 'You are sick of self-love, Malvolio, and taste with a distemper'd appetite.' Suffering from a kind of moral indigestion, Malvolio's true character is revealed in his involuted, Puritanic sensibility that allows of no appetites directed outward. His rhetoric is full of the Devil; it is full of humors and elements as well. No other character tends to mention these save in jest, for it is only Malvolio who believes in them. Yet real, exterior fluids of all kinds, wine, tears, sea-water, urine, and finally the rain of inevitability bathe the whole world of Illyria, in constant reference throughout the play.

The general concern of *Twelfth Night*, then, is *musica humana*, the Boethian application of abstract order and proportion to human behavior. The literalization of the universal harmony that is accomplished in comedy of humors, however, is unequivocally rejected. 'Does not our lives consist of the four elements?' catechizes Sir Toby. 'Faith, so they say', replies Sir Andrew, 'but I think it rather consists of eating and drinking.'

'Th'art a scholar', acknowledges Sir Toby. 'Let us therefore
eat and drink.' 'Who you are and what you would are out of
my welkin – I might say "element", but the word is over-
worn', says Feste, who, taking offense at Malvolio's characterization of him as a 'dry fool' touches off the whole proceedings
against the unfortunate steward. The plot to ridicule Malvolio
is more than the frolicsome revenge of an 'allowed fool'; it
serves both to put down the 'party-pooper' and to affirm the
psychology of appetite and fulfillment that governs the play.
To the degree that the *musica humana* of *Twelfth Night* involves the substitution of an alternative view to the fairly standard sixteenth-century descriptions of the order of the passions,
an application of the musical metaphor would be trivial, and
perhaps misleading. But the operation of practical music in the
plot, the amazingly naturalistic treatment of its various forms,
and the conclusions implied as to the nature and effects of
music in both the context of celebration and in the world at
large, all result in some musical speculation that remains one of
the play's unnoticed accomplishments.

The actual music in *Twelfth Night* starts and finishes the
play, occurring throughout on different occasions and in different styles. The presumably instrumental piece in which the
Duke wallows at the opening dampens his desire for it very
quickly, but that desire returns before long. Orsino's appetite
at the start of the play is purportedly for Olivia, who hungers
for, and indulges herself in, her own grief. The Duke's actual
love, too, is for his own act of longing, and for his own exclamations of sentiment. Both of these desires are directed outward
before the play is over. But until a peculiar musical mechanism, which will be mentioned later on, as has been set to work,
the Duke will hunt his own heart, and his desires, 'like fell and
cruel hounds', will continue to pursue him. The music in Act II,
scene iv, is of just such a nature to appease the Duke's extreme
sentimentality. Orsino makes it plain what sort of song he
wants to hear :

Now, good Cesario, but that piece of song,
That old and antique song we heard last night;
Methought it did relieve my passion much,
More than light airs and recollected terms
Of these most brisk and giddy-pacèd times. (ii iv 2–6)

This is a familiar sentimental attitude, the desire for the Good Old Song that nudges the memory, the modern request made of the cocktail pianist, the half-ironic translation in Bert Brecht's *Happy End*, where a singer tries to recapture better days by imploring '*Joe, mach die Musik von damals nach*'. Orsino's favorite song, he says,

is old and plain;
The spinsters and the knitters in the sun,
And the free maids that weave their thread with bones,
Do use to chant it; it is silly sooth,
And dallies with the innocence of love,
Like the old age. (ii iv 42–7)

Actually, the song that Feste sings him is a highly extravagant, almost parodic version of the theme of death from unrequited love. Its rather stilted diction and uneasy prosody are no doubt intended to suggest a song from an old miscellany. 'Come away' is a banal beginning, appearing at the start of four song texts in Canon Fellowes' collection. We may also presume that the setting employed was rather more archaic than that of the well-polished lute accompaniments of the turn of the century.

It is just one of these 'light airs and recollected terms', however, with which Sir Toby and Feste plague Malvolio in their big scene of carousal (ii iii). A setting of 'Farewell, dear heart' appears in Robert Jones' first book of airs, published in 1600. Of the other songs in the same scene, one is a round, a more trivial form of song, certainly with respect to its text, than the sophisticated and intricate lewdness of· the post-Restoration catch. The other is a 'love song' sung by Feste, and preferred by Sir Toby and Sir Andrew to 'a song of good life', perhaps with a pious text. It is of the finest type of Shakesperian

song that catches up the spirit of overall themes and individual
characters, ironically and prophetically pointing to the end of
a plot or bit of action. All of 'O mistress mine' is in one sense an
invocation to Olivia to put off her self-indulgent grief, her
courting of her dead brother's memory. In particular, the first
stanza refers to Viola, the boy–girl true love, 'that can sing
both high and low'.

Feste's songs to Malvolio in his madman's prison are both
of an archaic cast. The first is a snatch of a song of Wyatt's, 'A
robyn, joly robyn' that was set to music by William Cornish
during the reign of Henry VIII. The other one, a parting jibe
at Malvolio's cant about the Devil, suggests the doggerel of an
old Morality, invoking Malvolio as the Devil himself, and continuing the game of mocking him by appealing to his own
rhetoric.

All of these occurrences of practical music function in the
plot as well as with respect to the general theme of feasting and
revels. The one reference to *musica speculativa* is a very interesting one, however, and leads to the most important aspect of
the operation of music in *Twelfth Night*. Olivia is exhorting
Viola to refrain from mentioning the Duke to her, and imply-
ing that she would rather be courted by his messenger :

> I bade you never speak again of him ;
> But would you undertake another suit,
> I had rather hear you to solicit that
> Than music from the spheres. (iii i 104–7)

The citation of the music of the spheres here has the tone of
most such references during the later seventeenth century in
England. With the exception of poets like Milton and Marvell,
who used metaphors from the old cosmology for intricate poetic
purposes of their own, the music of the spheres became, in
Cavalier and Augustan poetry, a formal compliment, empty
of even the metaphorical import that the world view of the centuries preceding had given to it. Just as the word 'heavenly',

used in exclamations of praise, long ago became completely divorced from its substantive root, the music of the spheres gradually came to designate the acme of effective charm in a performer. It was often employed in compliments to ladies, for example, whose skill at singing made the spheres sound dissonant, abashed the singing angels, and so forth.

As in the case of Dryden's music that would 'untune the sky', references to the heavenly harmony had nothing to do with received ideas of music's importance during the later seventeenth century, which were more and more becoming confined to a rhetorical ability to elicit passion, on the one hand, and to provide ornament to the cognitive import of a text, on the other. Purcell likens music and poetry to beauty and wit, respectively; the former can unite to produce the same wondrous effects in song that the latter can in a human being, although the virtues of each are independent. The differences between music and poetry also tended to cluster about the celebrated rift between thought and feeling. Most important of all, traditional *musica speculativa* gradually ceased being a model of universal order, and was replaced by a notion of music as a model of rhetoric, whose importance lay in its ability to move the passions, rather than in its older role of the microcosmic copy of universal harmony. The Apollonian lute–harp–lyre constellation, once an emblem of reason and order, became an instrument of passion in the hands of Caravaggio's leering boys, and in the hands of Crashaw's musician who slew the nightingale by musically ravishing her, as even her avatar Philomela was never so ravished, to death.

With these considerations in mind, the crucial role of Viola as an instrument of such a rhetorical music becomes quite clear. It is unfortunate that we have no precise indication of an earlier version of the play, presumably rewritten when the superior singer Robert Armin entered Shakespeare's company, in which some of the songs may have been assigned to Viola. She declares herself at the outset :

> I'll serve this duke :
> Thou shalt present me as an eunuch to him;
> It may be worth thy pains, for I can sing
> And speak to him in many sorts of music,
> That will allow me very worth his service. (ɪ ii 55–9)

She will be the Duke's instrument, although she turns out to
be an instrument that turns in his hand, charming both Olivia
and himself in unexpected fashion. Orsino is given an excess
of music in Viola. As Cesario, she wins Olivia for her alter ego
Sebastian who is himself, in his few scenes, rhetorically effective
almost to the point of preciosity, and who is likened to the musician Arion who charmed his way to safety. Viola is the affec-
tive, instrumental, prematurely Baroque music in *Twelfth
Night*, and it is she whose charm kills off the gourmandizing
sentimentality in both Orsino and Olivia, directing their appetites of love outward, in fact, towards herself. Among the
characters to whom Malvolio refers as 'the lighter people', it
is Feste, the singer and prankster, whose pipe and tabor serve
as a travesty of Viola's vocal chords. The operation of Viola's
'music' involves charming by the use of appearances; the effects
of the trickery instigated by Feste are to make Malvolio appear,
until he is undeceived, to be Olivia's ridiculously amorous
swain. (It is, of course, the phrase 'To be Count Malvolio' that
appears on his lips after reading the forged letter.) Through
the mechanism of fooling, the travesty of music below stairs,
Sir Andrew is chastened, Sir Toby is soberly married to Maria,
Malvolio is made to act out the madness of which he falsely
accused Feste, and 'the whirligig of time brings in his revenges'.

The music that brings about the conclusion of the revels is
thus a figurative music. It pervades the symbolic enactment of
indulgence and surfeit in the plot as the actual music, rele-
gated to its several uses and forms with considerable eye to
details of practice in Shakespeare's own day, pervades the spectacle of *Twelfth Night*. The play is about revelry, and, in itself,
a revels; so too; there is music in it, and a working out of a theme

in speculative music that strangely coincides with later views on the subject. The *Ursprung* of Viola's music is certainly in the action of the play; it is not to be implied that *Twelfth Night* is anything of a formal treatise, and the music in Illyria all serves its immediately dramatic purposes. Within the context of the play's anti-Puritan, anti-Jonsonian treatment of moral physiology, the role of music seems to have become inexorably defined for Shakespeare. Set in a framework of what, at this point, might be almost coy to call a study in *musica humana,* practical music becomes justified in itself. Free of even the scraps of traditional musical ideology that had been put to use in the plays preceding it, *Twelfth Night* represents a high point in one phase of Shakespeare's musical dramaturgy. It is not until *Antony and Cleopatra* and the last romances that the use of an almost supernatural music, perhaps imported to some degree from the musical *données* of the masque, comes to be associated with the late, great themes of reconciliation and transformation.

SOURCE : *Sound and Poetry: English Institute Essays 1956* (1957) pp. 66–82

C. L. Barber

TESTING COURTESY AND HUMANITY IN *TWELFTH NIGHT* (1959)

. . . nature to her bias drew in that.

The title of *Twelfth Night* may well have come from the first occasion when it was performed, whether or not Dr Leslie Hotson is right in arguing that its first night was the court celebration of the last of the twelve days of Christmas on January 6, 1600–1601.[1] The title tells us that the play is like holiday misrule – though not just like it, for it adds 'or what you will'. The law student John Manningham, who saw it at the Middle Temple's feast on February 2, 1602, wrote in his diary that it was 'much like the Comedy of Errores, or Menechmi in Plautus, but most like and neere to that in Italian called *Inganni*'. Actually, Shakespeare used, in addition to Plautine devices with which he was familiar, not *Gl'Inganni* to which Manningham refers, but Rich's tale *Of Apolonius and Silla,* a romance perhaps derived indirectly from that Italian comedy. And he used no written source for the part Manningham specially praised : 'A good practise in it to make the Steward beleeve his Lady widdowe was in love with him. . . .'[2] So *Twelfth Night* puts together a tale from a romance, Plautine farce, festivity, and the sort of merry sport or 'practice' which Shakespeare customarily added from his own invention.

Shakespeare can be inclusive in his use of traditions because his powers of selection and composition can arrange each element so that only those facets of it show which will serve his expressive purpose. He leaves out the dungeon in which Rich's jealous Orsino shuts up Viola, as well as Sebastian's departure leaving Olivia with child; but he does not hesitate to keep such events as the shipwreck, or Sebastian's amazing marriage to a stranger, or Orsino's threat to kill Viola. It is not the credibility of the event that is decisive, but what can be expressed through it. Thus the shipwreck is made the occasion for Viola to exhibit an undaunted, aristocratic mastery of adversity – she settles what she shall do next almost as though picking out a costume for a masquerade :

> I'll serve this duke :
> Thou shalt present me as an eunuch to him;
> It may be worth thy pains, for I can sing
> And speak to him in many sorts of music . . . (1 ii 55–8)

What matters is not the event, but what the language says as gesture, the aristocratic, free-and-easy way she settles what she will do and what the captain will do to help her. The pathetical complications which are often dwelt on in the romance are not allowed to develop far in the play; instead Viola's spritely language conveys the fun she is having in playing a man's part, with a hidden womanly perspective about it. One cannot quite say that she is playing in a masquerade, because disguising *just* for the fun of it is a different thing. But the same sort of festive pleasure in transvestism is expressed.

It is amazing how little happens in *Twelfth Night,* how much of the time people are merely talking, especially in the first half, before the farcical complications are sprung. Shakespeare is so skillful by now in rendering attitudes by the gestures of easy conversation that when it suits him he can almost do without events. In the first two acts of *Twelfth Night* he holds our interest with a bare minimum of tension while unfolding a pattern of contrasting attitudes and tones in his several persons. Yet Shakespeare's whole handling of romantic story, farce, and practical joke makes a composition which moves in the manner of his earlier festive comedies, through release to clarification.[3]

'A MOST EXTRACTING FRENZY'

Olivia's phrase in the last act, when she remembers Malvolio and his 'madness', can summarize the way the play moves:

> A most extracting frenzy of mine own
> From my remembrance clearly banish'd his. (v i 273-4)

People are caught up by delusions or misapprehensions which take them out of themselves, bringing out what they would keep hidden or did not know was there. *Madness* is a key word. The outright gull Malvolio is already 'a rare turkey-cock' from 'contemplation' (ɪɪ v 28) before Maria goes to work on him with her forged letter. 'I do not now fool myself, to let imagination jade me' (ɪɪ v 145), he exclaims when he has read it, having been put 'in such a dream that when the image of it leaves him he must run mad' (ɪɪ v 173). He is too self-absorbed actually to run mad, but when he comes at Olivia, smiling and cross-gartered, she can make nothing else of it: 'Why, this is very mid-summer madness' (ɪɪɪ iv 53). And so the merry-makers have the chance to put him in a dark room and do everything they can to face him out of his five wits.

What they bring about as a 'pastime' (ɪɪɪ iv 132), to 'gull him into a nayword, and make him a common recreation' (ɪɪ iii 127), happens unplanned to others by disguise and mistaken identity. Sir Toby, indeed, 'speaks nothing but madman' (ɪ v 100) without any particular occasion. 'My masters, are you mad?' (ɪɪ iii 83) Malvolio asks as he comes in to try to stop the midnight singing. Malvolio is sure that he speaks for the countess when he tells Toby that 'though she harbours you as her kinsman, she's nothing allied to your disorders' (ɪɪ iii 93). But in fact this sober judgment shows that he is not 'any more than a steward' (ɪɪ iii 109). For his lady, dignified though her bearing is, suddenly finds herself doing 'I know not what' (ɪ v 292) under the spell of Viola in her page's disguise : 'how now ? / Even so quickly may one catch the plague?' (I v 278–9). 'Poor lady,' exclaims Viola, 'she were better love a dream!' (II ii 24). In their first interview, she had told the countess, in urging the count's suit, that 'what is yours to bestow is not yours to reserve' (I v 177). By the end of their encounter, Olivia says the same thing in giving way to her passion : 'Fate, show thy force! Ourselves we do not owe' (I v 294). And soon her avowals of love come pouring out, overcoming the effort at control which shows she is a lady :

> O, what a deal of scorn looks beautiful
> In the contempt and anger of his lip !
> A murd'rous guilt shows not itself more soon
> Than love that would seem hid : love's night is noon.
> Cesario, by the roses of the spring,
> By maidhood, honour, truth, and everything,
> I love thee so ... (III i 142–8)

A little later, when she hears about Malvolio and his smile, she summarizes the parallel with 'I am as mad as he, / If sad and merry madness equal be' (III iv 14–15).

The farcical challenge and 'fight' between Viola and Sir Andrew are another species of frantic action caused by delusion. 'More matter for a May morning' (III iv 136) Fabian calls it as they move from pretending to exorcise Malvolio's devil to pretending to act as solicitous seconds for Sir Andrew. When Antonio enters the fray in manly earnest, there is still another sort of comic error, based not on a psychological distortion but simply on mistaken identity. This Plautine sort of confusion leads Sebastian to exclaim, 'Are all the people mad?' (IV i 26). Just after we have seen 'Malvolio the lunatic' (IV ii 22) baffled in the dark room ('But tell me true, are you not mad indeed? or do you but counterfeit?' IV ii 109–10), we see Sebastian struggling to understand his wonderful encounter with Olivia :

> This is the air; that is the glorious sun;
> This pearl she gave me, I do feel't and see't;
> And though 'tis wonder that enwraps me thus,
> Yet 'tis not madness. (IV iii 1–4)

The open-air clarity of this little scene anticipates the approaching moment when delusions and misapprehensions are resolved by the finding of objects appropriate to passions. Shakespeare, with fine stagecraft, spins the misapprehensions out to the last moment. He puts Orsino, in his turn, through an extracting frenzy, the Duke's frustration converting at last to violent impulses toward Olivia and Cesario, before he discovers in the page the woman's love he could not win from the countess.

That it should all depend on there being an indistinguishable twin brother always troubles me when I think about it, though never when I watch the play. Can it be that we enjoy the play so much simply because it is a wish-fulfillment presented so skillfully that we do not notice that our hearts are duping our heads? Certainly part of our pleasure comes from pleasing make-believe. But I think that what chance determines about particular destinies is justified, as was the case with *The Merchant of Venice*, by the play's realizing dynamically general distinctions and tendencies in life.

'YOU ARE BETROTH'D BOTH TO A MAID AND MAN'

The most fundamental distinction the play brings home to us is the difference between men and women. To say this may seem to labor the obvious; for what love story does not emphasize this difference? But the disguising of a girl as a boy in *Twelfth Night* is exploited so as to renew in a special way our sense of the difference. Just as a saturnalian reversal of social roles need not threaten the social structure, but can serve instead to consolidate it, so a temporary, playful reversal of sexual roles

can renew the meaning of the normal relation. One can add
that with sexual as with other relations, it is when the normal
is secure that playful aberration is benign. This basic security
explains why there is so little that is queazy in all Shakespeare's
handling of boy actors playing women, and playing women
pretending to be men. This is particularly remarkable in
Twelfth Night, for Olivia's infatuation with Cesario-Viola is
another, more fully developed case of the sort of crush Phebe
had on Rosalind. Viola is described as distinctly feminine in
her disguise, more so than Rosalind:

> ... they shall yet belie thy happy years
> That say thou art a man : Diana's lip
> Is not more smooth and rubious; thy small pipe
> Is as the maiden's organ, shrill and sound,
> And all is semblative a woman's part. (i iv 30–4)

When on her embassy Viola asks to see Olivia's face and exclaims about it, she shows a woman's way of relishing another
woman's beauty – and sensing another's vanity: ' 'Tis beauty
truly blent. . . .' 'I see you what you are – you are too proud'
(i v 223, 234). Olivia's infatuation with feminine qualities in
a youth takes her, doing 'I know not what', from one stage of
life out into another, from shutting out suitors in mourning for
her brother's memory, to ardor for a man, Sebastian, and the
clear certainty that calls out to 'husband' in the confusion of
the last scene.

We might wonder whether this spoiled and dominating
young heiress may not have been attracted by what she could
hope to dominate in Cesario's youth – but it was not the habit
of Shakespeare's age to look for such implications. And besides,
Sebastian is not likely to be dominated; we have seen him
respond to Andrew when the ninny knight thought he was
securely striking Cesario:

Andrew. Now, sir, have I met you again? There's for you!
Sebastian. Why, there's for thee, and there, and there!

(IV i 24–5)

To see this manly reflex is delightful – almost a relief – for we
have been watching poor Viola absurdly perplexed behind her
disguise as Sir Toby urges her to play the man: 'Dismount
thy tuck, be yare in thy preparation. . . . Therefore on, or strip
your sword naked; for meddle you must, that's certain'
(III iv 214, 240). She is driven to the point where she exclaims in an aside: 'Pray God defend me! A little thing would
make me tell them how much I lack of a man' (III iv 286–7).
What she lacks, Sebastian has. His entrance in the final scene
is preceded by comical testimony of his prowess, Sir Andrew
with a broken head and Sir Toby halting. The particular im-
plausibility that there should be an identical man to take Viola's
place with Olivia is submerged in the general, beneficent realization that there is such a thing as a man. Sebastian's comment
when the confusion of identities is resolved points to the general
force which has shaped particular developments:

> So comes it, lady, you have been mistook.
> But nature to her bias drew in that. (v i 251–2)

Over against the Olivia–Cesario relation, there are Orsino–
Cesario and Antonio–Sebastian. Antonio's impassioned friendship for Sebastian is one of those ardent attachments between
young people of the same sex which Shakespeare frequently
presents, with his positive emphasis, as exhibiting the loving
and lovable qualities later expressed in love for the other sex.[4]
Orsino's fascination with Cesario is more complex. In the opening scene, his restless sensibility can find no object: 'nought
enters there, . . . / But falls into abatement . . . / Even in a minute' (I i 11–14). Olivia might be an adequate object; she at
least is the Diana the sight of whom has, he thinks, turned him
to an Acteon torn by the hounds of desires. When we next see

him, and Cesario has been only three days in his court, his entering question is 'Who saw Cesario, ho?' (I iv 10) and already he has unclasped to the youth 'the book even of [his] secret soul' (I iv 13). He has found an object. The delight he takes in Cesario's fresh youth and graceful responsiveness in conversation and in service, is one part of the spectrum of love for a woman, or better, it is a range of feeling that is common to love for a youth and love for a woman. For the audience, the woman who is present there, behind Cesario's disguise, is brought to mind repeatedly by the talk of love and of the differences of men and women in love. 'My father had a daughter loved a man . . .' (II iv 106)

> She never told her love,
> But let concealment, like a worm i' th' bud,
> Feed on her damask cheek. (II iv 109–11)

This supremely feminine damsel, who 'sat like patience on a monument', is not Viola. She is a sort of polarity within Viola, realized all the more fully because the other, active side of Viola does not pine in thought at all, but instead changes the subject: '. . . and yet I know not. / Sir, shall I to this lady? – Ay, that's the theme' (II iv 120–1). The effect of moving back and forth from woman to sprightly page is to convey how much the sexes differ yet how much they have in common, how everyone who is fully alive has qualities of both. Some such general recognition is obliquely suggested in Sebastian's amused summary of what happened to Olivia:

> You would have been contracted to a maid;
> Nor are you therein, by my life, deceiv'd:
> You are betroth'd both to a maid and man. (v i 253–5)

The countess marries the man in this composite, and the count marries the maid. He too has done he knows not what while nature drew him to her bias, for he has fallen in love with the maid without knowing it.

LIBERTY TESTING COURTESY

We have seen how each of the festive comedies tends to focus on a particular kind of folly that is released along with love – witty masquerade in *Love's Labour's Lost*, delusive fantasy in *A Midsummer Night's Dream*, romance in *As You Like It*, and, in *The Merchant of Venice*, prodigality balanced against usury. *Twelfth Night* deals with the sort of folly which the title points to, the folly of misrule. But the holiday reference limits its subject too narrowly : the play exhibits the liberties which gentlemen take with decorum in the pursuit of pleasure and love, including the liberty of holiday, but not only that. Such liberty is balanced against time-serving. As Bassanio's folly of prodigality leads in the end to gracious fulfillment, so does Viola's folly of disguise. There is just a suggestion of the risks when she exclaims, not very solemnly,

> Disguise, I see thou art a wickedness
> Wherein the pregnant enemy does much. (II ii 25–6)

As in *The Merchant of Venice* the story of a prodigal is the occasion for an exploration of the use and abuse of wealth, so here we get an exhibition of the use and abuse of social liberty.

What enables Viola to bring off her role in disguise is her perfect courtesy, in the large, humanistic meaning of that term as the Renaissance used it, the *corteziania* of Castiglione. Her mastery of courtesy goes with her being the daughter of 'that Sebastian of Messalina whom I know you have heard of' : gentility shows through her disguise as does the fact that she is a woman. The impact on Olivia of Cesario's quality as a gentleman is what is emphasized as the countess, recalling their conversation, discovers that she is falling in love :

> 'What is your parentage?'
> 'Above my fortunes, yet my state is well :
> I am a gentleman.' I'll be sworn thou art.

> Thy tongue, thy face, thy limbs, actions, and spirit,
> Do give thee fivefold blazon. Not too fast! Soft, soft!
> Unless the master were the man. (I v 273–8)

We think of manners as a mere prerequisite of living decently, like cleanliness. For the Renaissance, they could be almost the end of life, as the literature of courtesy testifies. *Twelfth Night* carries further an interest in the fashioning of a courtier which, as Miss Bradbrook points out,[5] appears in several of the early comedies, especially *The Two Gentlemen of Verona*, and which in different keys Shakespeare was pursuing, about the same time as he wrote *Twelfth Night*, in *Hamlet* and *Measure for Measure*. People in *Twelfth Night* talk of courtesy and manners constantly. But the most important expression of courtesy of course is in object lessons. It is their lack of breeding and manners which makes the comic butts ridiculous, along with their lack of the basic, free humanity which, be it virile or feminine, is at the center of courtesy and flowers through it.

Mr Van Doren, in a fine essay, observes that *Twelfth Night* has a structure like *The Merchant of Venice*. 'Once again Shakespeare has built a world out of music and melancholy, and once again this world is threatened by an alien voice. The opposition of Malvolio to Orsino and his class parallels the opposition of Shylock to Antonio and his friends. The parallel is not precise, and the contrast is more subtly contrived; Shakespeare holds the balance in a more delicate hand. . . .'[6] One way in which this more delicate balance appears is that the contest of revellers with intruder does not lead to neglecting ironies about those who are on the side of pleasure. We are all against Malvolio, certainly, in the great moment when the whole opposition comes into focus with Toby's 'Dost thou think, because thou art virtuous, there shall be no more cakes and ale?' (II iii 109–10). The festive spirit shows up the kill-joy vanity of Malvolio's decorum. The steward shows his limits when he calls misrule 'this uncivil rule'. But one of the revellers is Sir

Andrew, who reminds us that there is no necessary salvation in being a fellow who delights 'in masques and revels sometimes altogether' (i iii 106). There was no such ninny pleasure-seeker in *The Merchant of Venice*; his role continues Shallow's, the would-be-reveller who is comically inadequate. To put such a leg as his into 'a flame-coloured stock' only shows how meager it is. This thin creature's motive is self-improvement: he is a version of the stock type of prodigal who is gulled in trying to learn how to be gallant. As in Restoration comedy the fop confirms the values of the rake, Aguecheek serves as foil to Sir Toby. But he also marks one limit as to what revelry can do for a man: 'I would I had bestowed that time in the tongues that I have in fencing, dancing and bear-baiting' (i iii 87–9).

Sir Toby is gentlemanly liberty incarnate, a specialist in it. He lives at his ease, enjoying heritage, the something-for-nothing which this play celebrates, as *The Merchant of Venice* celebrates wealth – what he has without having to deserve it is his kinsman's place in Olivia's household:

> *Maria.* What a caterwauling do you keep here! If my lady have not call'd up her steward Malvolio and bid him turn you out of doors, never trust me.
> *Sir Toby.* My lady's a Catayan, we are politicians, Malvolio's a Peg-a-Ramsey, and [*sings*] 'Three merry men be we.' Am not I consanguineous? Am I not of her blood? Tilly-vally, lady.
>
> (ii iii 72–5)

Sir Toby has by consanguinity what Falstaff has to presume on and keep by his wits: 'Shall I not take mine ease in mine inn but I shall have my pocket pick'd?' (*1H.IV* iii iii 78–9). So Sir Toby is witty without being as alert as Sir John; he does not need to be:

> *Olivia.* Cousin, cousin, how have you come so early by this lethargy?
> *Toby.* Lechery? I defy lechery. There's one at the gate.

Olivia. Ay, marry, what is he?
    Toby. Let him be the devil an he will. I care not; give me faith,
say I. Well, it's all one. (I v 115)

Stage drunkenness, here expressed by wit that lurches catch-as-
catch-can, conveys the security of 'good life' in such households
as Olivia's, the old-fashioned sort that had not given up 'housekeeping'. Because Toby has 'faith' – the faith that goes with
belonging – he does not need to worry when Maria teases him
about confining himself 'within the modest limits of order'.
'Confine? I'll confine myself no finer than I am' (I iii 8–11).
In his talk as in his clothes, he has the ease of a gentleman whose
place in the world is secure, so that, while he can find words
like *consanguineous* at will, he can also say 'Sneck up!' to Malvolio's accusation that he shows 'no respect of persons, places
nor time' (II iii 90). Sir Toby is the sort of kinsman who would
take the lead at such Christmas feasts as Sir Edward Dymoke
patronized in Lincolnshire – a Talboys Dymoke.[7] His talk is
salted with holiday morals: 'I am sure care's an enemy of life'
(I iii 2–3). 'Not to be abed before midnight is to be up betimes'
(II iii 1–2). He is like Falstaff in maintaining saturnalian paradox and in playing impromptu the role of lord of misrule. But
in his whole relation to the world he is fundamentally different
from Prince Hal's great buffoon. Falstaff makes a career of
misrule; Sir Toby uses misrule to show up a careerist.

   There is little direct invocation by poetry of the values of
heritage and housekeeping, such as we get of the beneficence
of wealth in *The Merchant of Venice*. But the graciousness of
community is conveyed indirectly by the value put on music
and song, as Mr Van Doren observes. The Duke's famous
opening lines start the play with music. His hypersensitive
estheticism savors strains that have a dying fall and mixes the
senses in appreciation: 'like the sweet sound / That breathes
upon a bank of violets' (I i 5–6). Toby and his friends are more
at ease about 'O mistress mine', but equally devoted to music

in their way. (Toby makes fun of such strained appreciation as the Duke's when he concludes their praises of the clown's voice with 'To hear by the nose, it is dulcet in contagion', II iii 55–6.) Back at court, in the next scene, the significance of music in relation to community is suggested in the Duke's lines about the 'old and antique song' :

> Mark it, Cesario; it is old and plain;
> The spinsters and the knitters in the sun,
> And the free maids that weave their thread with bones,
> Do use to chant it. It is silly sooth,
> And dallies with the innocence of love,
> Like the old age. (II iv 42–7)

The wonderful line about the free maids, which throws such firm stress on 'free' by the delayed accent, and then slows up in strong, regular monosyllables, crystallizes the play's central feeling for freedom in heritage and community. It is consciously nostalgic; the old age is seen from the vantage of 'these most brisk and giddy-paced times' (II iv 6).

Throughout the play a contrast is maintained between the taut, restless, elegant court, where people speak a nervous verse, and the free-wheeling household of Olivia, where, except for the intense moments in Olivia's amorous interviews with Cesario, people live in an easy-going prose. The contrast is another version of pastoral. The household is more than any one person in it. People keep interrupting each other, changing their minds, letting their talk run out into foolishness – and through it all Shakespeare expresses the day-by-day going on of a shared life :

Maria. Nay, either tell me where thou hast been, or I will not open my lips so wide as a bristle may enter in way of thy excuse. (I v 1–3)

Fabian. . . . You know he brought me out o' favour with my lady about a bear-baiting here.
Toby. To anger him we'll have the bear again . . . (II v 6–8)

Fabian. Why, we shall make him mad indeed.
Maria. The house will be the quieter. (III iv 127–8)

Maria's character is a function of the life of 'the house'; she moves within it with perfectly selfless tact. 'She's a beagle true-bred', says Sir Toby : her part in the housekeeping and its pleasures is a homely but valued kind of 'courtiership'.

All of the merrymakers show a fine sense of the relations of people, including robust Fabian, and Sir Toby, when he has need. The fool, especially, has this courtly awareness. We see in the first scene that he has to have it to live : he goes far enough in the direction of plain speaking to engage Olivia's unwilling attention, then brings off his thesis that *she* is the fool so neatly that he is forgiven. What Viola praises in the fool's function is just what we should expect in a play about courtesy and liberty :

> This fellow is wise enough to play the fool ;
> And to do that well craves a kind of wit.
> He must observe their mood on whom he jests,
> The quality of persons, and the time . . . (III i 57–60)

It is remarkable how little Feste says that is counterstatement in Touchstone's manner : there is no need for ironic counterstatement, because here the ironies are embodied in the comic butts. Instead what Feste chiefly does is sing and beg – courtly occupations – and radiate in his songs and banter a feeling of liberty based on accepting disillusion. 'What's to come is still unsure . . . Youth's a stuff will not endure' (II iii 48, 51). In *The Merchant of Venice*, it was the gentlefolk who commented 'How every fool can play upon the word!' but now it is the fool himself who says, with mock solemnity : 'To see this age! A sentence is but a chev'ril glove to a good wit!' (III i 10–11). He rarely makes the expected move, but conveys by his style how well he knows what moves are expected :

(II v 48–50). His secret wish is to violate decorum himself, then relish to the full its power over others. No wonder he has not a free disposition when he has such imaginations to keep under! When the sport betrays him into a revelation of them, part of the vengeance taken is to make him try to be festive, in yellow stockings, and crossgartered, and smiling 'his face into more lines than is in the new map with the augmentation of the Indies' (III ii 74–5). Maria's letter *tells* him to go brave, be gallant, take liberties! And when we see him 'acting this in an obedient hope' (as he puts it later), he is anything but free : 'This does make some obstruction of the blood, this cross-gartering . . .' (III iv 20–1).

In his 'impossible passages of grossness', he is the profane intruder trying to steal part of the initiates' feast by disguising himself as one of them – only to be caught and tormented for his profanation. As with Shylock, there is potential pathos in his bafflement, especially when Shakespeare uses to the limit the conjuring of devils out of a sane man, a device which he had employed hilariously in *The Comedy of Errors*. There is no way to settle just how much of Malvolio's pathos should be allowed to come through when he is down and out in the dark hole. Most people now agree that Charles Lamb's sympathy for the steward's enterprise and commiseration for his sorrows is a romantic and bourgeois distortion. But he is certainly pathetic, if one thinks about it, because he is so utterly cut off from everyone else by his anxious self-love. He lacks the freedom which makes Viola so perceptive, and is correspondingly oblivious :

> *Olivia.* What kind o' man is he?
> *Malvolio.* Why, of mankind. (I v 141–2)

He is too busy carrying out his mistress' instructions about privacy to notice that she is bored with it, as later he is too busy doing her errand with the ring to notice that it is a love-token.

He is imprisoned in his own virtues, so that there is sense as well as nonsense in the fool's 'I say there is no darkness but ignorance; in which thou art more puzzled than the Egyptians in their fog' (IV ii 41–3). The dark house is, without any straining, a symbol: when Malvolio protests about Pythagoras, 'I think nobly of the soul and no way approve his opinion', the clown's response is 'Remain thou still in darkness'. The pack of them are wanton and unreasonable in tormenting him; but his reasonableness will never let him out into 'the air; . . . the glorious sun' (IV iii 1) which they enjoy together. To play the dark-house scene for pathos, instead of making fun out of the pathos, or at any rate out of most of the pathos, is to ignore the dry comic light which shows up Malvolio's virtuousness as a self-limiting automatism.

Malvolio has been called a satirical portrait of the Puritan spirit, and there is some truth in the notion. But he is not hostile to holiday because he is a Puritan; he is like a Puritan because he is hostile to holiday. Shakespeare even mocks, in passing, the thoughtless, fashionable antipathy to Puritans current among gallants. Sir Andrew responds to Maria's 'sometimes he is a kind of Puritan', with 'if I thought that, I'd beat him like a dog' (II iii 131–2). 'The devil a Puritan he is, or anything constantly', Maria observes candidly, 'but a time-pleaser' (II iii 137–8). Shakespeare's two great comic butts, Malvolio and Shylock, express basic human attitudes which were at work in the commercial revolution, the new values whose development R. H. Tawney described in *Religion and the Rise of Capitalism*. But both figures are conceived at a level of esthetic abstraction which makes it inappropriate to identify them with specific social groups in the mingled actualities of history: Shylock, embodying ruthless money power, is no more to be equated with actual bankers than Malvolio, who has something of the Puritan ethic, is to be thought of as a portrait of actual Puritans. Yet, seen in the perspective of literary and social history, there is a curious appropriateness in Malvolio's presence, as a kind of foreign body to be expelled by laughter, in Shakespeare's last free-and-easy festive comedy. He is a man of business, and, it is passingly suggested, a hard one; he is or would like to be a rising man, and to rise he *uses* sobriety and morality. One could moralize the spectacle by observing that, in the long run, in the 1640s, Malvolio *was* revenged on the whole pack of them.

But Shakespeare's comedy remains, long after 1640, to move audiences through release to clarification, making distinctions between false care and true freedom and realizing anew, for successive generations, powers in human nature and society which make good the risks of courtesy and liberty. And this without blinking the fact that 'the rain it raineth every day'.

OUTSIDE THE GARDEN GATE

Twelfth Night is usually placed just before *Hamlet* and the problem plays to make neat groupings according to mood, but it may well have been written after some of these works. In thinking about its relation to the other work of the period from 1600 to 1602 or 1603, it is important to recognize the independent artistic logic by which each play has its own unity. There are features of *Twelfth Night* that connect it with all the productions of this period. There is the side of Orsino's sensibility, for example, which suggests Troilus' hypersensitivity:

> Enough, no more;
> 'Tis not so sweet now as it was before. (I i 7–8)

> How will she love when the rich golden shaft
> Hath kill'd the flock of all affections else
> That live in her; when liver, brain, and heart,
> Those sovereign thrones, are all supplied and fill'd,
> Her sweet perfections, with one self king!
> Away before me to sweet beds of flow'rs! (I i 35–40)

Troilus carries this sort of verse and feeling farther:

> What will it be
> When that the wat'ry palate tastes indeed
> Love's thrice-repured nectar? Death, I fear me;
> Sounding destruction; or some joy too fine,
> Too subtle-potent, tun'd too sharp in sweetness,
> For the capacity of my ruder powers.
>
> (*Troi.* III ii 19–24)

Troilus' lines are a much more physical and more anxious development of the exquisite, uncentered sort of amorousness expressed by Orsino. But in *Twelfth Night* there is no occasion to explore the harsh anti-climax to which such intensity is vulnerable, for instead of meeting a trivial Cressida in the midst of war and lechery, Orsino meets poised Viola in a world of revelry. The comparison with *Troilus and Cressida* makes one notice how little direct sexual reference there is in *Twelfth Night* – much less than in most of the festive comedies. It may be that free-hearted mirth, at this stage of Shakespeare's development, required more shamefastness than it had earlier, because to dwell on the physical was to encounter the 'monstruosity in love' which troubled Troilus: 'that the desire is boundless, and the act a slave to limit' (*Troi.* III ii 79–80).

It is quite possible that *Measure for Measure* and *All's Well That Ends Well* did not seem to Shakespeare and his audiences so different from *Twelfth Night* as they seem to us. Both of them use comic butts not unlike Andrew and Malvolio: Lucio and Parolles are, each his way, pretenders to community who are shown up ludicrously by their own compulsions, and so expelled. Our difficulty with these plays, what makes them problem plays, is that they do not feel festive; they are not merry in a deep enough way. Part of our response may well be the result of changes in standards and sentiments about sexual behavior, and of alterations in theatrical convention. But the fact remains that in both plays, release often leads, not simply to folly, but to the vicious or contemptible; and the manipulations of happy accidents which make all well in the end are not made acceptable by the achievement of distinctions about values or by a convincing expression of general beneficent forces in life. Shakespeare's imagination tends to dwell on situations and motives where the energies of life lead to degradation or destruction :

> Our natures do pursue,
> Like rats that ravin down their proper bane,
> A thirsty evil; and when we drink we die.
> *(Meas.* I ii 122–4)

There's not a soldier of us all that, in the thanksgiving before meat, do relish the petition well that prays for peace.
> *(Meas.* I ii 14–16)

Pompey, you are partly a bawd, Pompey, howsoever you colour it in being a tapster. Are you not? . . .
Pompey. Truly, sir, I am a poor fellow that would live.
> *(Meas.* II i 207–11)

This sort of paradox is not brought home to us in *Twelfth Night.* In the problem comedies, vicious or perverse release leads to developments of absorbing interest, if not always to a satisfying movement of feeling in relation to awareness. But that is beyond our compass here.

We can notice here that the fool in *Twelfth Night* has been over the garden wall into some such world as the Vienna of *Measure for Measure.* He never tells where he has been, gives no details. But he has an air of knowing more of life than anyone else – too much, in fact; and he makes general observations like

Anything that's mended is but patch'd; virtue that transgresses is but patch'd with sin, and sin that amends is but patch'd with virtue. If that this simple syllogism will serve, so; if it will not, what remedy? (I v 40–4)

His part does not darken the bright colors of the play; but it gives them a dark outline, suggesting that the whole bright revel emerges from shadow. In the wonderful final song which he is left alone on stage to sing, the mind turns to contemplate the limitations of revelry: 'By swaggering could I never thrive. . . .' The morning after, the weather when the sky changes, come into the song:

> With tosspots still had drunken heads,
>   For the rain it raineth every day. (v i 389–90)

It goes outside the garden gate:

> But when I come to man's estate,
>   With hey, ho, the wind and the rain,
> 'Gainst knaves and thieves men shut their gate,
>   For the rain it raineth every day. (v i 379–80)

Yet the poise of mirth, achieved by accepting disillusion, although it is now precarious, is not lost:

> A great while ago the world begun,
>   With hey, ho, the wind and the rain;
> But that's all one, our play is done,
>   And we'll strive to please you everyday. (v i 391–4)

There is a certain calculated let-down in coming back to the play in this fashion; but it is the play which is keeping out the wind and the rain.

The festive comic form which Shakespeare had worked out was a way of selecting and organizing experience which had its own logic, its own autonomy: there is no necessary reason to think that he did not play on that instrument in *Twelfth Night* after making even such different music as *Hamlet*. Indeed, across the difference in forms, the comedy has much in common with the tragedy: interest in courtesy and free-hearted manners; consciousness of language and play with it as though a sentence were but a chev'ril glove; the use of nonsequitur and nonsense. Malvolio absurdly dreams of such a usurpation of heritage, 'having come from a day bed, where I have left Olivia sleeping', as Claudius actually accomplishes. The tragedy moves into regions where the distinction between madness and sanity begins to break down, to be recovered only through violence; the fooling with madness in the comedy is an enjoyment of the control which knows what is mad and what is not. The relation between the two plays, though not so close, is not unlike that which we have noticed between *Romeo and Juliet* and *A Midsummer Night's Dream*.

But there is a great deal in *Hamlet* which the festive comic form cannot handle. The form can only deal with follies where nature to her bias draws; the unnatural can appear only in outsiders, intruders who are mocked and expelled. But in *Hamlet*, it is insiders who are unnatural. There is a great deal of wonderful fooling in the tragedy: Hamlet's playing the all-licensed fool in Claudius' court and making tormented fun out of his shocking realization of the horror of life. For sheer power of wit and reach of comic vision, there are moments in *Hamlet* beyond anything in the comedies we have considered. But to control the expression of the motives he is presenting, Shakespeare requires a different movement, within which comic release is only one phase. After *Twelfth Night*, comedy is always used in this subordinate way: saturnalian moments, comic counterstatements, continue to be important resources of his art, but their meaning is determined by their place in a larger movement. So it is with the heroic revels in *Antony and Cleopatra*, or with the renewal of life, after tragedy, at the festival in *The Winter's Tale*.

SOURCE: *Shakespeare's Festive Comedy* (1959) chap. 10

NOTES

1. In *The First Night of 'Twelfth Night'* (1954), Dr Hotson has recovered, once again, documents that are astonishingly *à propos*. The most exciting is a long letter home written by a real nobleman named Orsino, who was Elizabeth's honored guest when she witnessed a play 'in the Hall, which was richly hanged and degrees placed round about it'. Don Virginio Orsino's account to his Duchess of the way he was honored gives a vivid picture of the Twelfth Day occasion at court, which Mr Hotson skillfully supplements with other evidence, much of it also new, so as to give us the most complete and graphic description we have of the circumstances of a dramatic performance at a court holiday. The Duke's candid letter reports that 'there was acted a mingled comedy, with pieces of music and dances' (*una commedia mescolata, con musiche e balli*). But then it adds 'and this too I am keeping to tell by word of mouth'. What maddening bad luck! Here, and everywhere else, the clinching proof eludes Dr Hotson, despite his skill and persistence. He himself cannot resist regarding it as a fact that *Twelfth Night* was the play in question on January 6, 1600–1601. But a sceptic can begin by asking where, in *Twelfth Night,* are those *balli* which Don Virginio witnessed – the play is notable, among Shakespeare's gay comedies, for its *lack* of dances. One could go on to ask whether it would not be more likely that the name Orsino would be used sometime *after* the great man's visit, when the elegant ring of it would still sound in people's ears but no offense be done. A devil's advocate could go on and on, so rich, and so conjectural, is Dr Hotson's book.

But it makes a real contribution, even if one is not convinced that the play on that night must have been *Twelfth Night,* and even if one rejects many of its sweeping conclusions about such matters as staging. Dr Hotson is a 'literalist of the historical imagination', to use Marianne Moore's phrase. He has produced something equivalent to an 'imaginary garden with real toads in' it – real circumstances and actions of Elizabethan life. He makes us aware of what the high day at court was like. And he describes and exemplifies many features of Twelfth Night custom in a fresh way, and so defines for us the *sort* of thing that Shakespeare refers to by his title. He also provides, from his remarkable knowledge of the period, a wealth of useful incidental glosses to hard places in the play.

But useful as his book can be, whether literally right or not, it is very misleading in one respect. For he writes as though the festive quality of *Twelfth Night* were wholly derived, on a one-to-one sort of basis, from its being commissioned for a court revel. He neglects the fact that, whatever its first night, the play was designed to work, also, on the public stage, so that it had to project the spirit of holiday into forms that would be effective everyday. He also ignores the fact that by the time Shakespeare came to write *Twelfth Night*, festive comedy was an established specialty with him.

2. E. K. Chambers, *William Shakespeare*, II 327–8.

3. I hope that a reader who is concerned only with *Twelfth Night* will nevertheless take the time to read the generalized account of festive comedy in Chapter I of *Shakespeare's Festive Comedy*, for that introduction is assumed in the discussion here.

4. The latest treatment of this motif, in *The Two Noble Kinsmen* (especially Act I, scene iii), is as generously beautiful as the exquisite handling of it which we have examined in *A Midsummer Night's Dream* (*Shakespeare's Festive Comedy*, pp. 129–30).

5. *Shakespeare and Elizabethan Poetry*, chap. ix.

6. *Shakespeare*, p. 161.

7. The whole encounter between Talboys Dymoke's revellers and the Earl of Lincoln is remarkably like that between Sir Toby's group and Malvolio. See *Shakespeare's Festive Comedy*, chap. 3, pp. 37–51. The parallels are all the more impressive because no influence or 'source' relationship is involved; there must have been many such encounters.

8. See *Shakespeare's Festive Comedy*, pp. 46–8.

Bertrand Evans

THE FRUITS OF THE SPORT (1960)

In the world of *Twelfth Night*, as in the worlds of the comedies just preceding, the spirit of the practiser prevails. Seven of the principal persons are active practisers, and they operate six devices. All action turns on these, and the effects of the play arise from exploitation of the gaps they open. During all but the first two of eighteen scenes we have the advantage of some participant; in seven – an unusually high proportion – we hold advantage over all who take part. In the course of the action, every named person takes a turn below our vantage-point, and below the vantage-point of some other person or persons : in this play neither heroine nor clown is wholly spared. Although Viola shares the great secret with us alone, Shakespeare early establishes our vantage-point above hers, and once even makes her the unwitting victim of another's practice. Although Feste is either 'in' on most practices or unaffected by them, he, with all Illyria, is ignorant of the main secret of the play, the identity of 'Cesario'. Here, then, even heroine and clown stand below us, and below them the others range down to the bottom, where sit Aguecheek and Malvolio in chronic oblivion. Though also victims of others' practices, neither needs deceiving to be deceived – Nature having practised on them once for all.

But if all are exposed at some time in ignorance of their situations, yet all but Orsino and Malvolio have compensatory moments when they overpeer others : even Aguecheek, though a fool the while, briefly enjoys advantage over Malvolio. The awarenesses in *Twelfth Night* are so structured that an overpeerer gloating in his advantage is usually himself overpeered by another participant or by us : thus Sir Toby exults in his advantage over 'Cesario', knowing that Sir Andrew is

not the 'devil in a private brawl' he would have 'Cesario' believe – but at the same time 'Cesario' holds advantage over him
in knowing that 'Cesario' is a fiction; and the last laugh is
ours, on Sir Toby, for even he would hardly have made his
jest of a duel had he known 'Cesario' truly. From much use of
such arrangements, in which a participant's understanding is
inferior with respect to some elements of a situation and superior
with respect to others, emerge the richest effects of *Twelfth
Night* and some of the finest in Shakespeare.

Of the six practices, the central one is of course the heroine's
masquerade. It is the longest, and, in its relations with the
play as a whole, the most important such masquerade in the
comedies. Julia's practice in *The Two Gentlemen of Verona*
affects only two important scenes, and the only person whose
ignorance of it is exploited is Proteus. Rosalind's impersonation of 'Ganymede' in *As You Like It* lasts longer than Julia's,
but it, too, is exploited in only two major scenes, and the only
victims whose ignorance of it greatly matters are Orlando and
Phebe. Portia's disguise in *The Merchant of Venice* is worn
during only one act, and its consequences furnish the substance
of another. Helena's masquerade in *All's Well that Ends Well*
makes the central incident of the plot, but its only victim is
Bertram. Imogen's practice in *Cymbeline*, though it yields spectacular effects in the climactic moments, is one among a
multitude of intrigues in that play. But the force of Viola's
masquerade in *Twelfth Night* prevails in all but the opening
scenes and relates to every incident and person. Though it most
affects two victims, Viola's is truly a practice on the whole
world of Illyria, as Duke Vincentio's is on the world of *Measure
for Measure*, and as, in tragedy, Iago's is on his world and as
Hamlet's antic disposition is on the whole world of Denmark.
Viola rightly belongs in this company of most notable mas-
queraders in all the plays.

Viola takes up her masquerade with somewhat less urgency
and altruism than moved Portia, but with somewhat more of

both than moved Rosalind to perpetrate her fraud in the Forest of Arden. Washed up on the shore of Illyria, she goes to work at once. Quickly ascertaining the name of the place, the name of its ruler, and the fact that he is still a bachelor, she makes up her mind:

> I'll serve this duke.
> Thou shalt present me as an eunuch to him.
> It may be worth thy pains, for I can sing
> And speak to him in many sorts of music
> That will allow me very worth his service.
> What else may hap, to time I will commit,
> Only shape thou thy silence to my wit. (i ii 55-61)

This speech creates at one stroke the discrepancy in awarenesses which will endure until the closing moments of the play, giving advantage to us and disadvantage to all Illyria. And as swiftly as he creates the gap, Shakespeare begins its exploitation. When next we see Viola, in man's attire, after three days at Orsino's court and already his favourite, Valentine's remarks give first expression to the general Illyrian error:

> If the Duke continue these favours towards you, Cesario, you are like to be much advanc'd. He hath known you but three days, and already you are no stranger. (i iv 1-4)

But a stranger, of course, this 'Cesario' is to the Duke, and to all others. The Duke's unawareness is next exploited: 'Cesario,' he says, 'thou know'st no less but all' – and so she does, more than he dreams. When Orsino directs her to bear his lovesuit to Olivia, his remarks come near enough to strike sparks from the truth, and these flashes of irony are the first to result from the great discrepancy:

> ... they shall yet belie thy happy years,
> That say thou art a man. Diana's lip
> Is not more smooth and rubious; thy small pipe

> Is as the maiden's organ, shrill and sound;
> And all is semblative a woman's part. (Ibid. 30–4)

As the scene ends, the basic exploitable gap is opened wider; says Viola,

> I'll do my best
> To woo your lady, – (*aside*) yet, a barful strife!
> Whoe'er I woo, myself would be his wife. (Ibid. 40–2)

As suddenly as her adoption of disguise created the first discrepancy, this confession creates a second. Henceforth her advantage, and ours, over the Duke is double: the secret of her right identity and the secret of her love.

The first major clash of the discrepant awarenesses of Viola and Illyria occurs, however, not in the Duke's court but in Olivia's house. Before meeting the recluse, Viola has encountered, in succession, Maria, Sir Toby, and Malvolio, who must be accounted first in the household to fall victims of her disguise even though the meetings are only reported; thus Malvolio: 'Not yet old enough for a man, nor young enough for a boy; as a squash is before 'tis a peascod, or a codling when 'tis almost an apple.' But the principal exploitation occurs in the interview with Olivia, whose attitude changes in the course of 100 lines from haughty scorn to flirtatious interest and finally to love. The effect of exploitation of the difference between our understanding and Olivia's is here not merely comic, although that is certainly part of the total. Though the play is not yet a full act old, the dramatist has already packed our minds with so much that simple laughter is an inadequate response. In this respect the meeting with Olivia contrasts with the comparable incident in *As You Like It*, when Phebe falls in love with 'Ganymede', and the contrast becomes even more marked in the later interviews of Viola with Olivia and with Orsino, which we are required to watch with minds packed with sympathy that forestalls laughter.

Until the end of this scene, when Olivia, moved by a passion she thinks futile to resist – not knowing how futile it is to succumb – dispatches Malvolio to run after 'that same peevish messenger' and give him a ring – 'He left this ring behind him / Would I or not' – Shakespeare had established only two levels of awareness. These are Viola's, shared with us, and Illyria's ignorance of 'Cesario's' identity. Two levels sufficed in *As You Like It*, even during the climactic scenes, when Rosalind's view is equivalent to ours and Orlando's represents that of all the Forest. But this relative simplicity is abruptly abandoned at the opening of Act II in *Twelfth Night* with the introduction of Sebastian. The instant effect of Sebastian's appearance, safe and sound on the very coast where Viola had inquired 'What country, friend, is this?' and been advised 'This is Illyria, lady' is the creation of a third level, a vantage-point above Viola's, to be held by ourselves alone until the end of Act III – and possibly but not probably until the last moments of Act V.

The placement of the scene informing us of Sebastian's survival and immediate destination – 'I am bound to the Count Orsino's court' – is a notable example of Shakespeare's way of handling the awarenesses. It is the more significant for being conspicuously early in the action, and the more conspicuous for its rather awkward interruption of the expected sequence of incident. Our notification of his rescue and arrival in Illyria might readily have been postponed until Act IV, when, in front of Olivia's house, the Clown mistakes Sebastian for 'Cesario'. Or he might have been introduced inconspicuously between almost any two scenes in either Act II or Act III. Instead, he is thrust between Viola's departure from Olivia's house and her meeting with Malvolio on the street. Ordinarily, no scene would intervene in this space, as is demonstrable many times over in the plays. The closest parallel occurs in *The Merchant of Venice.* At the end of the court scene Bassanio sends Gratiano to overtake Portia and give her a ring; the very next scene shows Portia and Nerissa on the street, overtaken by

Gratiano after Portia has spoken only four lines to mark the passage of an appropriate period of time. In contrast, the introduction of Sebastian splits the sequence with a scene of some fifty lines that entails also a shift from the vicinity of Olivia's house to the sea-coast. From the first history play onward, Shakespeare's method avoided violence to the normal order of action unless there was something special to be gained. By the time of *Twelfth Night*, certainly the only disruptions of sequence are calculated ones. In the present case the dramatist evidently wished us to learn as early as possible that Sebastian is alive, and, more precisely, to learn it *just before Viola discovers that Olivia has fallen in love with her.*

In short, Sebastian's introduction is our assurance that all is well and will end well, an assurance which contradicts Viola's distress on recognising what seems a hopeless entanglement :

> She loves me, sure. . . . If it be so, as 'tis,
> Poor lady, she were better love a dream.
> Disguise, I see thou art a wickedness
> Wherein the pregnant enemy does much. (II ii 23–9)

When we saw her leave Olivia's house, her vantage-point was ours. Now, overtaken by Malvolio – who is himself wrapped in fourfold ignorance – she has slipped below, for we have seen Sebastian. She is nevermore quite the match of Rosalind, who overpeered all and was never overpeered. Yet her mind is packed with almost as much understanding as ours : she realises, by the ring, that Olivia, ignorant of 'Cesario's' sex, has fallen in love; she recognises that Malvolio, besides being a fool, is ignorant also of her sex and of his mistress's meaning in sending the ring; and certainly she observes irony's bright flashes about his head when, with intolerable condescension, he announces that Olivia has commanded 'Cesario' to come no more 'unless it be to report your lord's taking of this' – thereupon tossing Olivia's, not Orsino's, ring on the ground.

But her mind is chiefly on Orsino and his oblivion, which includes ignorance of her identity, of her love for him, and of the fact that just now his beloved has given her heart to 'Cesario' :

> My master loves her dearly;
> And I, poor monster, fond as much on him;
> And she, mistaken, seems to dote on me.
> What will become of this? (Ibid. 34–7)

By making Viola voice dismay for the several matters that burden her awareness, Shakespeare bids our own be alert; he comes as near as a dramatist can to saying : 'Bear this in mind, and this, and yet this.' He prods our remembrance also with utterances that illuminate the newly opened gap between our understanding and Viola's :

> As I am woman, – now alas the day! –
> What thriftless sighs shall poor Olivia breathe!
>
> (Ibid. 39–40)

And, finally :

> O time! thou must untangle this, not I.
> It is too hard a knot for me t' untie! (Ibid. 41–2)

Viola's distress should be ours also – but we have just seen Sebastian, in the shape of another 'Cesario', and his words still sound in our ears: 'I am bound to the Count Orsino's court.' Olivia's sighs therefore need not be thriftless : the knot is looser than Viola thinks, and time is, indeed, capable.

Sebastian's introduction is thus a strategic move, giving us assurance that all is and will be well. But it is also a tactical move, multiplying the possibilities of exploitation. Sebastian's unawareness – exploitable the instant he appears on the seacoast, weeping for a 'drowned' sister who is in fact doing quite well for herself in Illyria – provides one such possibility. All Illyria's unawareness that Sebastian is not 'Cesario' – who, of course, is not 'Cesario' either – provides another. Add to these

the possibilities already in existence, including the main secret
of Viola–'Cesario' and the subordinate ones born of Aguecheek's and Malvolio's chronic oblivions, and it is evident that
by the start of Act II the exploitable potentiality is enormous.

Although Sebastian's appearance gives us advantage over
Viola, her demotion is hardly damaging to her prestige as
herione and prime practiser. Her ignorance that her brother
is at hand does not expose her to ridicule or pity, for the truth
that she cannot see is better than the appearance. Though the
heroines of comedy always look about them with a wider sweep
of the eye than others enjoy, Shakespeare occasionally cuts off
their view of a segment of the full circle; only Rosalind and
Portia escape such limitation of their vision. Other heroines,
though momentarily blind to some specific aspect of a situation,
usually retain a commanding view of all else and in any event
are spared exposure to laughter. Beatrice is an exception; but
she is a secondary heroine, and besides, like Benedick's, her
nature invites corrective effect. Later heroines, Isabella,
Imogen, and Perdita, are blind to significant facts of their
situations, but their ignorance does not make them vulnerable
to laughter. Viola stands between these and Beatrice; she is
caught in a condition of laughable unawareness during two
incidents in Act III.

During Act II, however, except that she does not know
about Sebastian, Viola escapes unawareness and enjoys an
advantage over Orsino that matches Rosalind's over poor
Orlando and Portia's over Bassanio. Indeed, her advantage
grows during this period. When she left for her first interview
with Olivia, Orsino was ignorant only of her identity. When
she returns, he is still ignorant of that, of the fact that she loves
him, that she is loved by Olivia, and that therefore his suit to
Olivia is truly hopeful. His fourfold ignorance is the exploitable
substance of the second Viola–Orsino interview. Shakespeare
capitalizes the opportunity fully but tenderly, and the result is
an artistic triumph. Lacking the complexity of some later

scenes, in which stair-stepped levels of awareness provide the structure for dazzling cross-play, the scene nevertheless makes a powerful demand for simultaneous conflicting responses. Luxuriating in melancholy, loving love, affecting the agony of the disdained lover, feasting on music and song that aggravate his craving, Orsino stands naked to laughter – a foolish plight for a hero, like that into which Shakespeare previously thrust Orlando, rehearsing with 'Ganymede' his love for Rosalind.

Like Orlando's, then, a brutally ludicrous representation of romantic masculinity, Orsino's exposure should inspire roaring laughter. Yet as the scene moves on laughter becomes inappropriate and is perhaps finally made impossible by the force of a contradictory impulse. The latter force is enhanced by the music, song, and poetry of the scene – but its original stimulation is the presence of Viola, whose quality is as right for this moment as are the qualities of Rosalind and Orlando for their wooing scene. Whereas Orsino sees nothing, Viola sees too much; her mind is burdened with understanding. 'Thus far I will boldly publish her', said Sebastian; 'she bore a mind that envy could not but call fair.' If she could know that Sebastian lives, that the solution to her dilemma is even now on the road to Orsino's court, her distress would be lightened and the pain of the scene would be eased. Everything that she does know, beyond Orsino's knowledge, hurts her; and what she does not know – that the dramatist has taken care to have *us* know – hurts her also. Deliberately, with a psychologically shrewd manœuvre, Shakespeare has balanced our own awareness between laughter and pain.

These contradictory impulses, equal in power, stimulated by complex awareness, do not cancel each other out, leaving indifference; they battle for supremacy, and the intensity of their struggle determines the degree of our involvement. Shakespeare's way in the great scenes is to involve us deeply, by packing our minds with private awarenesses that confer a sense of personal responsibility toward the action.

Duke. My life upon't, young though thou art, thine eye
  Hath stay'd upon some favour that it loves.
  Hath it not, boy?
Vio.   A little, by your favour.
Duke. What kind of woman is't?
Vio.   Of your complexion.
Duke. She is not worth thee, then. What years, i' faith?
Vio. About your years, my lord. (ii iv 24–9)

Here the Duke's oblivion, illuminated by each line he speaks, is
laughable – but opposing it is Viola's too-feminine awareness,
reaching to every corner of the situation, shining brightly in her
every utterance, demanding our concern. Toward the end
of the scene, when the same sort of exchange is repeated, with
the same tension of opposed awareness sustained, the dialogue is
laden with pathos :

Duke. What dost thou know?
Vio. Too well what love women to men may owe.
  In faith, they are as true of heart as we.
  My father had a daughter lov'd a man,
  As it might be, perhaps, were I a woman,
  I should your lordship.
Duke.   And what's her history?
Vio. A blank, my lord. She never told her love,
  But let concealment, like a worm i' th' bud,
  Feed on her damask cheek. She pin'd in thought,
  And with a green and yellow melancholy
  She sat, like Patience on a monument,
  Smiling at grief. Was not this love indeed?
  We men may say more, swear more; but indeed
  Our shows are more than will, for still we prove
  Much in our vows, but little in our love.
Duke. But died thy sister of her love, my boy?
Vio. I am all the daughters of my father's house,
  And all the brothers too; – and yet I know not. (ii iv 107–24)

Although the exchange glitters with irony, to describe the total
effect as that of irony is to leave its rarer metals unassayed. The
effect is compounded of many simples; elements of the comic

and elements of the pathetic are exquisitely blended, with the final unity conferred by the alchemy of poetry. Innately rich, vibrant, the lyric voices gather resonance from the sounding-board of awareness which the dramatist, with calculated art, constructed and fixed in our minds before the start of the duet. Perhaps Shakespeare never achieved a richer tone – though he rises to this once more in *Twelfth Night* – than with these voices reverberating over the chasm between the speakers' awarenesses.

In the interim between this scene and Viola's second interview with Olivia occur the beggings, along with much else, of Maria's practice on Malvolio. But it is best to postpone discussion of the antics of the clowns, wits, and dolts who make up Olivia's household, both in order that these may all be examined together and in order that we may follow the progress of the heroine and come at once to a scene which is closely knit to that just reviewed.

In the second Viola–Olivia interview, Shakespeare deals gently with Olivia's unawareness. Here, if he chose, he might cause a lady to look as ridiculous as Orlando rehearsing for 'Ganymede'. It is not so : we are required to pity Olivia, for she has caught the plague. With Phebe, suddenly smitten by passion for 'Ganymede', the dramatist dealt otherwise, making her ignorance of Rosalind's sex a means of mockery. But though Phebe stands to 'Ganymede' as Olivia to 'Cesario', Phebe and Olivia are contrasting spirits. Phebe's contemptuous treatment of the shepherd who follows her with doglike devotion demands that she be exposed to laughter; she deserves Rosalind's sharpest barbs : 'Sell when you can; you are not for all markets.' Olivia, though she has rejected Orsino, has not treated him contemptuously, and her 'cruelty' is only a figment of Orsino's music-fed imagination; nor, certainly, has she rejected him suddenly, at first sight of a seemingly better match, as Phebe did Silvius. Derisive exploitation of Olivia's disadvantage would be discordant here, and there is none. Moreover as Phebe differs from Olivia, Viola differs from Rosalind. To Rosalind the masquerade in the name of Jove's page is mocking, malicious, high-holiday sport. She relishes her advantage, exploits it with a conscienceless zest for the game that makes boobies of her victims. As the action continues, her exhilaration mounts; appropriating a magician's reputation, promising to make all things even at last, she enjoys astonishing all Arden. No practiser has a more glorious time of it. Devastating in her thrusts at Phebe, perhaps she would claw even Olivia, though not deeply, if that unfortunate were at her mercy. It is otherwise with Viola, who would deal tenderly even with Phebe.

Viola did not take up the masquerade for the love of mockery. Hers is not a mocking nature. The thing she starts threatens to get out of hand almost at once. Hopelessly wooing Olivia for Orsino, hopelessly loving Orsino, hopelessly loved by Olivia, ignorant that Sebastian is alive to make all right at last, she is caught in what is to her a frightening dilemma such as Rosalind would never be caught in – for Rosalind is superior to dilemmas. It is in accord with her nature that Viola bears her advantage mercifully in the second interview, and the gap between the pair is exploited tenderly : 'A cypress, not a bosom, / Hides my heart', Olivia begins, and Viola replies, 'I pity you'. These are not Rosalind and Phebe, the one exuberantly mocking, the other brazen-bold; these are Viola and Olivia, the one bearing her advantage as if it had suddenly become a cross, the other so deeply stricken that laughter at her condition would be gross. Exploitation is concentrated in one principal exchange that finds what is hilarious girt round with pathos :

Oli. Stay !
   I prithee, tell me what thou think'st of me.
Vio. That you do think you are not what you are.
Oli. If I think so, I think the same of you.
Vio. Then think you right. I am not what I am.
Oli. I would you were as I would have you be ! (iii i 149–54)

Olivia's confession of love is a compulsive outburst of such frankness as only rudeness could laugh at :

> Cesario, by the roses of the spring,
> By maidhood, honour, truth, and everything,
> I love thee so, that, maugre all thy pride,
> Nor wit nor reason can my passion hide. (Ibid. 161–4)

Yet the frame of the situation is comic, even grotesque : the reversal of roles, the woman wooing the man, an incongruity in society if not in nature, is a perennial subject of jest; and the fact that this 'man' is not even a man adds a joke to what is already a joke. But within this laughable frame the presentation of human qualities stifles laughter. Olivia's nature conflicts with her plight; her genuineness disarms laughter. And the 'man' is not only a woman, but a woman of rare sensitivity, who carries her masquerade with uncertainty, in a sprightly manner but with rising alarm and forced bravado. Earlier heroines – Julia, Portia, Rosalind – had no such difficulty with this role. Besides the fact that their capabilities were greater, they had female companions to confide in : before donning men's clothes Julia jests with Lucetta, Portia with Nerissa, Rosalind with Celia. They carry their roles with a certain elation. But in her disguise Viola is as much alone in the great world as when she floundered in the sea. Acutely feminine, she finds the role hard, is distressed by it, comes soon to wish she had not undertaken it : 'Disguise, I see thou art a wickedness / Wherein the pregnant enemy does much.'

The emotional conflict which rises from this unlaughable treatment of a laughable situation, complex already, is further complicated by the force of the crowning fact in our superior awareness : our knowledge that Sebastian lives and must now be close at hand. If Olivia can love 'Cesario', she can love Sebastian. The 'thriftless sighs' that arouse Viola's pity and prevent us from laughing need not be thriftless; the hand that can free Olivia will also sever the knot that is too hard for Viola to untie. Thus while the laughter implicit in the situation is drowned in the sympathy demanded by the gentleness of both women, the struggle is also flooded with comforting assurance; all is well and will end well.

And there is more : the total effect of this scene is lightened by the character of the action which surrounds it. The scene which immediately precedes it has ended on a high note of promised hilarity as Maria speaks of Malvolio to her accomplices :

If you will then see the fruits of the sport, mark his first approach before my lady. He will come to her in yellow stockings, and 'tis a colour she abhors, and cross-garter'd, a fashion she detests; and he will smile upon her, which will now be so unsuitable to her disposition, being addicted to a melancholy as she is, that it cannot but turn him into a notable contempt. If you will see it, follow me. (II v 217–25)

This invitation is followed by the entrance of Viola, who matches wits with Feste, then proceeds to the interview with Olivia. *Maria's promise of the ludicrous spectacle that is to be the highest point of hilarity in all the action thus hangs over the tender scene.* Though both women are ignorant that a practice on Malvolio is under way and its exploitation imminent, Olivia is integral to it, for the practice on Malvolio is necessarily a practice on her also; hence her mere presence in the interview helps keep awareness of the promised hilarity alive, and this awareness lightens the effect of the interview.

Shakespeare's preparation of our minds for the climactic scene of the yellow stockings and cross-gartering has been long and elaborate. It has included introduction to the back stairs of that household in which Olivia – exhibited in a predicament as deliciously ironical as any in Shakespeare – has vainly vowed to walk for seven years in mourning veil 'And water once a day her chamber round / With eye-offending brine: all this to

season / A brother's dead love'. It is not only Orsino's suit that
threatens her solemn purpose; the stamp of futility is set on her
vow by the lunatic character of her household : vain dream, to
pass seven years in weeping under the same roof with Malvolio,
Maria, Belch, and Aguecheek! Before it is visited by Viola,
practising as 'Cesario', and before Maria devises her practice
on Malvolio, Olivia's house harbours another practice : Sir
Toby is revelling at Sir Andrew's cost, the bait being Olivia.
This practice was begun before the action of the play com-
mences, and it continues until the final scene when, after
Sebastian has half killed both the guller and the gull, Sir Toby
breaks it off abruptly :

> *Sir And.* I'll help you, Sir Toby, because we'll be dress'd to-
> gether.
> *Sir To.* Will you help? – an ass-head and a coxcomb and a
> knave, a thin-fac'd knave, a gull! (v i 210–13)

Though inconspicuous, this long-standing practice is central to
much action, for it precipitates both Maria's practice on Malvolio and Toby's practice on Sir Andrew and Viola–'Cesario'
which brings them near to duelling and very nearly ends Viola's
masquerade; indeed it underlies the entire secondary action,
which itself provides the comic environment for the main
'Cesario'–Olivia–Sebastian plot.

This initial practice is introduced to us before we are shown
Sir Andrew himself; in our first sight of Olivia's household, Sir
Toby alludes to it :

> *Mar.* I heard my lady talk of it yesterday, and of a foolish
> knight that you brought in one night here to be her wooer.
> *Sir T.* Who? Sir Andrew Aguecheek?
> *Mar.* Ay, he.
> *Sir T.* He's as tall a man as any's in Illyria.
> *Mar.* What's that to the purpose?
> *Sir T.* Why, he has three thousand ducats a year. (i iii 15–23)

Nightly, Sir Toby and Sir Andrew drink healths to Olivia:
'I'll drink to her', says Toby, 'as long as there is a passage in my
throat and drink in Illyria.' Toby's is a lucrative practice; much
later, he estimates the gross:

> *Fab.* This is a dear manikin to you, Sir Toby.
> *Sir To.* I have been dear to him, lad, some two thousand strong,
> or so. (III ii 57–9)

Before we see him, then, we hold advantage over Sir Andrew
in knowing that he is being gulled. At first sight, in I iii, we
gain another: we perceive at once that his ignorance of Toby's
practice is only an acute manifestation of a native condition.
Of the race of Bottom, Sir Andrew would be at a disadvantage
if he were not being gulled; being gulled, he is doubly 'out'.

The practice on Sir Andrew goes forward in back-room
caterwauling; and it is this caterwauling that precipitates the
practice on Malvolio, whose high-handed manner of relaying
Olivia's command that the bacchanal cease provokes the wrath
of the revellers and inspires Maria's genius: 'If I do not gull
him into a nayword, and make him a common recreation, do
not think I have wit enough to lie straight in my bed.' Her
device is adapted precisely to that singular lack of self-perspec-
tive which is Malvolio's whole vice and whole virtue:

> ... it is his grounds of faith that all that look on him love him;
> and on that vice in him will my revenge find notable cause to
> work. (II iii 163–6)

Besides other attributes, Maria has a gift for forgery: 'I can
write very like my lady your niece.' Says Toby,

> He shall think, by the letters that thou wilt drop, that they
> come from my niece, and that she's in love with him.
> (Ibid. 178–80)

Such is the practice which places Maria and her accomplices, with ourselves, on a level above Malvolio and Olivia. Our advantage over Malvolio, however, like that over Sir Andrew, is double. Possibly Malvolio's pit is the darker, since Sir Andrew has moments when he apprehends the possibility that he lacks wit : 'I am a great eater of beef and I believe that does harm to my wit.' Though foolish enough to dream of Olivia's hand, he is scarcely hopeful. He adores Olivia, with an adoration that is hardly bolder than Slender's remote and silent worship of sweet Anne Page. If Toby did not egg him on – 'Send for money, knight. If thou hast her not i' the end, call me cut' – he would lose all hope and go home; if Toby had not first prompted him he would never have aspired. Sir Andrew, then, is deceived, and foolish, but not self-deceived.

Malvolio, on the other hand, is self-deceived before he is deceived. Sir Hugh Evans and Justice Shallow together cannot arouse real hope in Slender's breast; Sir Toby's assurances do not allay Sir Andrew's grave doubts. But Malvolio's fire is the product of spontaneous combustion, and his sense of worthiness is unalloyed by misgivings. Shakespeare makes this fact clear by exhibiting the man's vainglory just before he finds the forged letter : 'To be Count Malvolio !' and, again :

> Having been three months married to her, sitting in my state.
> . . . Calling my officers about me, in my branch'd velvet gown,
> having come from a day-bed, where I have left Olivia sleeping. . . .
> (II v 49–55)

This exhibition of self-deception continues until Malvolio picks up the letter, when deception is welded to self-deception by a gaudy flash of irony : 'What employment have we here ?' The 100 lines that follow, during which Malvolio manages to find his own name in the letters M, O, A, I, and arrives at confirmation – 'I do not now fool myself, to let imagination jade me; for every reason excites to this that my lady loves me' – make simultaneous exploitation of deception and self-deception :

M, O, A, I; this simulation is not as the former. And yet, to crush this a little, it would bow to me, for every one of these letters are in my name. (Ibid. 151–4)

Exhibiting the seduction of a mind eager to be seduced, the scene surpasses everything resembling it in Shakespeare. In comedy the nearest to it is the scene in which Falstaff hears the wives' propositions recounted by Mistress Quickly; yet Falstaff hears with astonishment and believes in spite of himself so that deception prevails over self-deception. And in tragedy, the nearest is the witches' initial winning of Macbeth – which leaves him, however, not yet wholly committed.

'Observe him, for the love of mockery', said Maria to her accomplices. Hidden in the box-tree, they hold a triple advantage over Malvolio, in that they watch him when he does not suspect, recognize his self-kindled folly, and, of course, know that the letter which sets him ablaze is forged. Yet the master practiser here is Shakespeare, whose way it is to set participants where they overpeer others while they are also overpeered. The practisers do not suspect, as we are privately reminded when Maria describes Olivia as 'addicted to a melancholy', a disposition which will render Malvolio's smiles intolerable to her. The fact is that Olivia is not now addicted to a melancholy, but is in love with 'Cesario' – and her world has changed. Hence even Maria, knowing nothing of the change, drops below our level. As for Sir Andrew, Shakespeare does not let us forget that the man is a fool all the while he joyously overpeers Malvolio – and that, besides, he is practice-ridden. Maria has just described her scheme to gull Malvolio when we are reminded that Andrew's own gulling continues:

Sir To. Let's to bed, knight. Thou hadst need send for more money.
Sir And. If I cannot recover your niece, I am a foul way out.
Sir To. Send for money, knight. If thou hast her not i' the end, call me cut. (II iii 198–203)

And while he is most enjoying his advantage over **Malvolio**, Sir Andrew is made to expose the depth of his congenital unawareness :

> *Mal.* 'Besides, you waste the treasure of your time with a foolish knight,' –
> *Sir A.* That's me, I warrant you.
> *Mal.* 'One Sir Andrew,' –
> *Sir A.* I knew 'twas I; for many do call me fool. (ii v 85–90)

Maria's invitation to see 'the fruits of the sport', which is the final word of preparation for the climactic scene of the yellow stockings, thus carries even higher promise than she intends, since the gullers as well as their gull will, in our perspective, contribute to the fun.

The climactic scene does not follow immediately : Maria's promise, suspended, conditions the environment of three scenes before it is fulfilled. The first of these, the pathetic interview of 'Cesario' with Olivia, totally encircled by past, continuing, and promised hilarity, has already been examined. Sentimentally conceived, permeated with emotion, Olivia's declaration of love demands sympathy : yet placed where it is, it gathers an echo from Malvolio's affair : Olivia's passion for 'Cesario' is as preposterous as Malvolio's for Olivia. The second scene (iii ii) is affected also, but differently : Sir Toby, assisted by Fabian, puffs up Sir Andrew's collapsing hopes of winning Olivia, and Sir Andrew, foolish and practice-ridden, fails to see in Malvolio's delusion the very portrait of his own. At the same time that it exploits the old practice on the brainless knight, this scene also prepares a new one; says Toby,

> Challenge me the Count's youth to fight with him; hurt him in eleven places; my niece shall take note of it; and assure thyself, there is no love-broker in the world can more prevail in man's commendation with woman than report of valour. (iii ii 36–41)

The new practice is in fact born of ignorance, not only Andrew's but the practisers', for Toby and Fabian do not guess that the 'favours' which Andrew reports he saw Olivia do 'the Count's serving-man' in the orchard were expressions of true love – or that they were misspent, this youth being no man at all. 'For Andrew', says Toby, 'If he were open'd and you find so much blood in his liver as will clog the foot of a flea, I'll eat the rest of the anatomy.' Fabian's reply flares up in irony that marks a hit of error upon truth : 'And his opposite, the youth, bears in his visage no great presage of cruelty.'

The third scene set between Maria's promise and its ful-filment shows Sebastian on a street in Illyria and confirms our long-held comforting assumption that the solution to Viola's 'insoluble' problem is at hand. Placed between the announce-ment of Sir Toby's practice (the challenge) which will surely terrify 'Cesario', and the exploitation of multiple practices in the climactic scene, Sebastian's declaration that he will walk abroad to view the town is our reassurance that all is well. It comes just as the climactic scene of the yellow stockings begins and is the dramatist's last bid to make certain that all useful information is in our minds.

And it is truly an enormous bundle of awarenesses that we must carry into this scene, during the action of which all nine of the persons present are blind to some part of the situation. Though not the first of Shakespeare's scenes in which everyone stands below our vantage-point, it is the most complex of such scenes until the climactic portion of *Cymbeline*. Four principal situations comprise the scene : first, that in which Malvolio's delusion is central; second, that in which Olivia's unawareness of 'Cesario's' identity is central; third, that in which Viola and Sir Andrew's unawareness of Toby's practice is central; fourth, that in which Antonio's mistaking of 'Cesario' for Sebastian is central. Yet these are only the basic situations. The total context which has been established in our minds and from which the action draws its full meaning is beyond explicit description; yet it is in the totality that the cream of the jest – or of four jests – lies.

First up for exploitation is Malvolio's unawareness – but Shakespeare delays Malvolio yet again, until we have been reminded of the state of Olivia's mind. Her remarks stand like the topic sentence for what follows :

> (*Aside.*) I have sent after him; he says he'll come. How shall I feast him? What bestow of him? For youth is bought more oft than begg'd or borrow'd. (III iv 1–3)

Not Malvolio, as he thinks, or her dead brother, as Maria and her accomplices suppose, but 'Cesario' fills her mind : *we are not to be allowed to forget, even at the very edge of it, that Malvolio's outrageous performance before his lady is set within the frame of Viola's masquerade.* Remembrance of Olivia's vain love thus is made to hang darkly over the hilarious spectacle very much as, earlier, Maria's promise of this hilarity hung brightly above the tender and embarrassed interview of Viola and Olivia. The second fold of Olivia's ignorance is next exposed :

> Where is Malvolio? He is sad and civil,
> And suits well for a servant with my fortunes.
> Where is Malvolio? (III iv 5–7)

Malvolio's gulling is also Olivia's; says Maria :

> Your ladyship were best to have some guard about you, if he come; for, sure, the man is tainted in 's wits. (Ibid. 12–14)

Unaware of Maria's forgery, both servants and lady are victims of the practice. But Olivia stands on the higher level : mystification is up the scale from oblivion. Maniacally smiling, cross-gartered, yellow-stockinged, a veritable bodying-forth of ignorance, Malvolio is the central figure amid circles of error.

His smile, his garters, his stockings are unawareness rendered visible; his words, unawareness rendered audible. Orlando's unawareness of 'Ganymede' and Orsino's of 'Cesario' are exploited mainly by words whose flares illuminate the space between their depths and our height. But Malvolio's is ignorance not so much of another person as of himself, hence is aptly exhibited not only by words but by physical signs – like Bottom's superadded head and Falstaff's horns. 'His very genius', says Sir Toby, when the incident is past, 'hath taken the infection of the device.' The smile, the garters, the stockings – the immediate effects of Maria's practice on him – are ultimately the signs of Malvolio's practice on himself.

Here and in Feste's later practice (iv ii) Malvolio's exposure to derision is well deserved. Not only is his aspiration self-kindled, lacking the excuse that it was set going by an external practice, but it is contemptible in its nature. Sir Andrew, with Toby's prompting, aspires to Olivia's hand because, in his booby fashion, he loves her. But Malvolio sees Olivia as means to Great Place. Shakespeare exhibits four such deceived, futile aspirants: Sir Andrew and Malvolio of *Twelfth Night*, Slender of *The Merry Wives of Windsor*, and, in the tragic case, Roderigo of *Othello*. Sir Andrew's aspiration is nearest Slender's in its innocence; Malvolio's, tainted with self-love and social ambition, nearest Roderigo's, which is lust.

Though a climax in itself, Malvolio's scene is framed by the main situation: it opens with Olivia awaiting the arrival of 'Cesario' to dine with her; 'Cesario', not Malvolio, is foremost in her mind then and thereafter – and Malvolio's performance, in her perspective, is only an odd episode which occurs while she is waiting. Moreover, the comic effect of Malvolio's scene arises partly from his ignorance of 'Cesario's' identity and of Olivia's misspent passion; indeed, in this ignorance Malvolio stands on the same level as his tormentors, for even Maria believes Olivia still to be grieving for her brother. And Toby incites Andrew to challenge 'Cesario', not because he thinks there are grounds for his gull's jealousy but merely for the love of the game. Amid preparations for Toby's newest practice, Shakespeare sets the third interview of 'Cesario' and Olivia, which reminds us – should the several interludes have obscured the fact – that Olivia's passion is real enough. Though brief, the interview is indispensable : it looks before and after, and its twenty lines bind together the four episodes of this very long climactic scene.

The third of these episodes, which primarily exploits Sir Andrew's ignorance, is at once the result of Sir Toby's old practice on him and of 'Cesario's' practice on all Illyria. The episode parallels that of the yellow stockings : his aspiration fed by Maria's practice, Malvolio makes a spectacle of himself before Olivia; his aspiration fed by Sir Toby's practice, Sir Andrew makes a spectacle of himself by challenging 'Cesario'. 'Marry', says Toby, when the opponents are brought front to front, 'I'll ride your horse as well as I ride you.' Even Malvolio is not so practice-ridden as is Sir Andrew at this moment. Victim, first of all, of nature's practice, he has next been deceived by Sir Toby into supposing that Toby's dry gullet is the way to Olivia's heart; next, he is deceived by Viola's practice into supposing that 'the Count's serving-man' is a serious rival; next, edged on to challenge 'Cesario', he is abused when his foolish letter is replaced by Toby's description of his ferocity : 'this letter, being so excellently ignorant, will breed no terror in the youth; he will find it comes from a clodpole'; and, finally, he is abused by Toby's exaggerated report of his adversary : 'Why, man, he's a very devil; I have not seen such a firago. . . . They say he has been fencer to the Sophy.' The densest concentration of the Illyrian fog which rolled in from the sea with Viola here settles about the head of Sir Andrew. Of the total, infinitely complex situation which the dramatist has spread out plainly to our view, he sees nothing in its right shape, colour, or dimension. 'So soon as ever thou seest him, draw,' Sir Toby has directed him; 'and, as thou draw'st, swear horrible.' When the time comes, Sir Andrew's resolution is shattered by the terrifying images looming through his wall of fog : 'Let him let the matter slip, and I'll give him my horse, grey Capilet.'

If it concerned him alone, the effect of the episode would be purely comic. But Sir Toby's device makes sport of 'Cesario' also : 'This will so fright them both that they will kill one another by the look, like cockatrices.' For the very first time, yoked with a booby as the butt of a joke, Viola is in danger of looking ridiculous. Hitherto our only advantage over her has been our knowledge of Sebastian's survival – an advantage that has provided comforting assurance but given no cause for laughter. Yet again, as in the case of Olivia stricken with passion for 'Cesario', though the plight is laughable the victim is not. It bears repeating that Viola is one of the most feminine of Shakespeare's heroines. No other heroine is less suited to brave it in man's role – unless it were Hero, who would not dare. To Viola, a duel with a warrior such as Sir Toby describes is unthinkable :

He is knight, dubb'd with unhatch'd rapier and on carpet consideration; but he is a devil in private brawl. Souls and bodies hath he divorc'd three; and his incensement at this moment is so implacable, that satisfaction can be none but by pangs of death and sepulchre. Hob, nob, is his word; give 't or take 't.

(III iv 257–63)

Rosalind could manage this Aguecheek; but even if Viola knew the truth about him, duelling would not be for her. 'I am one that had rather go with sir priest than sir knight', she tells Fabian; 'I care not who knows so much of my mettle.' Shakespeare has balanced the scales delicately between laughter and tears, and Viola's exquisite femininity keeps them so; capable Rosalind would destroy the tension. From the outset the trials in which Viola's disguise involves her have been hard; this one frightens her nearly to surrendering her secret : 'A little thing would make me tell them how much I lack of a man.'

The line prods our awareness at a crucial moment: the grotesque basis of the duel, the blubbering terror of Sir Andrew, and the swaggering, gross humour of Sir Toby would assuredly tip the scales to the side of hilarity if we should momentarily forget what 'Cesario' is. Further, this particular line of Viola's, being set just after Sir Toby's loudest exhortation to the reluctant duellists, subtly reminds us that Sir Andrew and Viola are not the only butts of this joke: they are the butts in Sir Toby's perspective, but Sir Toby is the butt in ours. If Sir Andrew is ignorant that 'Cesario' is not 'a very devil . . . a firago', and if 'Cesario' is ignorant that Sir Andrew is all hare and no lion, yet Toby is ignorant that 'Cesario' is Viola. This is the cream of the cream: that the boisterous manipulator, perpetrator of multiple practices on Sir Andrew, overpeerer also of 'Cesario' by virtue of his better acquaintance with the silly knight's valour, absolute master, in his own perspective, of all elements in the situation, as self-assured as Malvolio in his utterances – should be all the while ignorant of the most important fact in the entire action. 'Marry', he tells us confidentially of Aguecheek, 'I'll ride your horse as well as I ride you.' But Shakespeare has enabled us to ride Sir Toby.

Perhaps, then, Viola gets off free here, when her unawareness invites laughter at her expense. But in the final episode of the scene, though she escapes laughter, she is exposed under an unflattering light. The fault, of course, is not hers, but Antonio's, in mistaking her for Sebastian. In a sense, Antonio's level is lower than Illyria's, for Orsino, Olivia, and others have only supposed Viola to be 'Cesario', while Antonio, ignorant alike of 'Cesario' and Viola, takes her to be Sebastian. Yet in another sense Illyria's error is deeper, for 'Cesario' is a fiction, whereas Sebastian is a fact.

For this episode the dramatist has so arranged the awarenesses that they set contradictory responses fighting for supremacy. Here again, also, the initial preparation lies far back, in the scene which first shows us Sebastian. Antonio has saved him from the sea, weeps with him for his drowned sister, is solicitous for his welfare, begs to serve him, and, finally, braving old enemies in Orsino's court, insists on accompanying him : 'I do adore thee so / That danger shall seem sport, and I will go.' When next we see the pair, the expression of Antonio's regard for his young friend is emphatic to the point of being conspicuous; what is more, it is backed up by action : 'Hold sir, here's my purse.'

Perhaps Shakespeare remembered another Antonio, who risked his flesh for his friend Bassanio : had the sense of that Antonio's goodness not been established in our minds, our anxiety for him while danger increased would hardly have been stirred, and the tensions that make the court scene great would have been flabby. Sebastian's magnanimous Antonio is like Bassanio's; hence, when he mistakes 'Cesario' for Sebastian, is arrested, asks return of his purse – 'It grieves me / Much more for what I cannot do for you / Than what befalls me' – is stared at and refused, our knowledge of his kindness compels sympathy for him – and resentment towards the cause of this sudden shock given to his nature :

> Will you deny me now?
> Is 't possible that my deserts to you
> Can lack persuasion? (Ibid. 381–3)

It is a moment shrewdly wrought, which brings into conflict two urgent awarenesses – of Antonio's selflessness and of Viola's femininity and perfect innocence. Though we know Antonio to be in error and Viola blameless, yet in the eyes of this kind man she is terribly guilty. Shakespeare's devotion to such moments of extreme tension sometimes leads him to the edge of psychological calamity; perhaps here he goes too near, and his heroine, despite our awareness that she is innocent and despite her eagerness to do what she can for Antonio – 'My having is not much. / I'll make division of my present with you' – is singed by an involuntary flash of our resentment.

The incident closes the scene. Presenting four interlocked episodes all the relationships of which are constantly exposed to our Olympian view; parading forth nearly all the persons of the play in their relative states of ignorance, none understanding all, and some – Malvolio, Aguecheek, Olivia, Antonio – understanding nothing that is going on; moving from the hilarious exhibition of Malvolio's delusion to the painful representation of Antonio's sudden disillusionment with humankind, it is, from the point of view of the creation, maintenance, and exploitation of multiple discrepant awarenesses, the most remarkable achievement in Shakespearian comedy before *Cymbeline*.

The brief scene which follows is the very cap atop the action of the play, the tip of the summit. In short space are exploited the gaps between the several levels – all inferior to ours – of the six persons who enter. In Shakespeare's comedies, almost infallibly, two contrasting moments make the great peaks : first, the moment in which, errors having been compounded and various lines of action brought to a central point, confusion is nearest universal, visibility nearest zero; second, that in which confusion is dispelled. In the present scene, the first movement is marked by Feste's doubly ironical expostulation with Sebastian :

No, I do not know you; nor I am not sent to you by my lady, to bid you come speak with her; nor your name is not Master Cesario; nor this is not my nose neither. Nothing that is so is so.

(IV i 5–9)

So speaks the Clown, wise enough to *play* the fool, yet lost like the others in the Illyrian fog. He is the first of five who in quick succession mistake Sebastian for 'Cesario'. The formula is the same on which the entire action of *The Comedy of Errors* is based, but it is here used with a difference. In the early play, when Adriana mistakes Antipholus of Syracuse for her hus-

band, she is only once removed from the truth apparent to us
– for there is indeed an Antipholus of Ephesus. But the 'Cesario'
for whom Sebastian is mistaken is himself a fiction. All five
persons, thus, being twice removed from truth, hold a level
even lower than Sebastian's. For Sebastian, though he has
come from outside into a situation of which he is totally
ignorant – knowing neither that Viola lives nor that she poses
as 'Cesario', that Olivia loves this 'Cesario', or that Sir Andrew
is jealous of him – is nevertheless well enough aware that he is
himself Sebastian and no other; not seeing the illusion that
blinds the others, he is nearer reality than they. Oblivion is
a lower level than mystification; they are oblivious, and he is
mystified :

> What relish is in this? How runs the stream?
> Or I am mad, or else this is a dream. (Ibid. 64–5)

His mystification continues through his next scene, when it
contrasts with Olivia's blissful error as she draws him home in
the company of a priest. In all Shakespeare's comedies, only
the twin brothers of *The Comedy of Errors*, masters and servants, remain longer in this precise degree of awareness; indeed,
among the enormous number of persons in the comedies shown
ignorant of their situations, only a few are truly mystified. For
a moment or two in *Love's Labour's Lost*, upon their return to
the ladies after posing as Russians, the King and his companions stand in this condition. Briefly also, Bassanio and
Gratiano, in *The Merchant of Venice*, are mystified when
Portia and Nerissa suddenly show the rings earlier presented
to the 'doctor' and the 'clerk'. In *Much Ado About Nothing*
Hero is briefly mystified by Claudio's harsh indictment of her
honour. In *The Merry Wives of Windsor* Ford is twice mystified by his failure to find Falstaff in his wife's company. In the
later comedies, as we shall note, moments in which a participant's mystification is exploited are similarly rare and brief. In

both intensity and duration, Sebastian's mystification comes nearest that of Antipholus of Syracuse; thus, after his first meeting with Olivia:

> This is the air, that is the glorious sun,
> This pearl she gave me, I do feel 't and see 't;
> And though 'tis wonder that enwraps me thus,
> Yet 'tis not madness. (IV iii 1–4)

His relation to the illusion-ridden city of Illyria differs in one particular from that of Antipholus of Syracuse to Ephesus. Until Antipholus and his Dromio arrived, no illusion existed in Ephesus; what follows is all of their own making. But when Sebastian came out of the sea to Illyria, Viola had preceded him, bringing in the fog that now engulfs everyone. 'Madman, thou errest', the Clown tells Malvolio in the continuing practice on this most extreme case of the Illyrian affliction. 'I say, there is no darkness but ignorance, in which thou art more puzzl'd than the Egyptians in their fog.' Malvolio best represents also the Illyrians' inability to perceive their illusion: 'I tell thee, I am as well in my wits as any man in Illyria.' In contrast, coming from outside into all this, Sebastian knows enough to be mystified; though he cannot see through the fog, he can see that it is there; 'There's something in 't / That is deceivable.'

At the opening of Act V the burden of the context which preceding acts have established in our minds is staggering. *During Acts* II, III, *and* IV *no fully aware person except Viola has appeared before us* – and during part of this time she too has lacked full vision. At precisely what moment she rejoins us in our omniscience is the final question to be considered; indeed, the question of the state of Viola's awareness during the last two acts is the great question of the play.

At the close of Act IV we saw Olivia and Sebastian go to be married. We therefore hold advantage over Viola and Orsino upon their entrance in Act V. Over Orsino, of course, we hold other advantages also – the same that we have held for three acts. But are we to suppose that we hold any additional advantage over Viola? She is ignorant that her brother – in a state like that of shock – is now repeating the marriage oath before Olivia's priest. But is she still ignorant that he escaped drowning and has arrived in Illyria?

At the end of Act III, when Antonio interrupted her match with Sir Andrew, the cause of his error was as open to her as to us. That she then perceived the truth there can be little doubt:

> Methinks his words do from such passion fly
> That he believes himself; so do not I.
> Prove true, imagination, O, prove true,
> That I, dear brother, be now ta'en for you!
>
> (III iv 407–10)

And again:

> He nam'd Sebastian. I my brother know
> Yet living in my glass; even such and so
> In favour was my brother, and he went
> Still in this fashion, colour, ornament,
> For him I imitate. (Ibid. 414–18)

But now, at the opening of Act v, with Orsino, again meeting Antonio, she speaks with wide-eyed amazement:

> He did me kindness, sir, drew on my side,
> But in conclusion put strange speech upon me.
> I know not what 'twas but distraction. (v i 69–71)

'That most ingrateful boy there by your side, / From the rude sea's enrag'd and foamy mouth / Did I redeem', asserts Antonio. The sea captain who had saved Viola had told her:

> I saw your brother,
> Most provident in peril, bind himself,
> Courage and hope both teaching him the practice,
> To a strong mast that liv'd upon the sea;

> Where, like Arion on the dolphin's back,
> I saw him hold acquaintance with the waves
> So long as I could see. (1 ii 11–17)

And she had replied :

> Mine own escape unfoldeth to my hope,
> Whereto thy speech serves for authority,
> The like of him. (Ibid. 19–21)

From the first she had entertained hope; then Antonio had mistaken her and named Sebastian, whom she imitated in her masquerade; and, finally, Antonio describes a sea-rescue that accords with other evidence of Sebastian's survival. When Antonio has finished his account of the rescue and his three-months' life with Sebastian, Viola could, with few words, disabuse the tormented fellow, whose experience with ingratitude is maddening him. Instead, wide-eyed as before, she inquires, 'How can this be?'

That is to say, she holds to her masquerade in spite of all at this crucial moment – and even, in feigning ignorance, grafts a new practice on the old. Why does she do so? A damning answer is that Shakespeare is willing to sacrifice plausibility in order to preserve to the last moment the richly exploitable gap between Illyria's oblivion and Viola's awareness, so that when all lines have converged upon that moment, he can achieve a spectacular denouement, with Illyria's awareness shooting up like a rocket when Sebastian and 'Cesario' come face to face. That Shakespeare always set a high rate on exploitable gaps and that he here forces the situation to yield its utmost effect before he explodes it is unquestionable. But that he sacrifices plausibility in doing so is not so sure.

At the opening of Act v Viola is yet ignorant of one fact : that Olivia and Sebastian are married. *If she knew that*, she would know that time, on which she early set her hope – 'O time! thou must untangle this, not I' – has already solved her problem. Not knowing it, and being Viola, feminine as no other, she maintains her old fiction and compounds a new one of silence and innocence. Like Portia and Rosalind, Vincentio and Prospero in that she plays the role of chief practiser and controlling force, she is unlike these in her attitude toward it. She has found no joy in the role; she has been tempted to abandon it: 'A little thing would make me tell them how much I lack of a man.' More significantly, whereas the other controlling forces manipulate persons and contrive practices to bring their ends about, she has contrived nothing beyond her initial disguise. Though her goal – implied in 'He was a bachelor then' at her arrival in Illyria and shortly thereafter confirmed in 'Whoe'er I woo, myself would be his wife' – has always been to catch this Duke, she has played fair with both him and Olivia, serving faithfully, twisting nothing to her own purpose, striving only to stay out of trouble – and waiting on time. When trouble came, in the form of Olivia's passion and Sir Toby's practice, she rode it out despite embarrassment, pity, and even terror. When at last Antonio's terror advised her of her brother's survival, her hope took ecstatic new life: the end was in sight. Being Viola, she could not then break faith with time, even to save the good Antonio from misanthropy. Feminine in her patient waiting, she is no less so in her persistence: it is not enough that the end is in sight; it must actually be reached. When the Duke berates her, even threatening death, she opposes her patience to his fury:

> And I, most jocund, apt, and willingly,
> To do you rest, a thousand deaths would die. (v i 135–6)

The final silent moments of her masquerade are the hardest.

So great is her subtlety at the last that it is difficult to identify the instant at which she perceives that time has performed its final chore in her behalf. But she must be fully aware by the time of Olivia's exclamation: 'Cesario, husband, stay!' Never-

theless, to the Duke's enraged 'Her husband, sirrah!' she replies with a wide-eyed denial that we should perhaps take
instead as a victory whoop: 'No, my lord, not I.' The priest
confirms Olivia's word that 'Cesario' is her husband. Sir
Andrew and Sir Toby berate 'Cesario' for hurting them. Still
Viola keeps silent, except to deny the charges. Then follow fifty
lines of dialogue in the course of which Sebastian enters and
astonishes all Illyria except herself. And she speaks never a
word. The arrival of Sebastian cannot be a surprise to her; his
tender greeting of Olivia can be none. The long, superb silence,
more wonderful that the Illyrians' ejaculations of amazement,
is almost but not quite the extremest demonstration of her
femininity. That demonstration comes only after Sebastian has
subjected her to direct questioning, when she replies with wide-
eyed and incredible incredulity:

> Such a Sebastian was my brother too;
> So went he suited to his watery tomb.
> If spirits can assume both form and suit,
> You come to fright us. (Ibid. 241–3)

In this last instant before giving over her long masquerade, she
thus devises a final fiction: neither husband, brother, nor sister-
in-law will ever learn from her lips anything other than she
had been ignorant, *until this instant*, of her brother's survival,
his arrival in Illyria, and his marriage. This shred of a great
secret she will never give up, that she had ridden her masquerade to the very end, biding time – 'O time! thou must
untangle this, not I' – until it took Olivia off her hands and
gave her Orsino.

SOURCE: *Shakespeare's Comedies* (1960) chap. iv

Porter Williams, Jr

MISTAKES IN *TWELFTH NIGHT* AND THEIR RESOLUTION (1961)

A study of the significance of the mistakes in *Twelfth Night*, like the study of any important aspect of Shakespeare's art, must be made upon several levels, for mistakes by the protagonists are both a part of the superficial fabric of the plot and a subtle means of revealing underlying themes that often manifest themselves only indirectly below the surface action. This is not to say that the artificial devices of disguises and mistaken identities, all timeworn devices, are nothing more than a mere plot framework for the profundities that lie beneath. Rather, as Miss Bradbrook expresses it, there is an 'interdependence of the natural and the artificial, the human and the literary'.[1] The ridiculous mistakes that control the plot are therefore like Freudian slips which incite their superficial laughter and at the same time reveal subconscious patterns of human behavior. It is these slips, the mistakes of all the leading characters, that we must follow into the thematic material of the play, for it is on this level that they become of most interest.

Twelfth Night, then, on its superficial level is based upon familiar patterns, suggesting Plautus and Italian Renaissance comedy. Characters are symmetrically grouped, there are disguises, a twin brother and sister, a fool, and scarcely believable deceptions.[2] Added to this is something of the comic spirit of the Twelfth Night Feast of the Epiphany in which the world is turned topsy-turvy. Traditionally in such celebrations, servants change places with their masters and say what they please, jests and pranks may be carried out with impunity, and the Fool becomes enthroned as the Lord of Misrule.[3] All of this

Italian artificiality and the happy Twelfth Night nonsense can be felt as a background in Shakespeare's play, though they have been transformed into something that is sophisticated and even profound, possibly designed for a learned audience at the Inns of Court or to be acted before the Queen, as Leslie Hotson would have it.[4] Thus the maskings, deceptions, and the foolery may suggest the celebrations of the traditional Masks and Revels, or even hint at the seriousness behind such religious holidays, but they have been 'translated into an entirely different idiom'.[5] Nevertheless, disguises and deceptions of one sort or another dominate the play, and the errors to be studied spring from them. These disguises may be merely physical, as with Viola dressed as a page or Feste dressed as Sir Topas, or they may be psychological, as with Orsino and Olivia who have deceived themselves into believing that they have been overwhelmed with love or with grief. Such disguises may fool others or only the deceiver. Out of this emerges the full richness of one of Shakespeare's finest romantic comedies.

Superficially, the plot may be seen to develop in terms of Exposition, Complication, and Resolution, which might be described as masking, the resulting deceptions and errors, and a final unmasking. But the significant developments and revelations of character, and even the resolution of the errors, take place beneath this sparkling surface of disguises. The play opens to reveal Orsino and Olivia at an impasse, and both wear psychological masks, for one is foolishly determined to renounce love and grieve seven years for the loss of a brother; while the other, overcome with love melancholy, is determined that he can love only the woman who rejects him. Orsino's melancholy is reminiscent of the sadness that lengthens Romeo's hours while he is away from his unresponsive Rosaline. These are the two great mistakes opening the play, for Olivia and Orsino are self-deceived, both assuming false personalities and unaware that by all the rules of romantic comedy and love psychology, they are destined for marriage, though not to each other. The

Complication of the play begins with the entrance of Viola
disguised as the page Cesario, the central deception of the
play; and the action of the main plot as well as of the sub-plots
may be said to proceed as a series of thwarted suits for the hand
of Olivia or the love of Orsino. Mistakes control the direction
of the action throughout. Viola cannot obtain Orsino's love
as long as she is mistaken for Cesario and as long as Orsino
mistakes the object of his love; while Olivia, though abandon-
ing one error, that of a seven years' grief, still cannot love
Orsino and can never win the disguised Viola. Olivia's other
suitors, Sir Andrew Aguecheek and Malvolio, hopelessly deceived into playing the roles of lovers, are each fooled to the
top of his bent until unmasked before all by Sir Toby, Maria,
and their associates in the sub-plot. The action reaches its
turning point with the cleverest 'disguise' of all and the happiest deception. Sebastian, appearing as himself and hence
unwittingly disguised as Cesario, his masked sister, accepts the
hand of Olivia, now most truly herself and yet most completely
deceived. Only unmasking can follow after this, with the pair-
ing off of the lovers and the dismissal of the thwarted. Feste,
the wisest fool of them all, is left alone to frame the action in
Time.

It has already been suggested that mistakes, besides being at
the center of the superficial and hardly believable fabric of
disguises and deceptions that activate the plot, are also at the
center of the rich psychological revelations that represent the
important themes of the play and supply a believable kind of
motivation. Errors on this level supply startling insights into
patterns that run through many of Shakespeare's plays. On
this level, deceptions, or the effort to deceive, and the mistakes
they produce, all tend to reveal rather than to hide human
nature. There is a danger here, of course, of losing sight of the
specific problem of mistakes by merely repeating what has
already been discussed so admirably by such critics as Professor
H. B. Charlton, Miss M. C. Bradbrook, and Professor

J. R. Brown. In a sense, most of the themes that are implicit in all of Shakespeare's comedies cross the pattern of mistakes in *Twelfth Night*. Our problem here will be to show not so much that the comedies are informed by Shakespeare's 'attitude to life and, in particular, to love and personal relationships',[6] but to show that the mistakes themselves have an intimate bearing upon the revelation of these themes of love and personal relationships. It is through his mistakes that we can see a character in the play either find or avoid what for him is a right relationship. For example, Olivia's spontaneous love for Cesario, a mistake on most levels, unconsciously prepares her heart for a happy union with Sebastian, just as it also reveals the fallacy of contemplating an unnatural seven years' grief. Likewise, Sebastian, thrust into a world of misconceptions but sensing his own occasion mellow, accepts an offer of marriage in complete ignorance and fully aware only 'That this may be some error' (iv iii 10).

The examples above lead naturally to a control point for a discussion of mistakes – the marriage of Olivia and Sebastian, the happiest and most important error in the play. Superficially, it is a daring and spontaneous act, suggestive even of the 'too rash, too unadvis'd, too sudden' betrothal in *Romeo and Juliet* (ii ii 118). Olivia is aware of her haste and anxiety :

> Plight me the full assurance of your faith,
> That my most jealous and too doubtful soul
> May live at peace. (iv iii 26–8)

Likewise, Sebastian is enwrapped in 'wonder', aware of the possibility of 'error' or even 'madness', and ready to 'distrust' his eyes and 'wrangle' with his reason (iv iii 1–21). And yet these mistakes are fortunate ones of the mind rather than the heart, even though Olivia thinks that she is marrying Cesario. Intuition, not reason, is at work. Unlike Malvolio, they find happiness because they know what it is 'To be generous, guiltless, and of free disposition' (I v 89–90). Such impulses can bring tragic disaster, especially if fiery Tybalts or jealous Iagos are about; but given a world this side of tragedy, then the generous impulses of open natures are the surest way to happiness. A willingness to love and, something more, perhaps the gift to recognize a kindred spirit and to risk all, are the touchstones to Shakespeare's serious world of romantic comedy. Olivia's words, 'Love sought is good . . . but given unsought is better' (III i 153), seem to be the dominant note for those who win happiness in terms of love and friendship, but such giving and receiving must be done without counting the cost or measuring the risk. Viola gives her love unsought to Orsino, while on a more material level a surprising quantity of money and rings is given generously throughout the play, sought and unsought. Viola awards the Sea Captain gold without being asked, and she is quite willing to share what she has with the perplexed Antonio. Antonio gives unasked to Sebastian, and all pour coins into the open hands of the Fool.[7] Seldom in a play does money flow so freely or so readily symbolize generous love and friendship. Olivia specializes in sending rings and pearls to those she loves, though not quite so spontaneously as to be unaware that 'youth is bought more oft than begg'd or borrow'd' (III iv 3); and even the irritable Orsino sends to inform his 'sovereign cruelty' that neither her 'quantity of dirty lands' nor her fortune interests him,

> But 'tis that miracle and queen of gems
> That Nature pranks her in attracts my soul. (II iv 84–5)

Perhaps his love should have gone deeper than the 'gem' of her beauty, though surely the note of generosity is there. In sharp contrast to these generous lovers is Malvolio, who is rebuked by Olivia for being neither 'generous' nor 'free' (I v 87–9), not to mention Sir Toby's obvious abuse of friendship in his typical reminder to Sir Andrew that 'Thou hadst need send for more money', or Sir Andrew's equally mercenary reply, 'If I cannot recover your niece, I am a foul way out' (II iii 171–4). Shakespeare makes it clear enough that such self-love and such mercenary friendship lead nowhere, for all three are used according to their desert. These are their mistakes. The secret of true love and friendship, therefore, is a subtle and delicate relationship, depending upon uncalculating generosity and spontaneous impulses. Professor H. B. Charlton links this idea to the Elizabethan discovery that man was 'a much less rational and a much more complex creature than he had taken himself to be'. More than this, man had discovered that his instincts, intuitions, and emotions were 'often a much more exciting and satisfying part of his nature than was his sober intellect'. For the express purpose of comedy, man was becoming intellectually aware that 'the tumultuous condition of his being which followed his falling in love and urged him on to woo, was in fact no mean and mainly physical manifestation of his personality; it was, in fact, the awakening in him of the fuller capacities of his spirit'.[8] Shakespeare was particularly adept at underlying the awakening of these spiritual capacities by revealing them while the reason was perplexed with error, with the very mistakes that threatened well laid plans opening the way for intuitive solutions. Olivia's marriage to Sebastian, a farcical mistake of her intellect, nevertheless allows Shakespeare to explore with sympathy 'the subtle flow of unacknowledged attraction between man and woman'.[9] The very tone of the poetry conveys the spiritual quality of Olivia's 'most extracting frenzy' as she goes with Sebastian to the priest who is to marry them :

> Then lead the way, good father; and heavens so shine
> That they may fairly note this act of mine ! (IV iii 34–5)

Sebastian also takes his 'fair hour' with equal rapture. The verse alone informs us that all is well :

> This is the air; that is the glorious sun;
> This pearl she gave me, I do feel 't and see 't,
> And though 'tis wonder that enwraps me thus,
> Yet 'tis not madness. (iv iii 1–4)

Add to this the solemn words of the priest as he mistakenly testifies to having performed the holy ceremony of wedlock between Olivia and Cesario, and we see the richest fulfillment of spiritual capacities under the surface of error. With the thoughts of the jealous Duke ripe in mischief, the Priest announces

> A contract of eternal bond of love,
> Confirm'd by mutual joinder of your hands,
> Attested by the holy close of lips,
> Strength'ned by interchangement of your rings;
> And all the ceremony of this compact
> Seal'd in my function, by my testimony. (v i 150–5)

The Priest's confusion, even if it should be a moment for laughter, is also the final blessing of the marriage of Olivia and Sebastian. Unmasking after this can only reveal what has already been fulfilled under the 'darkness' of error.

Further light can be thrown on the subtle flow of attraction between man and woman by examining some of the unhappy errors in the play, the errors of the unsuccessful suitors. These errors reveal no redeeming capacities of the spirit. Malvolio's 'rapture' has nothing to do with love, and Sir Andrew's hopes draw on nothing more than the recollection that he 'was ador'd once too' (ii ii 170). Malvolio loves only the selfish vision of 'Count Malvolio' with all the coveted trappings of officers, velvet gowns, rich jewels, and the 'prerogative of speech' (ii v 24 ff.). He would like to think that Olivia 'did affect' him, but there is no underlying love to redeem his error of exposing to the world his impossible ambition of becoming Count Malvolio:

I will be proud, I will read politic authors, I will baffle Sir
Toby, I will wash off gross acquaintance, I will be point-devise
the very man. I do not now fool myself, to let imagination jade
me; for every reason excites to this, that my lady loves me.

(II v 142–5)

This selfish dream was too large for a mere steward and could
not stand the test of reality. Once he had imagined his dream
to be real, the real world took its harsh revenge. Similarly, Sir
Andrew came to grief by trying to rise to the dignified role of
knighthood. Deceived into believing that he was loved, he
made a fool of himself as he bought Sir Toby's friendship and
bargained for a fortune. He leaves the stage fleeced and
unloved, redeemed by no spiritual capacities, and content once
again to be Sir Toby's drinking companion.

Orsino, a more dignified suitor, presents the same kind of
complexities as Olivia. Like Olivia, he too had a spirit capable
of being awakened, but like her he made the mistake of assuming a false mask, that of a self-centered melancholy delighting in
the luxurious inactivity of unrequited love. His finer nature is so
mesmerized by self-indulgence that he almost forgets to seek
the object of his love except in the dream world of rich music.
'Instead of seeking opportunities to "give and hazard", he
passively takes what seeming pleasures can be his.'[10] This is his
mistake, and like Olivia he must be tricked into awakening by
another's fresh, spontaneous love. This is the work of Viola.

Viola, both protagonist and catalyst in the central action of
the play, suffers and triumphs through the mistakes of others.
She too must take part in masking and deceit, and yet she is
the least deceived of the three. Her mask is a physical disguise
and not one of the spirit, for she knows herself always to be
'one heart, one bosom, and one truth' (III i 155). Her mistakes rise out of her inability to foresee all of the consequences
of her disguising, not from any self-deceit, but this is enough
to bring her close to disaster and to force her to respond with

all the chords of her rich personality. Again, superficial farce reveals the inner depths of human psychology. Her first unexpected difficulty arises when she finds that in the role of Cesario she must against her own good unfold the passion of Orsino's love to Olivia, a task she undertakes so honorably that she ends by charming Olivia and winning her love. Already she has discovered the unexpected complications that can arise from deceit, however good one's intentions :

> Disguise, I see thou art a wickedness
> Wherein the pregnant enemy does much. (II ii 25–6)

Consequently she must continue to throw herself upon the mercy of time and the unknown :

> O Time, thou must untangle this, not I ;
> It is too hard a knot for me t' untie ! (II ii 38–9)

Other complications follow that draw heavily upon her reserves, for as Cesario she must face the unexpected 'rivalry' of Sir Andrew and the jealous rage of her own master, Duke Orsino. The first exposes her to a test of her courage and to ridicule, as well as to the accusations of ingratitude from Antonio; the second brings her close to death. She learns how truly difficult it is to pretend to be a man :

Pray God defend me ! A little thing would make me tell them
how much I lack of a man.   (III iv 286–7)

But left to the care of time, Viola's mistakes or miscalculations operate to clarify the mistakes of others. Her 'one heart' and her 'one truth' secretly bring about the resolution of all her problems, for she is not deceived about the essentials of love. In spite of her own difficulties, all the great mistakes of the play can be evaluated against her 'one truth'. This can best be seen by discussing her complex relationships to Orsino and Olivia.

In the very first scene of *Twelfth Night* we are presented with the two great mistakes of Orsino's lovesickness and Olivia's unnatural effort to 'keep fresh / And lasting, in her sad remembrance' all the wealth of a 'brother's dead love' (i i 31–2). Orsino unwittingly touches upon Olivia's mistake when he comments upon this 'debt of love but to a brother' and anticipates the wealth of love in her nature which she is trying to deny:

> How will she love when the rich golden shaft
> Hath kill'd the flock of all affections else
> That live in her ... (i i 35–7)

Olivia has yet to learn, in the words of the Fool, that 'beauty's a flower' subject to time (i v 46), and in the words of Viola, that 'what is yours to bestow is not yours to reserve' (i v 177). Here, again, is the Duke willing to console himself with music for seven inactive years, and a Countess willing to stifle her rich wealth of love for the same length of time in useless grief. A few lines later, in dramatic contrast to the themes of frustration and wasted time of the opening scene, Viola presents her first rich 'commentary' upon Olivia and Orsino. She too has lost a brother and feels the apathy of true grief: 'And what should I do in Illyria?' (i ii 3). Then quite spontaneously she thinks of her brother as happy in 'Elysium', though at the same time is willing to hope that 'Perchance he is not drowned' (i ii 5). Like her brother, 'Courage and hope both teaching him the practice' (i ii 13), she will make the best of what life offers: 'Mine own escape unfoldeth to my hope' (i ii 19). This hope unfolds itself with startling swiftness at the mention of Orsino's name and the words: 'He was a bachelor'then!' No bachelor duke is safe against a mind of this swiftness, however long the time to untangle events between the thought and the 'occasion mellow'. A final commentary on Viola's willingness to trust her-

self to time and to the responsive goodness in others can be
found in her words to the Captain :

> There is a fair behaviour in thee, Captain;
> And though that nature with a beauteous wall
> Doth oft close in pollution, yet of thee
> I will believe thou hast a mind that suits
> With this thy fair and outward character. (ɪ ii 47–51)

Viola's free and generous nature, though perhaps incautious, is
not a sign of naïve inexperience. As will be shown later, she
well knows that 'wickedness' can appear in 'disguise' (ɪɪ ii 27),
but she instinctively realizes that fulfillment of inner promise
involves commitment to events :

> What else may hap to time I will commit;
> Only shape thou thy silence to my wit. (ɪ ii 60–1)

The errors of Olivia and Orsino stand sharply revealed here.
In terms of the fulfillment of love's wealth, 'In delay there lies
no plenty' (ɪɪ iii 49).

Once Viola enters the stage as Cesario, fully involved in the
action herself, she continues to offer her 'commentary' upon the
error of denying love's fulfillment. Like Rosalind in *As You
Like It,* she teaches others the true meaning of love – the kind
of love that would bring a woman down upon her knees to
'thank heaven, fasting, for a good man's love' (*As You Like It,*
ɪɪɪ v 57–8). Phebe and Orlando profit from such instruction,
as do Olivia and Orsino, though Viola's subtle lessons must
thread their way through more complex obstacles. But the
instruction is persuasive, for the teacher speaks from her own
heart, and error itself helps point the way to truth. Olivia
abandons the error of seeking a 'brother's dead love' only to
mistake Viola as an object of her new love. But this mistake,
though perhaps begun by her being charmed with Cesario's
fair 'outside' (ɪɪ ii 16), soon leads to an intensity of love that

is far deeper than the pain of Orsino's 'Unstaid and skittish' love (II iv 18). Nevertheless, the error of being mistaken in the object of her love bears for Olivia its own rich reward, for it has prepared her to love Sebastian at first sight. We have here an interesting variation of the Platonic doctrine of 'elective affinity', for we see Olivia fall in love with Viola and then Sebastian at first sight, while at the same time we can also say that the mistake of loving Viola has really prepared Olivia for giving herself generously to Sebastian. In this sense, she loves Sebastian before seeing him because she has learned to love him through Viola. The psychology here is perhaps sounder than that of the lover in Donne's 'The Good-Morrow' who excuses his past conquests as a mere preparation :

> If ever any beauty I did see,
> Which I desir'd, and got, 'twas but a dream of thee.

Viola stood for something much more substantial than a mere dream of Sebastian, and the consequent marriage by mistake to Sebastian needs no apology. Similarly Orsino, not really profoundly in love with Olivia, learns in his subtle relationship with his page Cesario something of the depth of true love, and is therefore prepared through that aspect of Viola hidden in Cesario to accept the real Viola the instant she is unmasked. More than one meaning is revealed in Viola's beautiful lines,

> I am all the daughters of my father's house,
> And all the brothers too ... (II iv 119–20)

Among other meanings, at this point in her relationships to both Orsino and Olivia, she is creating as one person subtle ties that will become binding for her brother as well as for herself. It is the dénouement that must unmask Viola, reveal a brother and sister, and pair off lovers already destined for each other. The unmasked Viola will be no stranger to Orsino, nor Sebastian to Olivia. Like the sudden conversion of Beatrice and

Benedict in *Much Ado About Nothing,* the apparently superficial and hasty avowal of love has had its stormy preparation
in misunderstanding.

Above everything else, it is Viola's love for Orsino that
secretly teaches both Olivia and Orsino the true meaning
of love and emphasizes the ridiculous inadequacies of Malvolio, Sir Andrew, and even the affectionate Sir Toby. Viola's
love may have been disguised; it could not be entirely hid. In
sharp contrast is the introspective Duke, eloquent as he com-
pares the constancy of his own love to that of a woman's, but he
is not speaking from experience :

> There is no woman's sides
> Can bide the beating of so strong a passion
> As love doth give my heart; no woman's heart
> So big to hold so much : they lack retention.
> Alas, their love may be call'd appetite –
> No motion of the liver, but the palate –
> That suffer surfeit, cloyment, and revolt;
> But mine is all as hungry as the sea,
> And can digest as much. Make no compare
> Between that love a woman can bear me
> And that I owe Olivia. (ii iv 92–102)

The Duke is wrong; and Viola's answer, based upon her own
intense passion, is one that gives 'a very echo to the seat / Where
Love is thron'd' (ii iv 20–1). Viola knows only too well 'what
love women to men may owe' (ii iv 104). Here she tells her
own sad story to counter the Duke's argument :

> My father had a daughter lov'd a man,
> As it might be, perhaps, were I a woman,
> I should your lordship. (ii iv 106–8)

Unlike Olivia, only too well does she know the danger of wast-
ing time by sitting 'like Patience on a momument, / Smiling at
grief' (ii iv 113–14). This danger has been made all the more

intense by the unconscious cruelty of the Duke's earlier reference to time :

> For women are as roses, whose fair flow'r
> Being once display'd doth fall that very hour. (ii iv 37–8)

Knowing her own constancy, she can at least risk telling the
Duke some of the things about love that he does not yet know :

> We men may say more, swear more, but indeed
> Our shows are more than will; for still we prove
> Much in our vows, but little in our love. (ii iv 115–17)

Not until the last scene of the play does Orsino experience the
full truth in this, when he reveals his own divided heart and
threatens to kill, 'had I the heart to do it', both Olivia and
Viola. His language here betrays his own shifting devotion, for
he first threatens Olivia with the words, 'Why should I not . . .
Kill what I love' (v i 111–13); and then he turns upon Viola,
threatening her also, but at the same time using terms of affection that seem to warm into love :

> But this your minion [Cesario], whom I know you love,
> And whom, by heaven I swear, I tender dearly,
> Him will I tear out of that cruel eye. (v i 119–21)

Three lines later he is saying, 'I shall sacrifice the lamb *that I do
love*'. And shortly after this when Viola is unmasked, of course,
the Duke is fully prepared to call Viola 'Orsino's mistress, and
his fancy's queen' (v i 374). At last he finds his right love, but
surely not through the kind of constancy of which he had
bragged. Such constancy was Viola's alone, and there is no
more moving proof of this than the moment at which Viola
turns to follow the angry Duke to her own sacrifice :

> And I, most jocund, apt, and willingly,
> To do you rest, a thousand deaths would die. (v i 126–7)

Comedy here touches for a fleeting moment the pathos of tragedy. Viola's love would have endured a test as final as Desdemona's.

Olivia, too, receives her painful lessons about love from Viola. For example, Viola adopts the tone of the *Sonnets* in what comes close to being the kind of rebuke a Rosalind might have given in a courtly setting :

> Lady, you are the cruell'st she alive,
> If you will lead these graces to the grave,
> And leave the world no copy. (I v 225–7)

Later, Viola perhaps has herself in mind when she tells Olivia how she would love if she were Orsino :

> Make me a willow cabin at your gate,
> And call upon my soul within the house;
> Write loyal cantons of contemnéd love,
> And sing them loud even in the dead of night. (I v 252–5)

This almost parodies the language of an outworn code of love, but a fresh sincerity is in the speaker. Viola, to her surprise, reaps an unexpected reward for her sincere efforts when she undertakes Orsino's commission and finds herself beloved of Olivia. This is perhaps Viola's greatest error, but it serves to teach Olivia all she needs to know about herself and her waste of time, though more than once Viola must remind her 'That you do think you are not what you are' (III i 136). Such, then, are the deceptions and self-deceptions of Olivia and Orsino. It takes the love of Viola, knowing herself and trusting to time, to untangle the web of mistakes.

No one in *Twelfth Night* entirely escapes the darkness of ignorance, but at least those who come to know generous love and friendship escape time's harshest revenges. Those who escape make it clear why the others suffered, for comedy thrives on poetic justice. Viola is always the touchstone, though Feste may point the moral. Once Viola emerges from the sea, displays her courage and hope, and reveals her generous capacity for love, we have our standard by which to judge the others. Thus Sebastian reaps his fine reward by following his sister's path of open-hearted commitment to events. We can expect Antonio, the model of generous friendship, to find generosity in return, as will the Captain who helped Viola, though mistakes have been obstacles to them. Interestingly enough, some of the most important statements about friendship and generosity are made each time Viola and Antonio meet and quarrel over the vice of ingratitude. Either Viola or Antonio might have been given the following words as they confronted each other :

> I hate ingratitude more in a man
> Than lying, vainness, babbling drunkenness,
> Or any taint of vice whose strong corruption
> Inhabits our frail blood. (iii iv 338–41)

The words are Viola's, addressed to Antonio who has mistaken her for an ungrateful Sebastian. Neither of them is tainted with any of the vices listed in the passage, but the list may easily be related to the errors that lead the minor characters into the den of error. Malvolio's vanity, Sir Toby's drunkenness and unkindness, and Sir Andrew's foolish limitations, all show how far short they fall in human relationships.

In terms of the action of the drama, it is the appearance of Sebastian and Viola together that is the signal for the final resolution of all mistakes, although in another sense the appearance of Sebastian is merely a revelation of what has already been resolved earlier on a hidden level. The Duke's startled comment upon seeing Viola and Sebastian together for the first time makes clear to all that most of the problems have already been solved : 'One face, one voice, one habit, and *two* persons' (v i 208). In short, Olivia's mistaken marriage has already given her the right husband, and Orsino's unconscious love

for Cesario has made it clear where he is to find an adoring
wife. Antonio and the kind Captain need now fear no breach
in true friendship. And Viola finds a brother whose presence
she has already half suspected and a husband she already
loves. As for the injured parties, they come to see the cause of
their miseries, their own foolish errors. Sir Andrew experiences
the limitations of a shallow friendship, Malvolio the end of an
egotistical dream, and Sir Toby the end of at least one foolish
jest and his irresponsible bachelorhood. Virtue, open-hearted-
ness, and sense have prevailed, although no one has escaped
the perplexities of mistakes, and no one has escaped
being called a fool or mad. As the wisest of fools observes,
'Foolery, sir, does walk about the orb like the sun, it shines
every where' (iii i 36–7).

The wise and the generous, then, survive their foolish mistakes, and profit. Most important of all, there has been revealed a kind of wisdom of the heart that flourishes even while
the intellect is perplexed. Feste's remark that 'there is no darkness but ignorance' (iv ii 42–3) achieves its fullest meaning on
this deeper spiritual or psychological level. It is strange that a
study of mistakes, instead of restricting criticism to a discussion
of superficial farce, leads directly to the inner life of the play.
Every mistake may be a blemish of the mind, but the inner life
of the play reveals that only the blemishes of the heart destroy :

> In nature there's no blemish but the mind :
> None can be call'd deform'd but the unkind. (iii iv 365–6)

This is a note running through all of Shakespeare.

Beyond this point lie the tragedies, exploring again the problems of the heart, but presenting monstrous deformities and
disastrous mistakes. In this darker world, 'death would have
entered to measure the depth of Viola's love. It is enough for
the world of the comedies that *Twelfth Night* closes with Feste's
cryptic song after the happy talk of marriage to remind us once

again of time, mortality, and the passing of all things – a tragic theme that scarcely disturbs between the 'curtain' and the applause.

SOURCE: *PMLA*, LXXVI (1961) 193–9

NOTES

1. M. C. Bradbrook, *Shakespeare and Elizabethan Poetry* (1951) p. 228.

2. M. C. Bradbrook, *The Growth and Structure of Elizabethan Comedy* (1955) pp. 78, 86.

3. Leslie Hotson, *The First Night of 'Twelfth Night'* (1954) pp. 97–9. See also Sir E. K. Chambers, *The Mediaeval Stage* (1903) on Epiphany customs and the Feast of Fools.

4. Sir E. K. Chambers, *William Shakespeare* (1930) I 405, and Hotson, *The First Night of 'Twelfth Night'*.

5. Bradbrook, *Shakespeare and Elizabethan Poetry*, p. 230.

6. John Russell Brown, *Shakespeare and His Comedies* (1957) p. 160.

7. See I ii 18; I v 267; II iii 30; II iv 67; III i 41 ff.; III iii 39 ff.; III iv 324; IV i 18; IV iii 2; V i 24 ff.

8. H. B. Charlton, *Shakespearian Comedy* (1938) p. 281.

9. Bradbrook, *The Growth and Structure of Elizabethan Comedy*, p. 92.

10. Brown, *Shakespeare and His Comedies*, p. 164.

John Russell Brown

DIRECTIONS FOR *TWELFTH NIGHT* (1966)

After the first dozen *Twelfth Night*'s there are still surprises, new guises for the old masterpiece. Directors colour it golden, russet, silver or white; blue for dreams, and sometimes pink; or they allow red and even purple to dominate. They can make it sound noisy as a carnival, or eager, or melodious, or quarrelsome like children; it can also be strained and nervous. In 1958, Peter Hall at Stratford-upon-Avon hung the stage with gauzes and contrived what *The Times* called a 'Watteauesque light'. And critics report that a year previously, at Stratford, Ontario, Tyrone Guthrie contrasted Feste and Malvolio in 'psychological terms', allowing the final song of the 'wind and rain' to be 'as plaintive and wonderful as a Jewish lament'. Two years before that, at the English Stratford, Sir John Gielgud brought 'a faint chill to the air' of his production; the comics were on their best behaviour in deference to a pervasive 'charm'; *The Observer* said that the polite word for this would be 'formal', and the exact word 'mechanical'; it seemed as if, during rehearsals of the last scene, Sir John had stopped the actors and commanded, 'Be beautiful; be beautiful'.

This play might have been designed for an age when each director must make his name and register his mark. Yet there is one difficulty: in most productions some part of the play resists the director's control. In Sir John's elegant *Twelfth Night*, Malvolio yielded Sir Laurence Olivier a role in which to exploit his impudent and plebeian comedy, and in his last line – 'I'll be reveng'd on the whole pack of you' – an opportunity for the cry of a man unmade. The grey and urban setting of the Old Vic's production in 1950 was enlivened by an untrained ballet of sailors and riffraff, but Peggy Ashcroft's

clear, white voice was an unechoed reminder of other directions
the comedy can be given. More commonly, without such
trained stars to cross the director's intentions, robust comics
usurp more attention than their part in the last Act is allowed
to satisfy, or an intelligent Sebastian will deny his own words,
a too gentle Orsino devalue Viola's ardour. There is need for
vigilance : Margaret Webster, who sees *Twelfth Night* as 'filled
with impermanence, fragile, imponderable', has found that :

> The director will have to balance and combine his ingredients
> in carefully graded proportions, compensating for weaknesses,
> keeping a moderating hand on excessive strength. This play,
> above all, he must treat with a light touch and a flexible mind,
> keeping the final goal clearly in sight.[1]

What happened, one wonders, before there were directors to
give directions?

For if we refer back, from the theatre to the text of the play,
we shall observe a similar lack of simplicity and uniformity.
Malvolio can be a 'turkey cock', a common 'geck and gull' who
is told to 'shake his ears'; or a fantastic who asks what 'an alpha-
betical position portends' and speaks repeatedly 'out of his
welkin'. Yet Olivier's petty, ambitious vulgarian is also true to
the text when he addresses his mistress with 'Sweet lady, ho,
ho!' and with tags from popular ballads. Even Michael
Hordern's tortured Malvolio at the Old Vic in 1954, 'dried up,
emaciated, elongated . . . (as) an El Greco' – his hands, reaching out of the pit in the scene where Feste visits him as Sir
Topas, the curate, suggested to one critic 'the damned in the
Inferno' – is authorised by Feste's disguise, by his own first
words of 'the pangs of death' and 'infirmity', his account of
how 'imagination' jades him, and his physical and psychological isolation at the end. And yet again, Olivia's high regard
for Malvolio – she 'would not lose him for half her dowry' –
justifies Eric Porter's performance at Stratford-upon-Avon in

1960, as a solid, efficient steward waking with practical good sense to worlds unrealised.

Actors seeking to express their originality will find that 'new' interpretations rise unbidden from a straightforward study of the text, Sir Toby is usually a domesticated Falstaff, but at the Old Vic in 1958 with tumultuous 'gulps and shouts', he was seen as a plain 'boor'; and for this there is plenty of support in his name, Belch, and in his talk of 'boarding and assailing', making water and cutting 'mutton'. And the same year, at Stratford-upon-Avon, Patrick Wymark made him young and spry with a sense of style; for this, 'she's a beagle, true-bred' was most appropriate language, and his easy confidence in 'consanguinity' with Olivia and expertise in swordplay were natural accomplishments. One might imagine too, a melancholy Sir Toby, tried in true service and knowing from experience that 'care's an enemy to life': his tricks upon Sir Andrew would then be a compensation for his own retirement, his wooing – off-stage and presumably brief – of Maria, a just and difficult tribute to her service for him; lethargy comes with drunkenness and he 'hates a drunken rogue'; he needs company, even that of a fool, an ass, and a servant.

Olivia is another role which can be seen to be of different ages – either mature years or extreme youth; and she can be melancholy or gay. Maxine Audley at Stratford-upon-Avon in 1955 presented a gracious lady, truly grieving for the death of her brother and strong enough to recognise an absolute passion for a boy; this Olivia had the 'smooth, discreet and stable bearing', the majesty, to which Sebastian and Orsino testify. And three years later, at the same theatre, Geraldine McEwen presented her as kittenish and cute, saved from triviality by fine timing of movement and verse-speaking, the dignity of 'style'. And yet another Olivia may be suggested by the text: a very young girl, at first afraid of meeting the world and therefore living in a fantasy capable of decreeing seven years

of mourning; then a girl solemnly repeating old saws with a
new understanding of their truth :

> Even so quickly may one catch the plague? . . . I do I know not
> what, and fear to find Mine eye too great a flatterer for my mind.
> . . . What is decreed must be . . . how apt the poor are to be proud
> . . . youth is bought more oft than begg'd or borrowed,

and forgetting her 'discreet' bearing in breathless eagerness :

> *How* does he love me? . . . *Why,* what would you? . . . not too
> *fast* : soft, soft! . . . Well, *let* it be, . . . That's a degree to love.
> . . . Yet *come* again . . . *I* have sent after him : *he says* he'll come.
> . . . *What* do you say? . . . *Most wonderful!*

Feste, the fool, can be melancholy, or bitter, or professional,
or amorous (and sometimes impressively silent), or ˙self-con-
tained and philosophical, or bawdy and impotent. Sir Andrew
Aguecheek can be patient, sunny, feckless, gormless, animated
or neurotic. (In 1958 Richard Johnson gave an assured performance of this knight as a 'paranoid manic-depressive, strongly
reminiscent at times of Lucky in *Waiting for Godot*'.) Orsino
can be mature or very young; poetic; or weak; or strong but
deceived; or real and distant. The text can suggest a Viola who
is pert, sentimental, lyrical, practical, courageous or helpless.
Shakespeare's words can support all these interpretations, and
others; there are few plays which give comparable scope for
enterprise and originality. The characters, the situations and
the speeches are protean.

This is evident in a director's ability to alter the trend of his
production, even in the very last moments, to achieve what
Miss Webster has called his 'balance', to arrive at his chosen
'final goal'. If sentiment needs reinforcing, Viola (as Cesario)
can be given a down-stage position and a preparatory pause as
the arrangements for her duel with Sir Andrew grow to a comic
climax, and thus her 'I do assure you, 'tis against my will' can

be, not the usual laugh-line, but a reminder of her other full-
hearted struggles of will and passion; this momentary seriousness, the more impressive for its incongruous setting, was
managed with great grace by Dorothy Tutin at Stratford, in
Peter Hall's productions of 1958 and 1960. Still later in the
play, there is another opportunity for the strong re-emphasis of
Viola's depth of feeling: Peggy Ashcroft mastered this in 1950,
and J. C. Trewin has well described its effect in performance:

> At the end, as Sebastian faces his sister, he cries: 'What coun-
> tryman? What name? What parentage?' There is a long pause
> now before Viola, in almost a whisper (but one of infinite rapture
> and astonishment) answers: 'Of Messaline'. Practically for the
> first time in my experience a Viola has forced me to believe in her
> past. . . .[2]

More simply and without affecting any established character-
isation, the balance of a production can be altered by the
Priest's lines in the last scene, with their special idiom and
assured syntax and timing:

> A contract of eternal bond of love,
> Confirm'd by mutual joinder of your hands,
> Attested by the holy close of lips,
> Strength'ned by interchangement of your rings
> And all the ceremony of this compact
> Seal'd in my function, by my testimony;
> Since when, my watch hath told me, toward my grave,
> I have travell'd but two hours.

If these lines are spoken in a weighty and measured way, they
can restore a sense of awe, an awareness of general and time-
less implications, to a dénouement which has become too head-
long and hilarious for the director's taste. Or, at the last
moment, Orsino can give 'guts' to an over-pretty production:
the sight of Antonio permits an evocation of the 'smoke of war'
and 'scathful grapple', and can legitimately bring a harsh

quality to his voice which has hitherto been tuned to softer
themes. When he invites Olivia to live 'the marble-breasted
tyrant still' and turns to Cesario with :

> But this your minion, whom I know you love,
> And whom, by heaven I swear, I tender dearly,
> Him will I tear out of that cruel eye
> Where he sits crowned in his master's spite.
> Come, boy, with me; my thoughts are ripe in mischief :
> I'll sacrifice the lamb that I do love
> To spite a raven's heart within a dove

the director can call for physical as well as verbal violence
towards Viola. The lines imply that Orsino cares more for his
seeming boy than for the lady of his dreams and fancy, and
thus they may be acted fully and strongly; the release of passion
in a desire to kill Cesario shows the true object of that passion,
and its power. (This reading of the subtext is authorised by
Shakespeare, as by Freud and Stanislavski, for Orsino has just
acknowledged that a 'savage' jealousy 'kills what it loves', not
what it *thinks* it loves.) If the production is, at this stage of
the play, too solemn rather than too sentimental or hilarious,
there are opportunities in plenty for lightening the whole last
Act: Olivia's 'Where goes Cesario?', after Orsino's outburst,
can easily be spoken to invite laughter; and so can her 'Most
wonderful' as Viola and Sebastian confront each other. Nearly
all Sebastian's lines can be tipped the same way, as 'I do perceive it hath offended you' . . . 'Fear'st thou that, Antonio' . . .
and (about the mole on the brow of Viola's father) 'And so had
mine'. Antonio's 'An apple, cleft in two is not more twin' can
be directed so that it implies laughter rather than rapt amazement, and Orsino's final 'Cesario, come' can be a jest at the
whole contrivance of the last Act, or even at Viola's expense,
rather than recognition of his own long, half-hidden affection
for his bride-to-be.

The opportunities for swinging a production round into line

with a chosen mood – to make it 'what they will', to reverse roles as in a 'Twelfth Night' revel – have encouraged directors to tackle *Twelfth Night* and to experiment widely in the search for original interpretations. But a second practical consequence of the freedom of interpretation is of greater importance: this play challenges us to provide a longer and deeper study than is normally given to a text in the theatre. We may be assured that the diverse ways of playing the characters and controlling the mood are not finally irreconcilable. The experience of seeing many independent productions and reading about many more does not create a multitude of separate memories; each new revelation reflects on earlier ones and, in the mind, a single view of the play is continually growing in complexity and range, and in understanding. We may believe that a single production might, one day, represent to the full our single, developing awareness. Our knowledge of *Twelfth Night* and of human behaviour may assure us that an Olivia is both mature and immature, according to which side of her personality is in view; a Sir Toby energetic *and* melancholic, vulgar *and* well-schooled; and a Viola lyrical *and* practical, *and* helpless. The world of the play is gay, quiet, strained, solemn, dignified, elegant, easy, complicated, precarious, hearty, homely; the conclusion close to laughter, song, awe *and* simplicity. And this is an understanding which begs not to be hid, but to be realised on the stage.

Of course, in the theatre it is tempting to simplify too early, in order to be effective and make a 'strong' impression. But with such a play as *Twelfth Night* we are drawn by another possibility, a more demanding course: five years' study, a repeated return to its problems in a succession of productions under different conditions and for different audiences, might make possible a production which would be original, not by one-sidedness, but by answering more fully than before to Shakespeare's text and combining the excitement of many interpretations. The time necessary to make this attempt would

be an expensive investment; and it would be a risky one – for
the speculator may not be capable of living up to the developing demands of his enterprise. Yet the business is a practical
possibility, and must be considered. An exclusive pursuit of
immediate effectiveness and originality leads to immature and
insecure achievements, in theatres as in other fields of activity;
a play like *Twelfth Night* offers, therefore, an opportunity and
a challenge which it would be salutary merely to envisage,
regenerative to attempt. Shakespeare's stage-cunning, human
understanding and poetic imagination, which are all implicit
in the text, would be fine assets.

The necessary conditions for such an achievement would be a
concern for, and skill in, all the arts of the theatre – this is
required for any sort of theatrical success – but, more peculiarly, a constant return to the details of Shakespeare's text. Here
the popular misconception that close textual study is a dull
and pedestrian activity, restricting originality and encouraging
an exclusively verbal kind of drama – may inhibit the right
kind of work, and must be denounced : a prolonged and careful study of Shakespeare's text, in association with other theatre
skills, can awaken and enrich a production in all elements of a
play's life. If we trust Shakespeare's imagination, we know that
Twelfth Night was conceived as a whole with each apparently
discordant element reconciled to its opposite : and our only clue
to that original resolution is the printed words. Every opportunity for visual realisation or elaboration, for movement and
variation of grouping, for temporal control, for subtlety of elocution or stage-business, for creation of character and mood,
emotion and expression, that the text can suggest should be
searched out, tested, practically evaluated and, finally, given
its due place in the responsible and mature production which
each successive, partial and conflicting production of such a
play as *Twelfth Night* invites us to consider, and to hope that
one day we may help to stage or witness.

The combination, or growing together, of elements from new interpretations of roles is, perhaps, the best charted part of a difficult task; it calls for a developing sympathy and understanding, and a grasp of the progressive and formal presentation of character, but it does not require, at the beginning of rehearsals, a single limiting choice; moreover the actors are always in obvious contact with Shakespeare's words. Perhaps the problems of a textually responsible production will be most perplexing in choosing the stage setting, especially if the play is to be performed on a picture-frame stage with the full range of modern equipment.

Twelfth Night has received many visual interpretations : the elegant, controlled and overtly dramatic, as a Tiepolo fresco, is a common one; or domestic with dark shadows, like the Jacobean interiors in Joseph Nash's *Mansions of England in the Olden Times*; or Italianate, free and colourful in the fashion of the *commedia dell'arte*. Or the stage may be spacious and clean, like one modern notion of what an Elizabethan platform stage was like, or pillared, tiered and substantial, like another. Some designers have introduced the satins and laces of Restoration England, and others the boaters and billows of the theatre of *Charley's Aunt*. The main difficulty is that all these, and others, are in some degree appropriate, usually in different parts of the play; and yet it would be distracting to a modern audience to move from one to another during a single performance, even if this were technically possible. If a mature production of *Twelfth Night* is to be considered, this problem will have to be solved in a single way – the more urgently because the proscenium arches and lighting devices of modern theatres have made the visual embodiment of a play, in setting, costumes and effects, a dominating – often *the* dominating – element of a production.

A recourse to the text in the search for a comprehensive style and single stage setting does not involve the director in an antiquarian production which tries to reproduce original stage conditions; those are, in any case, irrecoverable, in their full complexity which involves specially trained actors and historically accurate audiences, as well as theatres which no longer exist. The study of the text can be of help in utilising the modern technical devices of a picture-frame stage, and in answering the expectations of any particular audience. The verbal imagery can, for example, give valuable help towards deciding which setting is most appropriate; it can tell the director the kind of visual images which were associated with the action and characters in the author's mind and which he may usefully transmit to the audience in visual stage terms.

Illyria, the world of *Twelfth Night*, is obviously a land of love, music, leisure, servants, a Duke and a Countess; it must have dwellings, a garden, a seacoast and a 'dark house' or temporary prison. Its institutions include a church and a chantry, a captain and officers of the law, an inn; and there must be doors or gates. Thus far the choice of a setting is not circumscribed; it might be English, Italian, French, Russian (before the revolution), or, with some adaptation, American or Utopian; medieval, renaissance or modern. But incidental details of speech and action at once limit the setting to something resembling, or representing, English countryside and domesticity. In the first scene there are mentioned a bank of violets, a hunt, sweet beds of flowers, and these are followed by wind and weather, a squash and a peascod, a willow, the hills, a beagle, roses, a yew, a cypress and box tree, and more flowers; familiar living creatures are a hart, a sheep-biter, a horse, a trout, a turkey-cock and a wood-cock, a raven, lamb and dove, and hounds; daylight, champaign (or open fields), harvest, ripeness, and oxen and wain-ropes easily come to mind; the songs of nightingales, daws and owls have been heard. The characters of the play do not talk of an elegant or fanciful scene, although the violets and beds of flowers might be interpreted in that way; their wain-ropes, sheep-biter and daws belong to a countryside that knows labour and inconvenience, as well as

delights. Speaking of horrors and danger, they are neither
sophisticated nor learned; they refer to tempests, the sea, fields,
mountains, barbarous caves, and hunger. The domestic note is
almost as persistent as that of the countryside : early in Act I,
canary-wine, beef, a housewife and a buttery-bar are mentioned; even the Duke, Orsino, speaks of knitters in the sun;
there is talk of pilchards and herrings (fresh and pickled) and
of vinegar and pepper. If a director is to attempt a responsible
production of the play, he should give substance to these references in his setting – not in an illustrative way which provides
objects for the actors to point at, but in a manner which echoes,
extends and, where appropriate, contrasts with the dialogue
and stage business. This is the mental and emotional world of
the *dramatis personae* as revealed by their language, and the
stage picture can help to establish this, not insistently, but with
subtlety.

It is the world of the play's action too, and its visual recreation will, therefore, aid the director towards an appropriate
rhythm and acting style : an Italianate setting, which is often
chosen, suggests the wrong tempo – the wrong temperature,
even – and insists on distracting contrasts between dialogue
and visual effect. An English summer takes three months to
establish itself, through April, May and June, and so does the
action of this play – as Orsino states explicitly in the last scene.
It would be convenient, therefore, to show this passage of time
in modifications to the setting during the course of the play :
the first Acts green and youthful, the last coloured with roses in
bloom and strong lights; the same setting but at different times
of the year. In the first scene Orsino would be seeking the
earliest violets; later 'beauty's a flower', 'women are as roses',
'youth's a stuff will not endure' would sound properly precarious in view of the visual reminder of the changing seasons;
a 'lenten answer' would seem more restrictive and 'let summer
bear it out' a fuller and more inevitable judgement. Orsino
might stand in white, as the young lover in Nicholas Hillyarde's

miniature (dated about 1590), over against frail, twining roses : this association represented for the painter his motto – '*Dat poenas laudata fides*', or 'My praisèd faith procures my pain' – and it might serve in much the same way today. 'Midsummer madness' and 'matter for a May morning', which are spoken of in Act III, would be in key with the setting, and the talk of harvest, the grave and the immutable yew-tree would sound in significant contrast.

The course of single days might also be suggested in the lighting of the stage picture. Talk of hunting in the first scene establishes the time as early morning. In the third, Maria's remonstrance to Sir Toby about returning late 'a'nights' belongs to the first meeting of a new day, and then coming 'early' by one's 'lethargy' implies prandial drinking. In II iii, the chaffing about 'being up late', Malvolio's chiding about 'respect of . . . time', and 'it's too late to go to bed now' all suggest midnight; so one 'day' is completed in due order. (Again Feste's song in this last mentioned scene, about 'present mirth' and 'what's to come' and 'youth's a stuff will not endure', will be more poignant if it seems indeed to have been sung before the 'night-owl', nature's reminder of death, is roused.) The following scene, II iv, is clearly a new day with its first lines of 'good morrow' and 'we heard last night'; and the truth that '. . . women are as roses, whose fair flower Being once display'd doth fall that very hour' is more fully expressed if spoken in the transitory light of dawn. The next scene, II v, beginning with 'Come thy ways . . .' and with news that Malvolio has been 'i' the sun practising behaviour to his own shadow this half hour', is still early morning. Act III, scene i, which follows with Feste speaking of the sun shining everywhere, may be at noon, and later, when Malvolio supposes Olivia invites him to bed, his outrageous presumption would be more apparent if it were obviously not that 'time of day'. At the end of IV ii, Feste visits Malvolio in prison and sings :

> I'll be with you again,
>   In a trice,
>   Like to the old Vice,
> Your need to sustain;
>
> Who, with dagger of lath,
> In his rage and his wrath,
>   Cries, Ah, ha ! to the devil. . . .

– here stage lighting could simulate a sudden, passing storm, such as interrupts an easy summer's afternoon in England; it might culminate in thunder. This would be an elaboration impossible to stage in an Elizabethan theatre, but it would be appropriate in a play which is continually concerned with the summer countryside of England, with 'beauty that can endure wind and weather', and which ends with a song of the rain that 'raineth every day'. Sir Toby and Maria could take shelter from the storm, while the fool is left to bear it out and 'pursue the sport'. The sun would shine fully again for Sebastian's 'This is the air; that is the glorious sun; This pearl she gave me . . .', and for the high afternoon of the ending of the comedy. Towards the close shadows might lengthen and, as the marriages are postponed till 'golden time convents', the sky might become golden with a sunset's promise of another fair day. Then as the other characters leave, to enter perhaps a lighted house, Feste might be left in the grey-green light of early evening to sing alone of time and youth, and of the beginning of the world and the conclusion of a play.

(There is in fact a double time scheme in *Twelfth Night*: three months for the development and fulfilment of the action, and two consecutive days for the sequence of scenes. The representation of both schemes in the setting and in the lighting may help an audience to accept this double sense of time which suits, on the one hand, the rapid fairy-tale transitions and the 'changeable' characterisations, and, on the other hand, the play's suggestion of the season's alterations and the endurance and maturing of affections.)

Such lighting effects require an outdoor setting for almost all the play. And this may be convenient for the action : Olivia's house might be shown to one side, with a terrace and garden before it, a main entrance and a way to the back door; and there might be a dovecote, small pavilion or gazebo on the other side of the stage to do duty as Malvolio's prison. There would be some inconvenience in staging the carousing scene between Feste, Sir Toby and Sir Andrew in a garden, but there is plenty of reference to outdoor affairs in its dialogue and the two knights could fall asleep around their table at the close of the scene and be discovered there next morning to be awakened by Fabian. The scenes at Orsino's court could also be in the open air, and could be set by bringing in tall cypress hedges to mask Olivia's house and garden, and to reveal part of the sky-cloth or cyclorama at the end of a long walk or vista in some spacious park. It would be appropriately affected for Orsino to seek the shade of such a walk in the early morning; there could be a stone seat on one side, and on the other a sculpture of Venus, or some such deity. For the brief scene outside Olivia's gate (ɪɪ ii) and for the Sebastian scenes, 'somewhere in Illyria' (ɪɪ i and ɪɪɪ iii), a 'wall' could be let down from the flies, with a gate in its centre : this would locate the action outside Olivia's estate and, if her house and the taller trees were visible over the top of the wall and through the gate, the audience would relish the physical proximity of Sebastian to his journey's end.

There remains one, apparently unrelated, scene (ɪ ii) which begins 'What country, friends, is this?' This might also be played 'outside Olivia's garden', but Viola's mysterious entry into the play from the sea asks for a different visual presentation. It would be possible to play it in front of gauzes let down to hide the transition from Orsino's park of ɪ i, to Olivia's garden of ɪ iii; these might be lightly painted and lit to suggest a seashore, touched, perhaps with fluorescent material low down, as if catching the surf of a strange sea. If Orsino had been contemplating a statue of Venus in the previous scene that figure might be caught by a higher light as the gauzes came down, and then, in a moment of darkness, Viola might take its place to rise from the sea as the stage is relit. If this were effected tactfully, this scene could easily take its place in the chiaroscuro : its sea-effects might be echoed later as Feste is also isolated in the 'storm' of his 'vice' song; and echoed differently at the end of the play, as he is isolated in the evening. Moreover the myth-like transition and transference would be in keeping with the 'romantic' attraction of the lovers and the solution of their stories – the dream, or fantasy element, of the play.

The colours of setting and costumes could be those of an early English summer : clear, light blues, greens, yellows and pinks, and plenty of white. The buildings could be the honey-coloured stone of the English Cotswolds, with marble ornaments for Orsino's park. Olivia would, of course, wear black while in mourning, and Malvolio always – the only character to take no colour from the sun.

Such is one solution of the visual problems of *Twelfth Night*, and one which tries to answer the demands of the text in terms of the realism of the picture-frame stage – which is perhaps the furthest removed from Elizabethan practice. Other stages and other visual styles would call for different solutions. This way of staging the play is worth consideration chiefly as an example : for if any production is to be undertaken with a belief in the unity and imaginative quality of Shakespeare's text, its choice of setting must answer the same demands and others like them, as more are revealed through further study of the text and further experiments in eccentric productions.

The quest for a responsible direction for *Twelfth Night* will not lead to a series of stereotyped productions : changing stage-conditions, actors and audiences will prevent that. Nor will we rest content with our achievements, for the 'idea' of the play, which grows in our minds as we meet it frequently in many guises, is most likely to remain several steps beyond our most truthful production. The desire for an authentic direction will not be satisfied easily, but those who try to respond to it will grow more aware of the wealth of Shakespeare's imagination and perhaps more expert in their attempts to give his masterpiece its theatrical life.

SOURCE: *Shakespeare's Plays in Performance* (1966)
pp. 207–19

NOTES

1. *Shakespeare Today* (1957) p. 205.
2. *John O'London's Weekly,* 8 December 1950.

D. J. Palmer

ART AND NATURE IN *TWELFTH NIGHT* (1967)

I

The improbable fictions which are the material of Shakespearian comedy have often embarrassed those who find
Shakespeare's genius in his truth to nature, but delighted those
who admire the plays above all for their formal qualities, for
their creation of a self-contained world that obeys only the laws
of imagination. Since delight is a surer guide than embarrassment to an understanding of the comedies, criticism that first
accepts the unreality of the comic world is usually more successful. The difficulty is to show why such unnatural and preposterous dramatic fictions should possess any meaning or
significance other than sheer fantasy. Yet, despite their far-
fetched plots, few of us would dismiss the comedies as absurd.
Northrop Frye recently addressed himself to this problem of
interpretation in his book, *A Natural Perspective* (1965), suggesting that 'in comedy and romance the story seeks its own
end instead of holding the mirror up to nature. Consequently
comedy and romance are so obviously conventionalized that
a serious interest in them soon leads to an interest in convention itself' (p. 8). It is true that Shakespeare's comic plots are
descended from the ancient conventions of romantic story-
telling, remote as they are from reality; but the divorce of art
from nature implied in Professor Frye's words misrepresents
the spirit of the comedies. For the question is not whether these
plays hold up the mirror to nature, but how they do so.

The story of *Twelfth Night* contains many conventional
elements: a shipwreck on a strange coast to initiate the action,

a pair of identical twins each believing the other dead, the consequent confusions of mistaken identity and the ironic situations arising from ·these, and from the additional complications of disguise, the cross-purposes of amorous intrigue, and the remarkable series of coincidences which eventually and conveniently bring about a happy ending. A plot of this kind, in *Twelfth Night* and the other comedies, certainly provides fullness and variety. It also produces a paradoxical effect of both artifice and artlessness. Highly artificial in its extravagant improbabilities, it is for the same reasons curiously naïve. The impression of a loosely-knit, apparently random sequence of events, following no natural laws of causality or necessity, is a basic feature of romance and of Shakespearian comedy. Although Professor Frye writes of 'the story seeking its own end', the imaginative experience of such a plot is not one of pressing forward to a conclusion, but rather the sense of a meandering and illogical succession of episodes which seem to take us further and further away from any feeling of inevitability. This is surely an important effect of dramatic composition, since it contributes significantly to what we feel as the liberating experience of Shakespearian comedy, the sense of life as a pastime. It also suggests that behind the apparently naïve artlessness of romance convention there lies a deliberate and sophisticated art. Such an effect would at any rate have met with the approval of the Elizabethan critic, George Puttenham, according to his own precepts :

We doe allow our Courtly Poet to be a dissembler only in the subtilties of his arte, that is, when he is most artificiall, so to disguise and cloake it as it may not appeare, nor seeme to proceede from him by any studie or trade of rules, but to be his naturall. . . . Therefore shall our Poet receave prayse . . . more by knowing of his arte then by unseasonable using it, and be more commended for his naturall eloquence then for his artificiall, and more for his artificiall well disembled then for the same overmuch affected and grossely or undiscretly bewrayed.

('The Arte of English Poesie', *Elizabethan Critical Essays,* ed.
G. Gregory Smith, II 186–7, 192)

In *Twelfth Night* the multiplicity of incident and the wayward progress of the plot not only serve to create the scope and
freedom of the comic world : what seem from one point of
view to be merely looseness of design and arbitrariness of event,
characteristic of romance narrative, here of themselves drama-
tise the play's concern with the instability and impermanence
of life. The dramatic form corresponds to the flux and
changefulness represented in each situation. Orsino's moody
restlessness is matched by the perversity of Olivia, who first
withdraws from life to mourn a dead brother, and then suddenly finds herself wooing her suitor's servant. Malvolio's
influence over his young mistress at the beginning of the play is
a kind of usurpation, an upsetting of the natural order, to say
nothing of the more outrageous ambitions he nourishes in her
direction. The clamorous revelry of Malvolio's enemies, Sir
Toby and company, constitutes a parallel source of unrest, for
they refuse to confine themselves 'within the modest limits of
order'. Feste, the ubiquitous fool, adds further to this unsettled
state of affairs in his restless wandering through the play.

Nothing is fixed or still in Illyria : an impression of capricious and elaborate artifice in the plot is directly related to a
major theme of the play, the theme of mutability. The confusions and accidents of romance convention, the circuitous
movement of events, are features of the structure that move us
to an immediate experience of what the play also states more
philosophically, that 'all is Fortune'. The unity of *Twelfth
Night* is therefore formulated in terms of its apparent lack of
unity as a romance, and an attempt to resolve its complex
harmonies into a single theme must be qualified by the
reminder that what we are aware of as we see or read the play
is not a neat, logical scheme being worked out, but an appar-

ently casual and random power controlling the fortunes of the characters it has brought together. Each of them may say with Sebastian, 'my determinate voyage is mere extravagancy', though we also discover that 'journey's end in lovers' meeting'.

II

The vicissitudes of fortune, translated into the kind of improbable circumstances conventional to romance, make life in Illyria an unstable and uncertain affair. Viola's first scene ensures that this at least is impressed on our minds:

> *Viola.* And what should I do in Illyria?
> My brother he is in Elysium.
> Perchance he is not drown'd – What think you, sailors?
> *Captain.* It is perchance that you yourself were saved.
> *Viola.* O my poor brother! And so perchance may he be.
> *Captain.* True, madam, and, to comfort you with chance,
> Assure yourself . . . (i ii 3–9)

Chance and fortune govern this world, where 'as giddily as Fortune' is a byword, and nature is subject to what Feste calls 'the whirligig of Time'.

We hear the word 'time' often enough in the course of the play. The muddle in which Viola finds herself between Orsino and Olivia is a knot which she says Time must untangle, and in time it does; for the waywardness of fortune is perfectly capable of producing Sebastian and so precipitating the happy ending. Sir Toby's drunken merry-making belies his claim that he keeps time in his catches; his anti-social hours send time topsy-turvy, and logic along with it: 'To be up after midnight, and to go to bed then, is early; so that to go to bed after midnight is to go to bed betimes.'

The confusions and disorders brought about by fortune and

time are exploited both for comedy and for the melancholy
lyricism which pervades the play. The general condition of
mutability produces situations of farcical absurdity, but it also
manifests itself in the more wistful sadness of Viola's reflections
on her situation, cast ashore believing her brother drowned,
and then impossibly in love with Orsino. Moreover, the giddi-
ness of fortune, it seems, can turn men's wits, and there is much
talk of madness in the play, from the innocent 'natural' folly
of Sir Andrew to the darker, crueller torments suffered by
Malvolio. Immediately after the scene of Malvolio imprisoned
in the dark, there comes Sebastian, lost in wonder at the strange
reception he has met with from Olivia :

> For though my soul disputes well with my sense
> That this may be some error, but no madness,
> Yet doth this accident and flood of fortune
> So far exceed all instance, all discourse,
> That I am ready to distrust mine eyes
> And wrangle with my reason, that persuades me
> To any other trust but that I am mad,
> Or else the lady's mad. (IV iii 9–16)

But it is not only in the wayward accidents of the romance
structure, or in the dramatic situations themselves, that the
changefulness of Illyria is revealed. The play has a remarkable
fluidity of mood, reflected in the ease with which shifts of feeling
and tension are made, even within a single scene. Music is of
great importance in creating and dissipating these dramatic
moods, and the lyrical texture of much of the verse similarly
gives an ethereal and dreamlike insubstantiality to these modu-
lations and changes of tempo. Indeed, language itself seems at
times to be swayed by the extravagant and mutable conditions
that govern in the play : Sir Toby appropriately displays an
inebriated state of speech in his fondness for pedantic and
exotic phrases, while Sir Andrew exposes his lack of wit and of

bravery in his verbal pretensions to them. Feste's quibbling and
punning show that words possess no more stability or fixity than
anything else in Illyria :

Feste. A sentence is but a chev'ril glove to a good wit. How
quickly the wrong side may be turn'd outward !
Viola. Nay, that's certain; they that dally nicely with words
may quickly make them wanton.
Feste. I would, therefore, my sister had had no name, sir.
Viola. Why, man?
Feste. Why, sir, her name's a word; and to dally with that word
might make my sister wanton. But indeed words are very rascals
since bonds disgrac'd them.
Viola. Thy reason, man?
Feste. Troth, sir, I can yield you none without words, and
words are grown so false I am loath to prove reason with them.
(III i 11–24)

III

Like Shakespeare's other comedies, *Twelfth Night* is a love
story. But love in this play participates in the waywardness and
impermanence that affects all things in Illyria. The lover's
mind is a microcosm, for, as Orsino says,

For such as I am all true lovers are,
Unstaid and skittish in all motions else
Save in the constant image of the creature
That is belov'd. (II iv 16–19)

And as if to prove his point, he changes his mind about the
same 'constant image' within the space of the next ten lines :

Let still the woman take
An elder than herself; so wears she to him,
So sways she level in her husband's heart.
For, boy, however we do praise ourselves,

> Our fancies are more giddy and unfirm,
> More longing, wavering, sooner lost and won
> Than women's are. (28–34)

Yet again, later in this same scene with Viola, Orsino shifts his
ground :

> There is no woman's sides
> Can bide the beating of so strong a passion
> As love doth give my heart; no woman's heart
> So big to hold so much; they lack retention.
> Alas, their love may be call'd appetite,
> No motion of the liver, but the palate –
> That suffer surfeit, cloyment, and revolt;
> But mine is all as hungry as the sea,
> And can digest as much. (92–100)

If the references to 'appetite' and 'surfeit' ironically recall
Orsino's description of his own feelings in the opening speech
of the play, the imagery of the sea, here and throughout the
play, relates the lover's changeful moods to the vicissitudes of
fortune. The sea as a mirror of nature's mutability, a metaphor of destruction and renewal, eternally ebbing and flowing
and therefore associated with the influence of time and fortune,
is familiar enough in Shakespeare's work from beginning to
end of his career; the associations he draws upon, both in poetic
imagery and in the action of his plots, were part of the common
property of the age. For instance, in one of the Italian plays
whose plots resemble that of *Twelfth Night*, Nicolo Secchi's
Gl'Inganni, printed in 1562, a servant tells his master :

> Maybe you will give up love for a time, but you will not hold
> firm; this gust of disdain will pass in a breath, and I foresee that it
> will be strengthened by a veritable hurricane, which will put you
> in peril, drive you ashore again, bring you to despair once more
> and so you will be worse off than ever. I know what I say.

There is no child so apt to change his mind.
No mist driven by the sun has life so brief;
The withered leaf is not so swift in flight,
Not so inconstant is the driven snow
Nor straw that from the stack the wind shakes off.
No dust is so unsure, feathers so light,
Not Spring itself flies with inconstant wing
So changeable as lover's fickle mind . . .

. . . These waves of love to which you commit yourself are so
full of rocks that you can hardly avoid them.
(G. Bullough, *Narrative and Dramatic Sources of Shakespeare,*
II 340)

At the beginning of *Twelfth Night*, before we hear of Viola's
shipwreck and fortunate survival, it is Orsino who introduces
this theme :

O spirit of love, how quick and fresh art thou!
That, notwithstanding thy capacity
Receiveth as the sea, nought enters there,
Of what validity and pitch soe'er,
But falls into abatement and low price
Even in a minute. So full of shapes is fancy,
That it alone is high fantastical. (I i 9–15)

Orsino's 'fancy', like the sea, is fluid and unconfined. He tells
Cesario, in representing his passion to Olivia, to 'Be clamorous
and leap all civil bounds', Just as these words remind us of Sir
Toby's refusal to confine himself 'within the modest limits of
order', so the sea imagery reaches towards Sir Toby in Feste's
comparison of the drunken man with the drowned man. Feste's
licensed wit also permits him to deliver this judgment on
Orsino :

Now the melancholy god protect thee; and the tailor make thy
doublet of changeable taffeta, for thy mind is a very opal. I would
have men of such constancy put to sea, that their business might
be everything, and their intent everywhere; for that's it that
always makes a good voyage of nothing. (II iv 72–9)

The latter part of Feste's riddle is rather obscure, but perhaps he refers to the hopelessness of Orsino's suit to Olivia. The Duke 'makes a good voyage of nothing', since, receiving no encouragement from the lady herself, he feeds on the 'high fantastical' 'shapes' of his imagination. Orsino's character is conceived as a study of a disordered fantasy, though not in any clinical sense; he is a prey to his passions, subject as these are to the vagaries of delusionary obsessions. Like Ovid's Actaeon, who gazed upon Diana,

> That instant was I turn'd into a hart,
> And my desires, like fell and cruel hounds,
> E'er since pursue me. (1 i 21–3)

His condition is that referred to by Puttenham in his description of the fantasy : 'And this phantasie may be resembled to a glasse, as hath bene sayd, whereof there be many tempers and manner of makinges, as the *perspectives* doe acknowledge, for some be false glasses and shew thinges otherwise than they be indeede, and others right as they be indeede, neither fairer nor fouler, nor greater nor smaller' (op. cit., p. 20).

Shakespeare seems to have developed a particular interest at this time in the aberrations of the fantasy, for within a year of 1600 he gave us Brutus, Orsino, and Hamlet, in each of whom, despite their very different situations, melancholy and an agitated fancy are mutually sustaining. Nobody in *Twelfth Night*, however, judges Orsino as severely as many critics have done, and while his egocentric lovesickness, projected upon Olivia, is akin to other types of madness in the play, he is more than the languid fop that he has often been made to seem. The ironic contrast between his unstable self-absorbed passion, and the selfless fidelity of Viola, certainly doesn't work in his favour; but at least, like Romeo's languishing for Rosaline, the very shallowness and unreality of this love prepares the ground for

transferring the affections to a more genuine object : 'Love is
not love which alters when it alteration finds.' Moreover,
Orsino is clearly invested with a certain aristocratic magnifi-
cence, and the lyrical voluptuousness of his melancholy contributes to the play a splendour and beauty that is not altogether
disqualified by his comic extravagance. Even at his most absurd,
yielding to a mistaken jealousy of his own servant, Orsino's
eloquence possesses grandeur and nobility, like an embryonic
Othello :

> Why should I not, had I the heart to do it,
> Like to th' Egyptian thief at point of death,
> Kill what I love? – a savage jealousy
> That sometime savours nobly. But hear me this :
> Since you to non-regardance cast my faith,
> And that I partly know the instrument
> That screws me from my true place in your favour,
> Live you the marble-breasted tyrant still;
> But this your minion, whom I know you love,
> And whom, by heaven I swear, I tender dearly,
> Him will I tear out of that cruel eye
> Where he sits crowned in his master's spite. (v i 111–22)

Such is the changeableness and confusion in Illyria, and in the
passion-tossed minds of the lovers, that delusions and the mistaking of false for true easily prevail in the love affairs of the
play. Orsino is kept apart from Olivia until the end of the play,
so that his love is inspired and fed by music and poetry, by art
rather than nature. And perhaps the 'silly sooth' of his favourite songs is truer, after all, than nature in this case. Olivia's less
courtly suitors are also led astray by their own false fancies : Sir
Andrew Aguecheek unconsciously parodies Orsino's words on
the 'high fantastical', as he decides to persist in his suit : 'I am
a fellow o' th' strangest mind i' th' world. I delight in masques
and revels sometimes altogether.' And of course Malvolio is betrayed by his own self-conceit when he suspects no trickery in

the outrageous invitations of the letter. 'Look how imagination blows him', says Fabian, but the steward co-operates in his own undoing: 'I do not now fool myself, to let imagination jade me, for every reason excites to this, that my lady loves me.' Maria took good stock, not only of Malvolio's proclivities, but of her mistress as well, or so it would appear, for the words that purport to come from Olivia in the letter Malvolio discovers bear a remarkable resemblance to what Olivia really says to another servant in a later scene. 'Be not afraid of greatness', reads Malvolio, 'thy Fates open their hands; let thy blood and spirit embrace them.' And Olivia, herself now deceived in the identity of her husband, tells Cesario,

> Alas, it is the baseness of thy fear
> That makes thee strangle thy propriety.
> Fear not, Cesario, take thy fortunes up;
> Be that thou knowst thou art, and then thou art
> As great as that thou fear'st. (v i 140–4)

Coincidences and echoes of this kind, which only the audience may be aware of, increase the sense of perplexity, and at the same time, like the strange accidents upon which the plot hinges, suggest the operation of a capricious Fortune.

If Orsino's passion is nourished by art, not nature, then Olivia's plight is no better, for she falls in love with a fiction, mistaking art for nature. 'Poor lady, she were better love a dream' says Viola, pitying the confusion her disguise has caused. But the dream proves true, for Cesario is an artificial copy of reality, and Olivia's marriage to Sebastian involves no change of her affections. To Sebastian, however, unaccustomed as he is to the waywardness of events in Illyria, this itself seems a dream, an abuse of his fantasy:

> Or I am mad, or else this is a dream.
> Let fancy still my sense in Lethe steep;
> If it be thus to dream, still let me sleep! (iv i 60–2)

When a full explanation later relieves his bewilderment, Sebastian comments on Olivia's passion for his sister, 'But nature to her bias drew in that'. He may mean that, unknown to any of them, Olivia was already loving him in Cesario, that her natural instinct was true, although she was mistaken about Cesario's identity. But the image, from the game of bowls, might also suggest that when like was drawn to like, in Olivia's unwitting love for another girl, nature's tendency to error and waywardness was at work. Certainly all the lovers in the play but Viola are drawn off course by their extravagant fancies, and in the seemingly hopeless predicament that is hers, even Viola's devotion to Orsino scarcely appears grounded upon reason.

Shakespeare not only drew the main events of his plot from his chief source, Barnabe Riche's 'Of Apolonius and Silla'; it was there, too, that he found the basis for his treatment of love in the play. The opening paragraph of Riche's tale contains the very spirit of Shakespeare's 'high fantastical' lovers :

There is no child that is borne into this wretched worlde, but before it doeth sucke the mother's milke it taketh first a soope of the cuppe of errour, which maketh us, when we come to riper yeres, not onely to enter into actions of injurie, but many tymes to straie from that is right and reason; but in all other thinges, wherein wee shewe our selves to bee moste dronken with this poisoned cuppe, it is in our actions of love; for the lover is so estranged from that is right, and wandereth so wide from the boundes of reason, that he is not able to deeme white from blacke, good from badde, vertue from vice; but onely led by the apetite of his owne affections, and groundyng them on the foolishnesse of his owne fancies, will so settle his likyng on such a one, as either by desert or unworthinesse will merite rather to be loathed than loved.   (G. Bullough, op. cit., II 345)

IV

While the confusions and caprices of the lovers are exploited for
comedy, the theme of mutability also assumes a more nostalgic,
elegiac form in the play's awareness of the transience of youth
and beauty. Such shifts of dramatic mood themselves create a
sense of changefulness, and like the imagery of the sea, relate
the lovers to a world whose very nature is impermanence and
vicissitude :

> *Orsino.* For women are as roses, whose fair flow'r
> Being once display'd doth fall that very hour.
> *Viola.* And so they are; alas, that they are so!
> To die, even when they to perfection grow !   (II iv 37–40)

This theme does not have to be explicitly stated before it is felt
as an undercurrent of wistful irony, for instance in Olivia's
banter as she first unveils her face to Cesario, using the terms of
art to describe an all too transitory nature :

> *Olivia.* But we will draw the curtain and show you the picture.
> Look you, sir, such a one I was this present. Is't not well
> done?
> *Viola.* Excellently done, if God did all.
> *Olivia.* 'Tis in grain, sir; 'twill endure wind and weather.
> *Viola.* 'Tis beauty truly blent, whose red and white
> Nature's own sweet and cunning hand laid on.
> Lady, you are the cruell'st she alive,
> If you will lead these graces to the grave,
> And leave the world no copy. (I v 218–27)

Viola's plea, like its counterpart in the opening sequence of
Shakespeare's sonnets, is a reminder that if all things in nature
are subject to transience and change, nevertheless such change
may bring renewal as well as decay : there is a continuity in
nature through change itself. Shakespeare converts into dramatic feeling the great Elizabethan commonplaces associated

with the theme of mutability. For commonplaces though they are, these ideas had a profound imaginative appeal to the Elizabethan sensibility, whether they found expression in the epic majesty of the fragments concluding Spenser's *Faerie Queene*, or in the lyric simplicity of songs like Peele's 'His golden locks time hath to silver turned'.

Behind the Elizabethan awareness of mutability there lies a long and complex tradition of medieval and classical though†, but there is one figure whose influence upon Shakespeare it would be difficult to exaggerate. This is Ovid, whose *Metamorphoses* seemed to the Elizabethans not only a delightful collection of mythological stories on the theme of transformation, but also a philosophical work dealing with the mutability of nature. According to his sixteenth-century translator, Arthur Golding, Ovid's meaning in these tales of mortals changed into beasts and birds and trees was

> That nothing under heaven doth ay in stedfast state remain,
> And next that nothing perisheth : but that each substance takes
> Another shape than that it had.

The famous passage from book xv of the *Metamorphoses*, in which Pythagoras expounds his doctrine, thus serves as a commentary on the sense of changefulness in *Twelfth Night* (I quote from Golding's version) :

> All things do change; but nothing sure doth perish. This same sprite
> Doth fleet, and fisking heer and there doth swiftly take his flight.
> From one place to another place, and ent'reth every wight,
> Removing out of man to beast, and out of beast to man;
> But yet it never perisheth nor never perish can.

And even as supple wax with ease receiveth figures
    strange,
And keeps not aye one shape, nor bides assured aye from
    change,
And yet continueth always wax in substance; so I say
The soul is aye the selfsame thing it was, and yet astray
It fleeteth into sundry shapes...
... In all the world there is not that that standeth at a
    stay.
Things ebb and flow, and every shape is made to pass
    away.
The time itself continually is fleeting like a brook,
For neither brook not lightsome time can tarry still. But
    look!
As every wave drives forth, and that that comes behind
Both thrusteth and is thrust itself, even so the times by
    kind
Do fly and follow both at once, and evermore renew ...
                            (lines 183–92, 197–203)

It is execrable verse, and Golding's awkward constrictions
may too often remind us of the old hermit of Prague, as cited
by Feste: 'That that is is'. But, although we might agree with
Malvolio concerning Pythagoras's opinion 'that the soul of our
grandam might happily inhabit a bird', Ovid's relevance to
our understanding of *Twelfth Night* extends beyond this conception of nature's flux and impermanence. The Ovidian
metamorphosis is a magical rather than a natural change, a
transformation to a more enduring plane of existence,
removed from the vicissitudes of time and fortune. As the
Elizabethans interpreted it, metamorphosis was a symbolic
change which altered the form in order to express its true
nature. For example, they understood the transformation of
Ulysses' sailors into swine to signify the domination of animal
appetites that yielded to Circe's temptation.

In *Twelfth Night*, the conception of metamorphosis informs
Shakespeare's use of disguise, and its function as a particular
kind of change in a world subject to changefulness is similar in

spirit to that of Ovid's stories. Viola, who is the constant and
unchanging heart at the centre of several shifting and unstable
attachments, first suffered an accident of fortune in the shipwreck, but survives in a changed shape as Cesario. Her disguise
adds to the delusions of those around her, but it seems to trans-
late her to an order of existence beyond the flux of nature.
Cesario is not of nature, but of art: a fiction in himself, he
nevertheless mirrors nature by expressing others' truth. Thus
to Orsino, Cesario embodies his suit to Olivia; to Olivia,
though she doesn't understand how until the end of the play,
Cesario embodies the man she loves and will marry; to Viola
herself, Cesario is a vehicle for the expression and revelation
of her love for Orsino. Cesario has no fixed identity of his own,
but changes his role chameleon-like in this world of ceaseless
change. He is a figure of change by renewal, the complement
to the theme of love's transitoriness and loss. Just as Viola survives in him, and in Orsino renews his courtship through him,
so Olivia is restored to the living from mourning the dead, when
she falls in love with him, and Sebastian also survives in him.
When the disguise is dropped, the termination of Cesario's
existence allows a new set of relationships to come into being,
based on truth and harmony.

Viola's is not the only metamorphosis in the play. Malvolio is
encouraged to 'cast off thy humble slough, and appear fresh',
and he dresses up in yellow garters, and puts on ridiculous airs,
to win his mistress Olivia. He is the antithesis of Viola, who
dresses as a boy to be Orsino's servant; moreover, while
adversity causes Viola to assume disguise, Malvolio thinks it is
his good fortune that tempts him to change his appearance.
But in his disguise, like Viola in hers, he is manifesting the true
nature of his secret desires and ambitions. Feste also disguises
himself at one point in the play, to act Sir Topas for the benefit
of the imprisoned Malvolio. In pretending to cast out the devil
possessing Malvolio, he speaks truth as jest, and jest as truth,
for in reality the fool is saner than Malvolio, whose madness

and delusion come from pride. The whole of this pantomime really is arranged to exorcise the devil from Malvolio, to purge him of his humour. Feste, however, *in propria persona*, is like Cesario : he reveals no personal emotions, and lives only in his art, his quibbles and his songs.

The poetry which most beautifully captures this pervading sense of transient nature transformed into art comes in Cesario's fiction of his dead sister, who is Viola herself :

> She never told her love,
> But let concealment, like a worm i' th' bud,
> Feed on her damask chêek. She pin'd in thought;
> And with a green and yellow melancholy
> She sat like Patience on a monument,
> Smiling at grief. (II iv 109–14)

The figure of Patience, the cherub above the grave, is a metamorphosis of love translated into a sphere beyond change and death, 'smiling at grief'.

V

Twelfth Night is a play in which art and nature are constantly changing places. It shows us nature becoming art, and at the end of the play we and the characters finally attain harmony, wholeness and completeness, that poise and balance which transcend mutability. These are the qualities of perfection felt too in the songs :

> What is love? 'Tis not hereafter;
> Present mirth hath present laughter;
> What's to come is still unsure.
> In delay there lies no plenty,
> Then come kiss me, sweet, and twenty;
> Youth's a stuff will not endure.

Both in its theme and in its form, this song holds in suspension all the fleeting transience and fragile beauty of the play. Insubstantial though it is, an interlude in a scene which is itself an interlude, the song fixes and holds by its highly-wrought art the fluidity and unconfined movement of feeling that 'leaps all civil bounds'. Thus while the play includes the song, the song also contains the play; just as the play, art itself, contains and orders the capricious mutability and confusion of nature.

SOURCE: *Critical Quarterly*, IX 3 (1967) 201–12

M. C. Bradbrook

ROBERT ARMIN AND *TWELFTH NIGHT* (1969)

I

Perhaps the most difficult problem for Shakespeare the dramatist was the control of the clown. 'In the days of Tarlton and of Kempe' clowns not only ad-libbed; they would 'kill' a scene by holding, as Brome testified, 'interlocutions with the audience'.[1] Very early popular merriments were largely mock-fights; such bantering from the courtly audience as Shakespeare evidently knew himself, to judge from *Love's Labour's Lost*, established a relationship highly provocative, not easily controlled. At the end of a public play came the clown's 'jig' or an improvised game of rhyming with the crowd. Clowns wrote their own plays – Tarlton's *Seven Deadly Sins* was successful; Kempe's *Knack to Know a Knave* is a robust merriment of the Wise Fools of Gotham. The unity of dramatic ensemble was completed only when the fool became absorbed in the group relations of the play itself.

The old level of exchange is suggested by a rhyme contest between Henry VIII and his jester Will Summers, which comes to conclude one of Rowley's plays. The Emperor is judge.

> *King.* Answer this, sir. 'The bud is spread, the rose is red, the leaf is green'.
> *Will.* A wench 'tis said Was found in your bed Beside the Queen.
> *Queen.* God a mercy for that, Will, There's two angels for thee. I' faith, my lord I am glad I know it. . . .
> *Emperor.* He's too hard for you, my lord, I'll try him. 'An Emperor is great, high is his seat, who is his foe?'

Will. The worms that shall eat His carcase for meat
Whether he will or no.

          (*When you See Me You Know Me,* 1605) Sig. L.I*v*

There were simple jests with custard pies and pints of beer for gormandizing clowns. By the late 1590s, certain sections of the audience were beginning to tire of this kind. There is a passage in the Bad Quarto – the actors' version – of *Hamlet,* that sounds like a warning. Hamlet is made to say :

> You have some again that keeps one suit of jests, as a man is known by one suit of apparel, and Gentlemen quote his jests down in their tables before they come to the play, as thus : Cannot you stay till I eat my porridge? and You owe me a quarter's wages, and My coat wants a cullison and Your beer is sower, and blabbering with his lips and thus keeping in his sinkapace of jests when God knows the warm clown cannot make a jest except by chance as the blind man catches a hare. (III ii 50 ff.)

Compare Lavache's universal answer that fits all questions in *All's Well* II ii : 'Oh, Lord, spare not me' (which is proved unserviceable by his mistress).

Tarlton, a robust and vigorous solo artist, improvisor and swordsman, with a line in 'blue' jokes, artfully pretended to be much simpler than he was. After his death in 1588, Will Kempe, a dancing and singing clown, had taken the lead. He joined the Lord Chamberlain's Men, and we know that he played Peter in *Romeo and Juliet* and Dogberry in *Much Ado About Nothing.* But in 1599 he left and it was then that Shakespeare met the congenial Robert Armin, for whom he created Touchstone, Feste, the gravedigger in *Hamlet,* Lavache in *All's Well,* and the Fool in *King Lear.*

The new feature about these parts is that they are dramatically interwoven with the central characters and the central feelings of the play; they demand an actor ready to play many parts, not just his own brand of clowning. It is a mark of confidence that Hamlet can dismiss the kind of clown who gags, and banish jigs and tales of bawdry from the repertoire he wants; if the new clown had liked such a style of acting, the lines would have produced a backstage row.

Armin's style may be deduced from the roles which Shakespeare created for him; but there is other evidence, for Armin was himself quite a prolific writer, though not of any permanent significance. Nevertheless, it seems curious that no one has looked at Armin's works, to try to measure how closely Shakespeare was conforming to the kind of humour that these shew to have been his speciality. I am going to consider these works in some detail, because I think they do throw light on Shakespeare's careful study of his clown's particular style; but first, perhaps, a word about Armin himself by way of introduction.

Robert Armin, son and brother of merchant tailors, and grandson of a fletcher, was born at King's Lynn, four years younger than Shakespeare; in 1581, at 13, he was apprenticed for eleven years to a famous London goldsmith, Master of Works at the Royal Mint.[2] Socially the Goldsmiths were a most exclusive craft; so Armin's parents must have been fairly wealthy and he must have been reasonably well educated. But next year his master died.

There is a jest-book story that claims 'Tarlton made Armin his adopted son to succeed him' because Armin, sent by his master to collect a debt from a man named Charles, who lodged with Tarlton, chalked up a verse on the defaulter's wall.

> O world, why wilt thou lie?
> Is this Charles the Great! that I deny
> Indeed Charles the Great before,
> But now Charles the less, being poor.

Tarlton read the lines and added some of his own:

> A wag thou art, none can prevent thee;

And thy desert shall content thee.
Let me divine. As I am,
So in time thou'lt be the same,
My adopted son therefore be,
To enjoy my clown's suit after me.

And see how it fell out. The boy, reading this, so loved Tarlton after, that regarding him with more respect, he used to his plays, and fell in a league with his humour; and private practice brought him to present playing, and at this hour performs the same, where at the Globe on the Bankside men may see him.

(*Tarlton's Jests,* 1611, ed. Halliwell Phillips, 1844, p. 22)

Armin became a pamphleteer and player with Lord Chandois' troupe; he also seems to have given private performances. He probably joined the Lord Chamberlain's Men in the autumn of 1599. Next year there appeared his rhyming jest book, of which only one imperfect copy in the British Museum survives, under the pseudonym of 'Clunnico del Curtanio Snuffe' – Snuffe, the Clown of the Curtain Theatre – where, you will remember, the company had to retreat after the Theatre had been evacuated. (Later works appeared by 'Clunnico del Mondo Snuffe', the clown of the Globe.) The Italian style reminds us that Armin knew that language – he published some translations from it – and as for the name 'Snuffe' he signs the dedication to the reader 'Thine own Snuffe, that takes it in snuff, not to be well used'. This little work parodies academic disputations by the method of question and answer, the answer being itself deflated by a concluding 'quip'.[3]

The very form of the little book therefore puts Armin with learned fools in the great tradition descending from Thomas More, patron of players, and from Erasmus, rather than the boisterous clowns of the countryside and the playing place. He was a vivid, peppery, stimulating jester; yet also nervous if spirited, and rather waspish. If Erasmus' *Praise of Folly*[4] gave supreme wisdom to the Fool, we know that Armin saw the whole world as Folly's subjects : he opens his book with a return to the origins of man, his first question being 'Who first began to live i' the world?'

The full title of his little blackletter octavo is very revealing:

Quips upon Questions; or a Clown's conceits on occasions offered, bewraying a moralised metamorphosis of changes upon interrogatories; shewing a little wit, with a great deal of will; or indeed, more desire to please in it than to profit by it. Clapt up by a clown of the town, in this late restraint, having little else to do, to make a little use of his fickle muse and careless of carping. By Clunnico del Curtanio Snuffe.

> Like as you list, read on and spare not,
> Clowns judge like clowns, therefore I care not.

or thus:

> Flout me, I'll flout thee, it is my profession
> To jest at a jester, in his transgression.

The mock dedication to 'His right worthy Sir Timothie Truncheon; Alias Bastinado, ever my part-taking friend' is an address to Harlequin's bat, and yet also a poignant reminder of the whippings and beatings that were the jester's lot both on stage and in great households. 'I salute thy Crab-tree countenance with a low congey being struck down by thy favour. Whereas I sometimes slept with you, in the fieldes, wanting a house o'er my head . . . guard me through the spittle fields I beseech you.' There follows an appeal to the Readers, ending with the famous 'Harlequin bow' – 'Readers, revilers, or indeed what not, to you I appeal . . . and so a thousand times making leg, I go backwards till I am out of sight, hoping then to be out of mind.' But this does *not* end the very elaborate introduction; there is an old-fashioned address of encouragement 'To the Book'.

There follow about forty questions, some ironic, some nonsensical, some sententious and some bawdy. This little catechism, with its mock academic form, shews how Armin enriched and changed the clowning tradition with rapid and nimble shifts of posture, acceptance of contradiction, flirts and fidgets of wit.

He had caught up, in his humble way, with the vogue of Paradoxes and Problems. The first question – 'Who first began to live i' the world?' – the answer being Adam, leads into a learned discussion of First and Last Men but ends with the 'quip' :

> Thou art a fool. Why? for reasoning so.
> But *not* the first or last, by many mo.

Other questions include : Why barks that dog? who sleeps in the grass? who's dead? who's the fool now? what's near her? what's a clock? are you there with your bears? where's Tarlton? These presumably formed part of Armin's repertory in his one-man shews or after-pieces.

There are several anecdotes about the theatre. Some are about tumults and the robbing of simpletons, 'Where's Tarlton?' leads to the story of a simple Collier 'that knew not chalk from cheese' who, although he had heard Tarlton was dead, went to the play and demanded to see him.

> Within the play passed was his picture used,
> Which when the fellow saw, he laught aloud :
> A ha, quoth he, I knew we were abusde,
> That he was kept away from all this crowd.
>   The simple man was quiet and departed,
>   And having seen his picture, was glad-hearted.

This leads into a bitter little disquisition on fame, identity and survival : the play mentioned must be *Three Lords and Three Ladies of London*, in which the picture of Tarlton is used in a scene written to mourn his death.

A malicious jest 'Can that Boy read?' might have been

directed on a member of the audience. The answer is 'Yes, he can read and write and cast accounts, and once his reading saved him from you-know-what' – a hanging. There must have been some moments when exchanges with the audience came near a David Frost show.

Armin himself was pathetically proud of his learning, and given to scraps of Latin. Shakespeare gives such a justifying tag to Feste: ' "Cucullus non facit monachum"; that's as much as to say, I wear not motley in my brains'.

Erasmus quotes Cato about the wisdom of playing the fool in due season, and so does Armin. He ends his little catechism with an ample apology :

> Gentles, whose gentleness in censuring
> Is to take pleasure in your pitying :
> Craftsmen, whose craft in cleanly covering
> Is to be crafty in your kindest cunning,
> To you I appeal; to whom in my appealing,
> I crave forgiveness, giving this hard dealing.

Armin's first question suggests not only Feste's song 'A great while ago the world begun', but the gravedigger's riddle about Adam in *Hamlet*. From the time that Armin joined the company Shakespeare very noticeably began to give his clowns the catechism as a form of jesting. Touchstone questions Rosalind and Celia in this way, and proves the damnation of the country yokel by a catechism; Feste catechizes Olivia on why she grieves and proves her a fool for doing so; later, in the guise of the curate, he catechizes Malvolio. Lavache plays the same kind of game with Helen and the Countess; the gravedigger uses it as his chief form of witticism. Lear's Fool uses riddles and questions to undermine or ridicule pretensions.

The very name of Touchstone is of course a reference to Armin's trade – the touchstone was the emblem of the goldsmiths, and the name is given to various characters who follow this trade, including the heavy father of *Eastward Ho!*

Armin took over Kempe's famous part of Dogberry, and was evidently proud to do so, for ten years later in a dedication he apologizes for 'the boldness of a beggar, who hath been writ down for an ass in his time, and pleads (under forma pauperis) in it still, notwithstanding his constableship and office'.

He was certainly not restricted to one line in clowning, for in his own play, *Two Maids of Moreclacke*, he doubled the parts of a clever servant Touch with that of a well-known London character, Blue-coat John, a poor idiot who was kept at Christ's Hospital and became a kind of public plaything. There is one point in the play where Touch (played by Armin) has himself to disguise as Blue-coat John. As a dramatist, Armin must have caused some embarrassment to his new colleagues, for his play is one of the most confused, overcrowded farces of multiple disguise to survive from the Elizabethan stage. Two girls and their lovers outwit parental opposition with the help of Touch:[5] It is the playhouse equivalent of a curious knotted garden, a thick tapestry, or the intricate embroidery of a lady's state dress. That Shakespeare had read or seen this play is plain from the capital he makes out of one of its scenes. In Feste's opening scene in *Twelfth Night* he says,

> I am resolv'd on two points.
> *Maria.* That if one break, the other will hold; or if both break, your gaskins fall.

This quibble on the tagged points or laces of Elizabethan breeches would recall to the audience a scene where Armin as Blue-coat John had played counters with one of the blue-coat boys.

> *John.* I ha' ne'er a counter.
> *Boy.* I'll give thee one for a point.
> *John.* Do, and I'll play hose go down. (C.3 v)

When John's nurse finds he had parted with the lace of his breeches she cries :

> I'll whip ye for it, take him up. Lose your point, lamb, fie! up with him, sirrah

and she slaps his bottom till he cries 'Good nurse, now, no more, truly, O, O'.

Nothing is more memorable than the clown getting a good thrashing, and this hilarious scene is what Shakespeare briefly recalls, to put the audience in the right frame of mind at the start.

Sir Topas's talk about transmigration exploits another interest of Armin who, from Straparola's *Piacevoli Notti*, translated a fairy tale about shape-changers. Another little item from *Quips upon Questions* suggests why Sir Toby should go drinking in his boots – because either his shoes or his stockings are too disreputable to be seen.

There are several characteristics of the roles of Armin which serve to distinguish him from the ordinary clown :

(1) He attends upon ladies, rather than on lords (Armin was devoted to Lady Mary Chandois and Lady Haddington). Touchstone, Feste, Lavache share this trait.

(2) He is often contrasted with a knave and he likes to prove that others are either fools, knaves or both, by means of catechism and other marks of the wise Fool.

(3) He underlines or calls attention to social gradations; although living outside the social order, he enforces it. (This is a characteristic of *Quips upon Questions*.)

(4) His wit is bitter and deflationary.

(5) He is given to music and song.

II

But what Armin seems to have provoked in Shakespeare (and membership of the company in Armin) was the integrated comic vision of an Erasmus or a More of the world of fools; the idea of what Erasmus had first termed the 'foolosopher' (a word picked up by Armin). 'He uses folly like a stalking-horse, and under the presentation of that he shoots his wit', defines Touchstone, in words close to Armin's own definition : 'Fools natural, are prone to selfconceit / Fools artificial with their wits lay wait.'

Feste is Malvolio's first and principal antagonist, parish clerk to Lady Folly.

He never uses such gross terms of familiarity as earlier clowns, but he can conjure money from old friends like the Duke or strangers like the twins; he invents wonderful mock authorities to edify Sir Andrew; he can parody the church service as readily as Erasmus himself.

Very early, he foresees the fate which overtakes Malvolio; 'God send *you*, Sir, a speedy infirmity for the better increasing of your folly' (I v 72–3).

At the end Feste recognizes the rounded and absurd perfection of the comedy – 'Thus the whirligig of time brings in his revenges'. There was a feeling that the clown ought to be able to deal with anything – perhaps from his taking on all comers – and in *Quips upon Questions* a faintly discernible notion of some grand inclusive plan can be guessed by the opening question on Adam, and others on the state of the world. It is really a medley incorporating some traditional jests, including one of Tarlton's in answer to the question 'What's fit?'; some little tales; some pieties ('Where does the devil keep Christmas?') and some 'blue' jokes. The new kind of wit depended on being able to adjust to a varied audience, to play a multiplicity of roles. The clown was losing his independence as an entertainer; he was no longer a challenger but a servant. As Viola recognizes, this asks sensitive responses to mood and company :

> This fellow is wise enough to play the fool;
> And to do that well craves a kind of wit.
> He must observe their mood on whom he jests,
> The qualities of persons, and the time;
> And, like the haggard, check at every feather
> That comes before his eye. This is a practice
> As full of labour as a wise man's art. (III i 57–63)

No confident jig for such a character – he ends with a melancholy song. And in his next appearance a household jester Yorick has long been dead, and Armin the clown is digging a grave. The association of the Fool and Death in the famous pictures of Hans Holbein had haunted Shakespeare's imagination since he wrote of the antic Death crouching within the hollow crown circling a king's brow (*Richard II,* III i 160–70).

Although his writings are broken and confused, and his history with the players too seems a broken and uncertain one, Armin's sympathetic *rapport* can be sensed in the full, gratified unity of conception that makes *As You Like It, Twelfth Night,* and *King Lear* each in so different a way macrocosmic, a complete world whose inhabitants live in a special glow, or light that suffuses them :

> Foolery, sir, does walk about the orb like the sun, it shines everywhere. (III i 36–7)

Perhaps as he spoke, Feste glanced round the orbed seats of the Globe Theatre, with a bow that included the audience in this observation.

In *Twelfth Night* we are transported by way of an old English festivity (Twelfth Night was the occasion for masques, fantastic happenings, the last of the great Christmas feasts, followed by St Distaff's Day and Plough Monday) to a sunny Mediterranean land where it is always afternoon. Except for his versatile page, the Duke's household is shadowy but at the Countess Olivia's we see life below and above stairs. We seem to be in a city with an Elephant Inn, but Olivia's country-style living belongs outside the walls where Christmas was kept as Shakespeare knew it – by a big generous, noisy, rapacious court, with Christmas cheer for all comers. Summer and winter, city and country, an old world of revels and a new one of social distinctions are somehow all united – the only discord being that ill-will which kills imagination.

To King Charles the play was known as *Malvolio*, and from an early admirer we learn that it was Malvolio the crowds went to see.[6] Van Doren says of Toby's attack on Malvolio, 'It is the old world resisting the new; it is the life of hiccups and melancholy, trying to ignore latter day puritanism and efficiency' and between his mood and the music of old manners it may be felt that Malvolio is 'dreadfully likely to prevail'. Certainly Olivia would not have this important and necessary officer miscarry for half of her dowry; but when he resents the quips of Feste, she diagnoses him acutely: 'O, you are sick of self-love, Malvolio, and taste with a distemper'd appetite'.

Self-Love, as many authorities from Erasmus to Ben Jonson bear witness, is the chief attendant on Folly; and Folly, as again Erasmus and other authors had made clear, held her rule in the world of fools by delegation from Fortune, or Lady Luck. The unity of this play comes from the Rule of Fortune over the lives of Orsino, Olivia and the twins, and the Rule of Folly over life below stairs. As a victim of Self-Love, Malvolio tries to climb the wheel of Folly's Mistress, Fortune. 'All is fortune' he remarks as he picks up the deceptive love letter from 'the fortunate-unhappy' (II v 21). But it is Folly that guides him – the penalty of his aspiration to be Count Malvolio is to be taken for a madman; when all is revealed, Olivia tacitly withdraws her offer to let him judge his own case – 'Alas, poor fool, how have they baffl'd thee!' Malvolio's 'obedient hope' was not exactly madness – since the Countess does marry one whom she takes to be a serving man; moreover in real life, as perhaps some of the audience would remember, that formidable royalty, the widowed Duchess of Suffolk, had married her youthful Master of the Horse. Eworth painted the termagant beside the slight lad who is nervously fingering just such a jewel as Malvolio covets.

On the other hand the deception practised on Malvolio is certainly no more vindictive than the jokes courtiers played on each other (or on actors). Fools would treat rival fools with even greater violence – Armin describes one who half-killed and put the eye out of a rival.[7] The tricking of Malvolio was specially commended as a 'good practice', i.e. a clever deception by a young lawyer who saw the play given at Candlemas 1602 in the Middle Temple Hall. 'Flout me, I'll flout thee' (remember), was one of Armin's mottoes.

The cross garters and yellow hose recommended to Malvolio were those of the henpecked husband in a popular song. 'Malvolio's a Peg-a-Ramsey', cries Sir Toby, and the chorus of this popular ditty was:

> Give me my yellow hose again,
> Give me my yellow hose,
> Forsooth my wife she follows me,
> See yonder where she goes.[8]

So Malvolio is drawn into the kingdom of folly. Ecclesiastes has said the number of fools is infinite, and the idea of a kingdom of, fools was familiar in carnival and sottie. Malvolio in fact performs a kind of little play to his appreciative stage audience, and when he is bound in the dark room, Feste performs one of the regular clowning acts by holding a dialogue in which he sustains both parts, demanding that Malvolio subscribe to the heretical doctrine of transmigration[9] and in his own person challenging the devil, now inhabiting Malvolio, to combat.

Sir Toby, if he had been a different sort of person, would have been Olivia's natural guardian; old houses harbour such buffoons as proof of their own antiquity and dignity. 'Am I not consanguineous? am I not of her blood?' he protests: 'Tilly-vally, lady.' He 'talks puffingly and explosively and is as full of wine as he is loud with song', but he belongs to a rough countrified society, and his place is below stairs with Fabian, who had got into trouble about a bear-baiting. Within the fantasy there is a very clear sense – an actor's sense, or a jester's – of precise social distinctions. The most poignant comes at the end of Feste's last song when he suddenly turns into Armin himself, as the wind and rain of January fall, the world returns to work again, ending foolish things and childish toys. For the Players' offerings, unlike those of the old households, *will* go on, as part of a workaday world.

> A great while ago the world begun
> With hey, ho, the wind and the rain,
> But that's all one, our play is done,
> And we'll strive to please you *every day*. (v i 391–4)

Here, the moment of comic truth is the moment when the old world of the revels turns into the new world of the theatre, and when the craft of the player is laid aside for a final bow as he turns to 'woo the twopenny room for a plaudite'. The new fool is a fool *deferring to an audience.*

The immediate effect of the play may have depended on Feste, but later King Charles was terming it 'Malvolio'. Such fools were out of fashion, and William Cartwright in 1647 dismisses them as part of Shakespeare's uneducated simplicity. 'Nature was all his art.'

> Shakespeare to thee [Fletcher] was dull, whose best jest
>   lies
> In the ladies' questions and the fools' replies;
> Old-fashion'd wit which walk'd from town to town
> In turn'd hose, which our fathers called the Clown.
>   (Verses prefixed to the Folio ed. of Fletcher, 1647)

For the fine social distinctions that are sustained by the world of love had been lost in the intervening years.

'Love and Fortune play in Comedies' had been an old adage of the stage,[10] and though the Lovers are partly in Folly's jurisdiction, they are ruled chiefly by her great Mistress, the Goddess Fortune.

In case it may be thought that such distinctions would not be immediately present to an ordinary attendance at the theatre, I should point out that there was quite a number of plays about fools in the years 1598–1604; that Armin's printer, William Ferbrand, brought out a number of books on fools, including one by Armin himself that categorized six different sorts of fool; and another that supplied fools culled from every county in England.[11] It would be possible to take *The Hospital of Incurable Fools* (1600), translated from the Italian of Tomaso Garzoni, and assign every one of the characters in *Twelfth Night* to one or other of the thirty different wards for different sorts of fool, each presided over by an appropriate God. Under the general patronage of Lady Fortune and presided over by Dame Folly, the Hospital would have accepted Malvolio among its 'malicious and despightful fools' who were placed for cure under the goddess Nemesis.

> Some men there be that inwardly have inserted to them such a spirit as if they happened at any time to be offended or injured by any one, with a foolish wilfulness at one time they began to contend with him....
> (The Thirteenth Discourse, *The Hospital of Incurable Fools*, 1600, pp. 56–60)

Orsino and Olivia might be placed among the 'solitary and melancholy fools', Toby as a 'drunken fool', Andrew a 'dottrel and shallow-pated fool' or a 'carpet and amorous fool' or perhaps even a 'gross and three-elbow'd fool'. At all events he is more of a fool than anyone else.

Feste on the other hand would be placed among the 'parasitical and scoffing fools' of whom it is said that they should not be enclosed in the hospital at all, but among the wise and under the special protection of God Mercury.

In the dedication of this book, Cato and Erasmus are joined as the upholders of wise fools.

The whole strength of Shakespeare's work lies in the fact that it is not analytic but directly and fully dramatic in its presentation. It does not carry even the amount of argument and ceremony that belongs to his earlier plays of the noble courtly life, still less such atrophied social grading as Jonson's unsuccessful *Cynthia's Revels*.[12] But on the other hand, the delicate relationships of Orsino, Olivia and Viola will reward the closest inspection; they are fully personal while fully dramatic. The Duke opens the play

> If music be the food of love, play on,
> Give me excess of it, that, surfeiting,
> The appetite may sicken and so die.
> That strain again! It had a dying fall;
> O, it came o'er my ear like the sweet sound
> That breathes upon a bank of violets,
> Stealing and giving odour! Enough, no more;
> 'Tis not so sweet now as it was before. (1 i 1–8)

In eight masterly lines, you have the tragi-comic Duke; absorbed in the sensation of love, he yet wants to be rid of it. The lines are so beautiful that one overlooks the suppressed violence that would kill by satiety. A susceptible young Italian who hardly wishes to know the beauty whose image drives him from one 'shape' of fancy to the next, he is exquisitely sensitive to

the perfume and suppliance of a minute and to the fine vari-
ations of his own mood ('O spirit of love, how quick and fresh
art thou!'), only to feel an immediate recoil. 'Now the tailor
make thy doublet of changeable taffeta,' says Feste, 'for thy
mind is a very opal.' This was a recognized state of lovesickness;
the Duke is meant to be a little mad – agreeably so, but percep-
tibly off-balance. Yet his servants tell us he is not inconstant
in his personal favour to them. And with Cesario he becomes
frank, sceptical, mocking, for of course, quite unaware of what
is happening, he is falling in love more reasonably and on the
way to a cure.

Viola is changeable as the Duke is, but changeable because
she is so ready to adjust to Fortune's whims; it is these, not
Folly, that toss her about. She remains charmingly prepared to
laugh at her own predicaments, plays at being Sebastian, in
fantasy restoring the brother she had lost by taking his shape.
He was seen binding himself to a mast as their ship went down
– 'courage and hope both teaching him the practice'; Viola too,
with courage, hopefulness and a readiness to improvise, accepts
her unwelcome mission, while perfectly clear about her own
wants.

> Whoe'er I woo, myself would be his wife. (1 iv 41)

She puts on an inflated style like a bad player

> Most radiant, exquisite, and unmatchable beauty – I pray you
> tell me if this be the lady of the house, for I never saw her. I would
> be loath to cast away my speech; for besides it is excellently well
> penn'd, I have taken great pains to con it. (1 v 160 ff.)

Olivia gives the expected cure for such a 'happening'; 'Whence
came you, sir?' and Viola breaks decorum again; 'I can say
little more than I have studied and that question's out of my
part'. 'Are you a comedian?' asks Olivia with a touch of scorn,
and Viola disclaims the professional role, which nevertheless

colours all the scene. After Olivia has unveiled the face which
is Orsino's 'Heaven on earth', complacently asking 'Is't not
well done?' the whole thing is deflated by the cool 'Excellently
done, if God did all!'

Then when the young messenger strikes the true note, as she
remembers what it is to feel the soul by love drawn out into
another's being, she moves out of her jesting, living her part so
effectually that Olivia is carried away too, suddenly overwhelmed by a part of herself she does not know. 'I do I know
not what' she says, 'Ourselves we do not owe', and from
mourning, she is plunged head over heels in love with mockery
and courage.

The whole situation being resolved by the appearance of the
twin, the play ends like a square-dance. The miracle of the
twins (it is described theologically)[13] dissolves that unreal inner
world, where the Duke had lived tormented by fancy and
Olivia by her own loneliness. Faced with a snub in public, the
Duke grows maddened by the 'ingrate' rejection of his
'devotion'. He knows he must kill somebody and knows he
loves both Cesario and Olivia.

> I'll sacrifice the lamb that I do love
> To spite a raven's heart within a dove. (v i 124–5)

The formal Petrarchan images make it quite unreal, but Viola
hears him say he loves her, and she cries at once :

> And I, most jocund, apt, and willingly,
> To do you rest, a thousand deaths would die. (v i 126–7)

At the end of comedies it was usual for a heroine to be exposed to an alarming risk; in one of Peele's plays, she is threatened
with being sawn in half. Here we have all the conventions – 'A
duke there is, and the scene is Italy as those things lightly we
never miss' – but now, when Orsino learns the very worst
treachery, he is suddenly jolted into sanity. There is no more

talk of killing when he thinks Olivia and Cesario married; take her, he says, but don't let us meet again.

And finally he is left with laughing, stumbling efforts to disentangle the boy Cesario from a new image that is beginning to form – his 'fancy's queen'.

All the elements of control in the story – the suffusive power of Fortune and Folly, the 'Italianate' compliments and the device of the twins – do not distract attention from the natural aspects of festivity and character as they evolve here.

'What's to come is still unsure.'

The comic version was more elusive than the tragic, but in *Twelfth Night*, it is fully embodied. To attribute this to the presence of a gifted clown rather than the presence of an Italian Duke (as Leslie Hotson would have it in *The First Night of 'Twelfth Night'*) implies that Shakespeare had left behind that ceremonious kind of drama which he perfected in *A Midsummer Night's Dream*, and that he was as deeply influenced by his fellow-actor as by his audience. A momentary compliment, a skilful improvisation might be part of the play; but the play itself had become a craft mystery.

Twelfth Night, because it was made for one company at one time by a master of craft, carries the self-adjustive elasticity of all great drama; being so complete and beautifully balanced in itself between the world of revels and the January cold, it absorbs the imbalance of those who would present or accept it.

That the solution to a dramatist's problem, which had been puzzling the stage since Sidney had complained of Clowns, should be a practical matter – a matter of temperaments and of occasion – is what might be expected of this social art. Even as the play succeeded in London, at Cambridge students were still shewing a clown drawn in on the end of a rope and told to extemporize :

Clowns have been thrust into plays by head and shoulders ever since Kempe could make a scurvy face . . . if thou canst but draw thy mouth awry, lay thy leg over thy staff, saw a piece of

cheese asunder with thy dagger, lap up drink on the earth I'll
warrent thee they'll laugh mightily....

The difference between this and the kind of inconsequence
that Feste may shew in a begging plea to the Duke ('the bells
of St Bennet, may put you in mind sir, one, two, three') is the
difference between Nature and Art; but, 'the Art itself is
Nature'.

SOURCE : *Shakespeare the Craftsman* 1969) chap. iv

NOTES

1. These quotations are from Richard Brome, *The Anti-
podes*, ɪɪ ii 45–8.
2. The best account of his life is that by Charles S. Felver,
Robert Armin, Shakespeare's Fool (Kent State University, Kent,
Ohio : Research Series v, 1961). See also his article on Armin as
Touchstone, *Shakespeare Quarterly*, vɪɪ (1956) 135–7. Armin's
life is also discussed by Leslie Hotson in *Shakespeare's Motley*
(1952) pp. 84–128.
3. *Quips upon Questions* may be treated as one of the minor
sources of *Twelfth Night*. It exists in a single imperfect copy in
the British Museum, two leaves CI and DI being missing. See
T. W. Baldwin, *Modern Language Notes*, xxxɪx (1924) 447–55,
who uses it to date *As You Like It*. This work was not previously
recognized as Armin's and *The Short Title Catalogue* ascribed
it, for some reason, to John Sharp. Armin's other works were
edited by Grosart (1880).
4. *The Praise of Folly* was englished by Sir Thomas Chaloner
in 1545 from Erasmus, *Moriae Encomium* of 1511. The world of
fools goes back beyond this to Brant's *Ship of Fools* (1494). In
France the world of wise fools was associated with law sports and
the *sottie*; see Enid Welsford, *The Fool* (1935) pt iii; and R. H.
Goldsmith, *Shakespeare's Wise Fools* (1958). He quotes the mock
sermon of Folly in *Ane Satyre of the 3 Estates,* and that of Gela-
simus in Grimald's *Archipropheta* (1547), a Latin play.
5. The play belongs to the same tradition as *John a Kent and
John a Cumber* and *Friar Bacon and Friar Bungay*; quick changes

and magic shows are part of the plots. There seemed to be a convention of the magician and the lovers which can be seen dimly reflected in Armin's very latest work. But *Two Maids of Moreclacke* must have depended almost entirely on Armin's mimicry of Blue-coat John.

6. Leonard Digges in the lines prefixed to Shakespeare's *Poems* (1640):

> Let but Beatrice
> And Benedick be seen, lo in a trice
> The Cockpit, Galleries, Boxes, all are full
> To hear Malvolio, that cross garter'd gull.

7. Robert Armin, *Fool upon Fool* (1605), ed. Grosart (1880) pp. 6–7. This violence was due to jealousy; but some masters seem to have tolerated extraordinary ill-behaviour on the part of their household fools, such as the one who stole a special dish for which a large party had been invited, jumped into the moat and stood in the water eating it that he might not be prevented.

8. Malvolio also quotes in all innocence the very dirty little ditty of Richard Tarlton, 'Please one and please all'. He must be presumed not to realize the point of this song which is the same as that of 'A little of what you fancy does you good'.

9. Transmigration denies the resurrection of the body, 'So, living in its liberty' adherents 'Commit foul treason, and villainy'. William Rankin, *Seven Satyres* (1598) p. 17.

10. From the prologue to *Soliman and Perseda* (1590). *The Rare Triumphs of Love and Fortune* shows the two in contest; it was played at court in 1582 by Derby's Men.

11. Rankin, the academic who wrote *Seven Satyres* against fools (1598), drew Skelton for Henslowe; Rowley's play on Summers is dated 1596; among later fools are Marston's Passarello (*The Malcontent*), the fools in *Volpone*, and Babulo in *Patient Grissell*. William Ferbrand, Armin's printer, also produced *Jack of Dover . . . his quest of Inquirie . . . his privy search for the veriest Fool in England* (1601/1614); a sequel was *The penniless Parliament of threadbare Poets* (1608), published, however, by William Barley.

12. Leslie Hotson connects *Cynthia's Revels* with *Twelfth Night* (*The First Night of 'Twelfth Night'*, 1954), only by way of contrasting its reception and aim. The identification of Jonson

with Crites is not accepted by O. J. Campbell, *Comicall Satyre* (1938) pp. 82–108.

13. 'One face, one voice, one habit and two persons', says the Duke (v i 208).

> Do I stand there? I never had a brother;
> Nor can there be that deity in my nature
> Of here and everywhere,

says Sebastian (v i 218–20).

SELECT BIBLIOGRAPHY

The play has been edited with a critical introduction and a stage-history by Sir Arthur Quiller-Couch and John Dover Wilson (New Cambridge Shakespeare: Cambridge University Press, 1926). More detailed commentary is provided in the edition by M. M. Mahood (New Penguin Shakespeare: Penguin Books, 1968), while the edition by Herschel Baker (Signet Classic Shakespeare: New American Library and New English Library, 1965) includes Riche's 'Of Apolonius and Silla' and reprints several critical essays on the play.

G. Bullough, *Narrative and Dramatic Sources of Shakespeare*, vol. II (Routledge & Kegan Paul and Columbia University Press, 1958). The standard study and edition of the source material, including Riche's 'Of Apolonius and Silla' and a translation of *Gl'Ingannati.*

Enid Welsford, *The Fool* (Faber & Faber, 1935; paperback edition, 1968). An informative history of the traditional role of jesters and professional fools.

Austin Gray, 'Robert Armine', *Publications of the Modern Language Association of America*, XLII (1927). An account of Armin's career in its bearing upon the role of Feste.

Paul Mueschke and Jeannette Fleisher, 'Jonsonian Elements in the Comic Underplot of *Twelfth Night*', *Publications of the Modern Language Association of America*, XLVIII (1933). Discusses the influence of Jonson's satirical 'humour' comedies upon the gulling of Malvolio.

Sylvan Barnet, 'Charles Lamb and the Tragic Malvolio', *Philological Quarterly*, XXXIII (1954. Shows that Lamb's influential conception of Malvolio was probably not derived from Bensley's stage-performance, as it purports to be.

L. G. Salingar, 'The Design of *Twelfth Night*', *Shakespeare Quarterly*, IX (1958). A close study of the play, its structure and themes, in relation to its sources and analogues.

John Hollander, '*Twelfth Night* and the Morality of Indulgence', *Sewanee Review*, LXVIII (1959). An interpretation of the play as a refutation of the Jonsonian theory of comedy, substituting the dynamics of 'appetite' for the static conception of 'humours'.

Clifford Leech, '*Twelfth Night*' *and Shakespearian Comedy* (University of Toronto Press and Oxford University Press, 1965). The chapter on *Twelfth Night* stresses the precariousness of happiness in Illyria, and the play's discomfiting elements.

Julian Markels, 'Shakespeare's Confluence of Tragedy and Comedy : *Twelfth Night* and *King Lear*', *Shakespeare Quarterly*, xv (1964). Explores the parallel between Feste's comic exposure of Malvolio's 'spiritual pride' and the Fool's relationship to Lear in the tragedy.

NOTES ON CONTRIBUTORS

C. L. BARBER. Professor of English at New York State University, Buffalo; the author of *Shakespeare's Festive Comedy,* one of the most influential of modern studies of the comedies.

M. C. BRADBROOK. Formerly Professor of English in the University of Cambridge, and Mistress of Girton College; her books include *Themes and Conventions in Elizabethan Tragedy, Shakespeare and Elizabethan Poetry, The Rise of the Common Player,* and *Shakespeare the Craftsman.*

A. C. BRADLEY. One of the greatest of Shakespearian critics, he held Chairs of English Literature in the Universities of Liverpool and Glasgow before becoming Professor of Poetry at Oxford. His *Shakespearian Tragedy* (1904) is a classic of character-interpretation.

JOHN RUSSELL BROWN. Professor of English in the University of Sussex, and Associate Director of the National Theatre; his books include *Shakespeare and his Comedies, Shakespeare's Plays in Performance, and* editions of *The Merchant of Venice* and *The Duchess of Malfi.*

H. B. CHARLTON (1890–1961). Formerly Professor of English Literature in the University of Manchester. *Shakespearian Comedy* (1938) is one of the first serious attempts to study the form and development of Shakespeare's comic art.

BERTRAND EVANS. Professor of English in the University of California at Berkeley. *Shakespeare's Comedies* focuses upon the dramatic exploitation of discrepant awareness between characters and audience.

JOHN HOLLANDER. Professor of English at Hunter College, New York; the author of *The Untuning of the Sky,* a study of musical ideas in Renaissance literature.

LESLIE HOTSON. His brilliant but often controversial exercises in literary detection include, in addition to *The First Night of 'Twelfth Night'*, *The Death of Christopher Marlowe*, *Shakespeare's Sonnets Dated*, *Shakespeare's Motley*, and *Shakespeare's Wooden 'O'*.

D. J. PALMER. Professor of English Literature in the University of Manchester; author of *The Rise of English Studies*.

JOSEPH H. SUMMERS. Professor of English at the University of Rochester, New York; his books include *George Herbert: His Religion and Art*, and *The Muse's Method: An Introduction to 'Paradise Lost'*.

PORTER WILLIAMS, JR. Professor of English at North Carolina State University; he has also published work on Conrad.

INDEX

AGUECHEEK, SIR ANDREW 29,
31, 32, 41–2, 64, 68, 75, 87,
90, 91–2, 105–6, 107, 110,
115, 117, 122, 137, 151–3,
154–6, 158, 159, 160, 161,
172, 174–5, 177, 185–6, 191,
208, 213
Alexander, P. 21
All's Well That Ends Well 12,
36, 66, 131, 138
ANTONIO 12, 13, 54, 89, 94,
115, 118, 161–2, 174, 185,
192
Antonio (*Merchant of Venice*)
12, 21, 162
Antony and Cleopatra 70 n,
111, 134
Armin, Robert 20, 109, 222,
223–40, 241–2 n
As You Like It 12, 19, 63,
75, 120, 138, 140, 141, 232,
241 n
Ashcroft, Peggy 189, 192
Audley, Maxime 190
Audrey (*As You Like It*) 63

Baldwin, T. W. 241 n
Barker, C. L. 19, 112–36
Barnet, Sylvan 17
Bassanio (*Merchant of Venice*)
120, 141, 162
Beatrice (*Much Ado About
Nothing*) 74, 144

Beckett, Samuel: *Waiting for
Godot* 191
BELCH, SIR TOBY 12, 31, 32,
40, 41, 45, 46, 51–2, 53, 63,
65, 67, 75, 89, 92, 94,
105–6, 107, 114, 119, 121–3,
137–8, 151–3, 155–6, 158–9,
160–1, 172, 174–5, 185–6,
190, 194, 206, 207, 208, 211,
233, 235
Bensley, Robert 17, 37–41
Boaden, James 17, 18, 48–51
Boethius 105
Bolingbroke (*Richard II*) 100
Bottom (*Midsummer Night's
Dream*) 75, 151, 158
Bradbrook, M. C. 20, 121,
170, 172, 187 n, 222–43
Bradley, A. C. 20, 63–71
Brecht, B. 108
Brome, R. 222, 241 n
Brown, J. R. 21, 173, 187 n,
188–203
Brutus (*Julius Caesar*) 101,
212
Bullough, G. 211, 215
Burnaby, William: *Love
Betray'd* 14–15, 25–8

Campbell, O. J. 242 n
CAPTAIN 89, 90, 113, 174
Caravaggio 109
Cartwright, W. 235–6

Castiglione, B. 78, 120
Cato 228
Celia (*As You Like It*) 66, 74
Cervantes 30
Chambers, E. K. 136 n,
  187 n
Charles I 14, 233
Charlton, H. B. 16, 19, 72,
  173, 175, 187 n
Coffin, Hayden 71 n
Coleridge, S. J. 55
Comedy of Errors 12, 25, 112,
  128, 163–5
Congreve, W. 30; *Love for
  Love* 47
Cornish, W. 108
Costard (*Love's Labour's Lost*)
  75
Countess (*All's Well That Ends
  Well*) 66
Crashaw, Richard 109
Cymbeline 138, 156, 163

Digges, Leonard 14, 25,
  242 n
Dogberry (*Much Ado About
  Nothing*) 75, 223
Don Quixote 40
Dryden, John 109

El Greco 189
Elizabeth I 11, 78–85, 135 n
Epictetus 64
Erasmus 20, 225, 228, 231,
  233, 241 n
Evans, Bertrand 137–69

FABIAN 36, 40, 115, 125, 156

Falstaff 12, 44, 77, 122, 123,
  154, 158
Felver, C. S. 241 n
FESTE 13, 20, 31, 32, 37, 41,
  50, 55, 59, 63–71, 89, 90,
  92, 95, 106, 107, 108, 110,
  125–6, 132–3, 137, 158,
  163, 165, 172, 174, 184,
  186, 191, 206, 209, 211,
  219, 228, 229, 230, 231–2,
  235
Freud, S. 170, 193
Frost, David 228
Frye, Northrop 204–5

Gervinus 63
Gielgud, Sir John 188
Gobbo (*Merchant of Venice*)
  70 n
Golding, Arthur 217–18
Goldsmith, R. H. 241 n
Gonzaga, Curzio 12
Granville-Barker, Harley 18,
  57–8, 71 n
Guthrie, Sir Tyrone 188

Hall, Peter 188, 192
Hamlet 121, 130, 133, 134,
  223, 228
Hamlet 72, 138, 212, 224
Hazlitt, William 15–16, 18,
  29–36
Helena (*All's Well That Ends
  Well*) 36, 138
Henry VIII 108, 222
Hillyarde, N. 198
Holbein, H. 232
Hollander, John 20, 98–111
Hordern, Michael 189

Hotson, Leslie   11, 78–85,
    112, 135–6 n, 171, 187 n,
    240, 241 n, 242 n
Hotspur (*Henry IV Part I*)   38

Iago   38, 138, 174
Imogen (*Cymbeline*)   138,
    144
Irving, Sir Henry   18, 54–5
Isabella (*Measure for Measure*)
    144

Jaques (*As You Like It*)   75
Jessica (*Merchant of Venice*)
    102–3
Johnson, Richard   191
Johnson, Samuel   14, 21, 29,
    31
Jones, R.   107
Jonson, Ben   14, 75, 111,
    233, 237
Jordan, Mrs   17, 36, 48–51
Julia (*Two Gentlemen of Verona*)
    12, 138, 149

Kempe, Will   222, 223, 229,
    240
King Lear   68, 232
Knight, G. Wilson   98

Lamb, Charles   16–17, 18,
    36–48, 128
Launce (*Two Gentlemen of
    Verona*)   70 n
Lavache (*All's Well That
    Ends Well*)   66, 70 n, 223,
    228, 230

Lear   45, 66
Lear's Fool   20, 63, 69, 70 n,
    223, 228
Lorenzo (*Merchant of Venice*)
    102–3
Love's Labour's Lost   120, 164,
    222

Macbeth   72, 154
McCarthy, Lillah   58
McEwen, Geraldine   190
MALVOLIO   13, 14, 16, 17, 18,
    19, 20, 25, 29, 31, 32, 34–5,
    37, 39–41, 52, 53, 54–5, 59,
    67, 73, 75, 77, 91, 95, 105,
    108, 110, 114, 121, 127–30,
    137, 142, 150, 151–5, 157–
    9, 165, 172, 174, 176–7,
    185, 186, 189, 206, 213–14,
    219, 233–5
Manningham, John   11, 12,
    14, 16, 25, 112
MARIA   11, 31, 32, 39, 40, 41,
    53, 63, 65, 66, 67, 91, 110,
    114, 125, 150, 151–3, 154–5,
    172
Marvell, Andrew   108
Masefield, John   18, 58–9
Measure for Measure   12, 121,
    131–2, 138
Merchant of Venice   12, 65,
    101–3, 116, 120, 121, 122,
    123, 125, 138, 141–2, 164
Merry Wives of Windsor   153,
    154, 158, 164
Midsummer Night's Dream   95,
    120, 134, 136 n, 240
Milton, John   103, 108
Molière   30, 52
Montégut, E.   51–4

Moore, Marianne 135
More, Sir Thomas 20, 225, 231
Much Ado About Nothing 164, 182

OLIVIA 14, 18, 29, 31, 32, 35, 36, 37, 39–40, 41, 51, 52, 54, 56, 57, 63–4, 66, 73, 75, 87, 88–9, 94, 104–5, 107, 108, 110, 114–15, 117, 118, 119, 120–1, 124, 140–1, 142, 147–50, 154, 155, 157–9, 164, 171–2, 173–4, 175–6, 179–81, 185, 190–1, 194, 206, 214–15, 233, 239
Olivier, Sir Laurence (now Lord) 188, 189
Ophelia 36
Orlando (*As You Like It*) 73, 86, 145, 147, 158, 180
ORSINO 36, 40, 41, 49–51, 57, 64, 66, 73, 75, 86, 87–8, 94, 104–5, 106–7, 110, 118, 121, 123–4, 130–1, 139, 144–6, 158, 171–2, 174, 177, 179, 182–3, 185, 191, 192–3, 198, 206, 209–13, 237–8, 239
Orsino, Don Virginio, Duke of Bracciano 11, 78–85, 135 n
Othello 70 n, 158, 213
Othello 38, 50, 72
Ovid 212, 217–18

Palmer, D. J. 204–21
Peele, George 217
Pepys, Samuel 14, 25

Perdita (*Winter's Tale*) 144
Petrarch 239
Phebe (*As You Like it*) 117, 140, 147–8, 180
Plato 102
Plautus 12, 25, 112, 115, 170
Porter, Eric 189
Portia (*Merchant of Venice*) 101–2, 138, 141–2, 144, 149, 168
PRIEST 192
Puck (*Midsummer Night's Dream*) 44, 45
Purcell, Henry 109
Puttenham, George 205, 212

Rabelais 52
Rankin, W. 242 n
Rehan, Ada 18, 55–7
Richard II 99–100, 232
Riche, Barnabe: 'Of Apolonius and Silla' 12, 112, 215
Romeo 171, 212
Romeo and Juliet 134, 173, 223
Rosalind (*As You Like It*) 73–4, 86, 117, 138, 141, 142, 144, 147–8, 149, 160, 168, 180
Russell, Sir Edward 54–5

SEBASTIAN 12, 13, 32, 52, 54, 64, 89, 90–1, 94, 110, 115, 117, 118, 119, 141–2, 143, 145, 149, 156, 160, 164–5, 172, 173–4, 175–6, 207, 208, 214–15
Secchi, Nicolo 12, 210

Shallow (*Henry IV Part II*) 122; see also *Merry Wives of Windsor*

Shylock 121, 128, 129

Sidney, Sir Philip 240

Spenser, Edmund 217

Stanislavski 193

Summers, Joseph 19, 86–97

Summers, Will 222

Taming of the Shrew 13

Tarlton, Richard 222, 223, 224, 227, 231, 242 n

Tawney, R. H. 129

Tempest, The 71

Tennyson, Alfred Lord 74

Tiepolo 196

Timon of Athens 70 n

Touchstone (*As You Like It*) 20, 63, 66, 70 n, 75, 125, 228, 230, 321

Trewin, J. C. 192

Trinculo (*The Tempest*) 70 n

Troilus and Cressida 130–1

Tutin, Dorothy 192

Two Gentlemen of Verona 12, 21, 138

Two Noble Kinsmen 136 n

VALENTINE 88, 139

Vanbrugh, Sir John 30

Van Doren, Mark 121, 123

Verges (*Much Ado About Nothing*) 75

Verlaine 98

Vincentio (*Measure for Measure*) 138, 168

VIOLA 12, 13, 15, 17, 18, 20, 21, 31, 32, 35, 36, 48–51, 52, 53, 54, 55–7, 64, 67, 73–4, 89–90, 93–4, 108, 109–10, 113, 114, 117, 118–19, 120, 126–7, 137, 138–40, 142–3, 144, 147–9, 151, 157, 158, 159, 160–2, 165–9, 172, 174, 177–84, 191, 194, 207, 219, 238–9

Watteau 188

Webster, Margaret 189, 191

Welsford, Enid 241 n

Williams, Porter, Jr 20, 170–87

Winter, Williams 18, 55–7

Winter's Tale 58, 70 n, 134

Wyatt, Sir Thomas 108

Wycherley, William 30

Wymark, Patrick 190